The Language of Mental Health

Series Editors
Michelle O'Reilly
The Greenwood Institute of Child Health
University of Leicester
Leicester, Leicestershire, UK

Jessica Nina Lester
School of Education
Indiana University Bloomington
Bloomington, IN, USA

This series brings together rich theoretical and empirical discussion at the intersection of mental health and discourse/conversation analysis. Situated broadly within a social constructionist perspective, the books included within this series will offer theoretical and empirical examples highlighting the discursive practices that surround mental health and make 'real' mental health constructs. Drawing upon a variety of discourse and conversation analysis perspectives, as well as data sources, the books will allow scholars and practitioners alike to better understand the role of language in the making of mental health.

More information about this series at
http://www.palgrave.com/gp/series/15193

Mary Horton-Salway · Alison Davies

The Discourse of ADHD

Perspectives on Attention Deficit Hyperactivity Disorder

palgrave
macmillan

Mary Horton-Salway
Independent Academic Consultant
Derbyshire, UK

Alison Davies
Independent Academic Consultant
Hertfordshire, UK

The Language of Mental Health
ISBN 978-3-030-09383-9 ISBN 978-3-319-76026-1 (eBook)
https://doi.org/10.1007/978-3-319-76026-1

Softcover re-print of the Hardcover 1st edition 2018

Cover credit: Diane Randell/Alamy Stock Photo

Printed on acid-free paper

This Palgrave Macmillan imprint is published by Springer Nature
The registered company is Springer International Publishing AG
The registered company address is: Gewerbestrasse 11, 6330 Cham, Switzerland

Preface

This volume is the third book in The Language of Mental Health book series (Eds. Michelle O'Reilly and Jessica N. Lester). We trace the discourse of Attention Deficit Hyperactivity Disorder (ADHD) across a range of perspectives to critically examine how its meaning has been constructed through the discourse of various standpoints, science, media, parents and personal experience. This will contribute to a growing area of studies that consider how mental health categories are constructed through discourse and will appeal to a wide readership, from health professionals, therapists and academics to social support organisations that have an interest in ADHD, and educationalists who work with children and adults who have special needs. We anticipate that this book will be a resource for postgraduate students with an interest in discourse analysis and also for those working on mental health projects. Although the book is primarily aimed at an academic and professional readership, the lay public have an interest in ADHD because of the debate about its meaning and legitimacy and the history of struggle for medical recognition.

The discursive approach used in this book is a distinctive and different approach to language, focusing on how the meanings and definitions of both the social and the natural worlds are defined and constructed through discourse and social practices. To this end, we aim to explore how science and medicine has defined ADHD in a variety of ways, how the media have taken up different ideas and represented them to the public as a controversy, and how families and individuals are affected by negative and stigmatising representations and definitions of ADHD and how they resist them. We conclude by analysing accounts of personal experience that help us to understand more about the consequences of ADHD, the difficulties arising from the unmet needs of children and adults, and the potential for more empowering, transformative and enabling narratives of lives and selves.

The themes arising from the ADHD debate are identified early in the book and are thereafter picked up as threads that run through all of the chapters. These are, the constructive power of discourse and culture, the social identities that support different representations of ADHD, the significance of gender in the meaning of ADHD, and the power of discourse as a form of social resistance. The processes we will describe in this book have an application to a wider context than ADHD discourse. We have taken the view that contested mental health conditions share common threads and an analysis of discourse can help us to understand how they have emerged, how they rely on cultural definition for their meaning, and how this has social consequences. We explore the following:

- How medical and mental health categories are defined in both science and lay discourse, and how this draws on cultural representations.
- How social identities that are all too often negative or stigmatic are constructed alongside mental health categories in discourse.
- How the meanings of categories such as ADHD can be defined through gendering.
- How the discourse of mental health is constructed through negative stereotypes of impairment that are both taken up and resisted in discourse.

ADHD as a mental health category has been shaped by a long history of controversy that allows us to explore more closely the 'battles over truth' that have produced its meaning in variable ways. This book aims to map out some of the cultural issues arising from the discourse of ADHD, and we put the case that people who are affected by mental health categories require greater public and professional understanding of how those categories have come about and how they have social consequences.

Derbyshire, UK — Mary Horton-Salway
Hertfordshire, UK — Alison Davies

Acknowledgements

In various parts of this book, we have referred to extracts from interviews with people who took part in research interviews. For these valuable accounts of personal experience and the opportunity to do this research, the authors would like to thank the following people. Parents of children with ADHD took part in Alison Davies's doctoral research, which was funded by *The Open University*. As participants in scholarly research, they kindly allowed anonymised extracts of interviews to be used in publications (see Chapters 4 and 5). We are also grateful to the women who shared their personal experiences of ADHD as part of a *British Academy*-funded research study hosted by *The Open University*. Without the people who generously gave their time to help us understand more about their personal worlds, we would be much less able to understand what ADHD means from their point of view. We are also grateful to Dr. Lindsay O'Dell of *The Open University* for her support and permission to include extracts of interview data from this study in Chapter 6 discussions.

During the process of writing this book, we have had some invaluable advice and critical feedback on earlier drafts of chapters. For this, we thank Associate Professor Rachael Gabriel, Dr. Andrea Garner,

Dr. Jessica Lester, Dr. Lindsay O'Dell, and Professor Adam Rafalovich. They have been generous with their time and expertise and provided constructive comments. We hope we have improved our writing because of this, but we acknowledge that any remaining errors are entirely our own.

Contents

Abbreviations

ADD	Attention Deficit Disorder
ADHD	Attention Deficit Hyperactivity Disorder
APA	American Psychiatric Association
BA	British Academy
BPS	British Psychological Society
CDP	Critical Discursive Psychology
DP	Discursive Psychology
DSM	Diagnostic and Statistical Manual of Mental Disorders
EBM	Evidence-Based Medicine
ECF	Extreme Case Formulations
GP	General Practitioner
ICD	International Classification of Diseases
MBD	Minimal Brain Dysfunction/Damage
ME	Myalgic Encephalomyelitis
MRC	Medical Research Council
MRI	Magnetic Resonance Imaging
NHS	The National Health Service
NICE	The National Institute for Health and Care Excellence (formerly The National Institute for Clinical Excellence)

NSPCC	The National Society for the Protection of Cruelty to Children
PET	Positron-Emission Tomography
SSK	Sociology of Scientific Knowledge

List of Figures

1
Introduction

Mary Horton-Salway and Alison Davies

Attention Deficit Hyperactivity Disorder (ADHD) has been one of the most debated medical categories affecting children in different parts of the globe. Increasingly this is recognised as a lifelong disorder that can continue into adulthood, a diagnosis that has been reflected by the incorporation of adult criteria into the American Psychiatric Association's *Diagnostic and Statistical Manual of Mental Disorders*, DSM 5 (APA 2013). The diagnosis and medical treatment of ADHD for both children and adults is rising and this is based on the view that ADHD has a biological, neurodevelopmental, genetic basis and, in the UK, it is typically identified by educational and health practitioners who refer to guidelines from the *National Institute of Clinical Excellence* on three areas of behavioural functioning: impulsivity, hyperactivity and inattention (NICE 2009).

Despite the classification of ADHD as a mental health category, there has been no absolute consensus historically and even currently about its status as a health condition, its meaning and causes which continue to be discussed, researched and debated by scientists and health practitioners, educationalists, multi-media and by members of the public. There have been claims, counterclaims and contributions to knowledge

M. Horton-Salway and A. Davies, *The Discourse of ADHD*,
The Language of Mental Health, https://doi.org/10.1007/978-3-319-76026-1_1

that have spanned over a century, ranging across perspectives of genetics and the biological sciences, to the psychological, social, educational and health sciences. Perspectives on ADHD and its previous labels have been followed up, summarised and debated in the media and further discussed by the public, families and individuals who are personally affected. This has given rise to a range of discourses about ADHD, constructed and contested through a long and chequered history that informs current understanding.

Science, Fact Construction and 'Ships in Bottles'

To give this a wider context, allow us to unpack one of the theoretical principles informing the analysis in this book. The meaning of any medical category is as much a product of social activity and culture as it is a scientific discovery. According to sociologists who study the production of scientific knowledge, any scientific fact (even an apparently uncontroversial one) can be understood as the product of social constructive practices. This process of fact construction has been demonstrated in studies of the discourse and practices of scientists. For example, Woolgar (1988) described how science came to be regarded as a superior form of knowledge that is set apart from other forms of knowledge and distinguished as a means of discovering objective truths. In the natural sciences essentialists assumed that 'scientific knowledge is determined by the actual nature of the physical world' which is out there waiting to be identified (Woolgar 1988: 27). The scientific method of discovery was developed to define science as a neutral and objective process and a superior and reliable form of positivist enquiry. This, they argued, resulted in scientists being able to describe and represent the nature of the real world of objects, events and phenomena. However, a new wave of relativist philosophers and sociologists of scientific knowledge (SSK) challenged these realist and essentialist views of the world and argued that representations of reality are underpinned by culture and produced through social practices. The task that SSK set for itself was to study and describe how scientific facts were constructed in the discourse and practices of scientists. This approach has queried positivist views of science that treat scientific discovery as a process of describing a reality that exists prior to scientists' representations.

In his seminal work, *Science the Very Idea*, Woolgar (1988: 32) pointed out that for any phenomenon it is 'always possible to nominate an alternative to any specific proposed meaning'. Elaborations of meaning will always refer back to some other meaning that cannot be fully explained without resorting to a further representation and so on. Woolgar contended that where science is concerned, we accept the status of its facts and representations because science has itself convinced us that its models and practices are reliable. As he put this; 'the perception of reliability is a consequence of its claimed superiority, not a cause' (Woolgar 1988: 32). Phenomenologist Merleau-Ponty also regarded classical science as 'a form of perception which loses sight of its origins and believes itself complete' (Merleau-Ponty 1945/1962). In a circular manner, the idea of science as an objective activity is itself dependent on perceptions that are derived from an ideological framework that supports the idea of positivist science and objective facts (Woolgar 1988). Where error or anomalies might arise in scientific activity and findings, these can be put down to 'technical difficulties' or to problems in the work of individual scientists so that these contingencies do not threaten the robustness of science as a whole (Gilbert and Mulkay 1984).

Woolgar's argument rests on the relativist philosophy criticising the underlying idea that *any* form of representation could be a reflection of a prior existing reality or an objective truth. Social constructionism is a way to explain the social processes that are involved in the construction of science facts and also the process of scientific change, such as the paradigm changes described by Thomas Kuhn (1962/1970). For example, Woolgar described the process of scientific change in the representation of 'unusual rapidly pulsating radio sources' that later became known as 'pulsars'. He describes how this 'discovery' was published in 1968 in *Nature* by Bell and colleagues at Cambridge University in the UK and, at the time of writing his thesis, Woolgar (1988: 64–65) traced the development of this discovery through its 'five separate incarnations', including 'unusual trace', 'interference' extra-terrestrial activity 'little green men', and a 'pulsating radio source'. Since naming the discovery as a 'pulsar', this was then defined as a 'white dwarf star', and became re-defined as a 'a rotating neutra star', a 'neutron star with a satellite', and 'the plasmic interaction between binary neutron stars' and so on. Woolgar went on to describe how the existence and character of the discovery had depended, not only on a social network of scientists, but also the culture of science for its meaning. The term 'discovery' implied that something was there and had now been found and named, but Woolgar contends that it was not possible to demonstrate this without representations that depend on other representations, and so on, for their meaning. In other words, to be represented in the first place, an object or phenomenon relies on a range of prior 'discoveries' and the current state of scientific knowledge that is treated as fact. Collins (1985) had earlier described such facts as appearing 'like a ship in a bottle'. It is difficult to unpack the processes of construction that built such a ship because it looks as if it has always been there. The existence of pulsars as a named phenomenon (a 'ship in a bottle') came into being through processes of construction that included observation, theorising, representation, re-presentation and fact construction within the framework and assumptions of positivist science. Woolgar's approach to understanding this process was to turn to the discourse and rhetoric of science to describe in detail how scientific discourse 'constitutes the nature of the object it claims to be merely reporting' (Woolgar 1988: 81).

The Context of Health and Illness

In a health context, a social constructionist analysis can help us to deconstruct the 'ships in bottles' of medically recognised categories. For example, coronary heart disease did not appear in official statistics as a cause of death until the 1920s and, as Alan Radley (1994) has observed, the discovery of degeneration in coronary arteries did not by itself make for a medical explanation. Degeneration was attributed to causes that were partly cumulative dietary, physical and lifestyle risk factors and these were theorised as factors having a specific link to congestion of the coronary arteries. Such theories about the part played by lifestyle risks have been further backed up by statistical epidemiological research and the significance of those findings for heart disease are continually being amended, updated, contested and argued about to this day. However, Radley pointed out how the discovery of degeneration in the coronary arteries had to be combined with explanatory theories about lifestyle risk factors to provide the specific diagnosis of coronary heart disease and a warrant for medical interventions. These interventions were pharmaceutical and increasingly social and psychological as discoveries were made about the relationship of lifestyles, diet and environment. How people experience and manage heart disease is dependent on these ideas and facts for its meaning. Congestive heart disease has now become like a 'ship in a bottle' that depends on a history of theory and positivist science 'discoveries' and validates medical intervention in lifestyles. We mostly take the causes of congestive heart disease for granted as objective truth. Lifestyle choices, diet and the details of public health policy are themselves an ongoing issue of contention, but congestive heart disease remains a medical fact.

Despite the solid appearance of medical facts as having an independent existence, prior to scientist's theories and representations, many phenomena that we know as health conditions only make sense within certain social and cultural contexts (see also Foucault 1973). The boundaries between definitions of disease and normal or social phenomena are far from clear or fixed. Many categories that have been afforded the label of disease might also have been interpreted as ageing. For example, the treatment of the menopause as a 'deficiency disease', rather than a natural stage of a woman's life, made sense not simply because a reduction of oestrogen in women after the menopause had been identified as a physiological fact. As Woolgar argued, there are always alternatives to any specific proposed meaning. The fact of a reduction in oestrogen was therefore not, by itself, 'enough to make this variation into a disease' (Radley 1994: 29). Radley argued that the case for oestrogen as a 'therapy' to correct a deficiency was based on a number of things. Oestrogen was considered effective in helping prevent deterioration of bones and congestion of arteries in older women, but the advantages of the 'therapy' were also grounded in currently held cultural ideas about the maintenance of youthful attractiveness, social worth and women's psychological well-being. The 'treatment' of menopause as a 'deficiency disease' was introduced despite some significant concerns about long term health risks of the 'therapy'. The clinical risks might easily have been represented as at least as great as the advantages for bone and artery health and for some women they were even greater. Making a case for oestrogen therapy was not the only clinical conclusion that could have been made and the deciding factor in the choice to medicate or not to medicate was, at the very least, a balancing act that was influenced by the social and psychological 'benefits' of the treatment as well as the relative risks to health.

The Social and Psychological Worlds as Medical Business

In addition to the power of natural science to provide representations of reality as fact, these examples of oestrogen 'therapy' and coronary heart disease indicate something of the potential power of the 'clinical-gaze' to define ever wider aspects of the social and psychological world as medical business (Foucault 1973). The origins of medical interest in the social and psychological world has evolved partly with the development of the social, psychological and health sciences that now inform the application of the biopsychosocial model in medicine.

The term biopsychosocial has been attributed to Grinker who introduced it in 1954 to psychiatry 'to emphasize the biologic against psychoanalytic orthodoxy' (in Alvarez et al. 2012: 173). George Engel (1977, 1980) later identified a crisis in medicine which he attributed to medicine's 'adherence to a model of disease no longer adequate for the scientific tasks and social responsibilities of either medicine or psychiatry' (Engel 1977: 589). This so called outmoded model was a traditional 'biomedical model' with its emphasis on the biological and natural sciences and the idea of measurable physical causal variables. This model of reductionist science was used 'by medical scientists for the study of disease' (ibid.: 589). When applied to the study of disease in human beings it implied a philosophy of mind-body dualism in which the body was separate from the mind (ibid.: 591). Not only does this assume that physiological variables can be explained by biology but also that behavioural ones can. Engel also described a simultaneous crisis in psychiatry as a 'question of whether the categories of human distress with which it is concerned are properly considered "disease"... and whether exercise of the traditional authority of the physician [applying the biomedical model] is appropriate for their help functions.' Paradoxically, the issue for physicians was the extent to which they needed to 'be concerned with psychosocial issues which lie outside medicine's responsibility and authority.' (1977: 589–590). Engel's original contention was that psychiatry had struggled to 'clarify its status within the mainstream of medicine... if indeed it belongs in medicine at all', meaning that they were not really applying the scientific biomedical model (ibid.: 591). Engel quoted one 'critical psychiatrist' (Ludwig 1975, cited in Engel 1977) as saying "psychiatry has become a hodgepodge of unscientific opinions, assorted philosophies and 'schools of thought', mixed metaphors, role diffusion, propaganda, and politicking for 'mental health' and other esoteric goals" (cited in Engel 1977: 589) and it appears that factions were taking up oppositional positions about the proper place of psychiatry in relation to medicine. One solution was to 'exclude psychiatry from the field of medicine, while the other would adhere strictly to the "medical model"...' (1977: 590). The medical model, Ludwig argued, was based on the premise that "sufficient deviation from normal represents *disease*, that disease is due to known or unknown natural causes, and that elimination of these causes will result in cure or improvement..." (cited in Engel 1977: 590, with Ludwig's italics). An article in *Psychiatric News* (19 August cited in Read 2005: 596–597) expressing concern at 'the over-medicalization of mental disorders and the over-use of medications' by psychiatrists, suggests that since then there had been an increased dependence on a 'quick fix' of medication treatment along with a reduction in psychotherapy. So it seems that the second solution described by Engel, that psychiatrists adhering to the biomedical model appears to have overcome dissenting voices that might have otherwise taken a different route. Writing in *The Psychologist*, John Read (2005) applauded the 'dissident viewpoint' expressed by the, then, president of the *American Psychiatric Association* who had the courage to challenge a model that made his profession appear to be 'mere pill pushers and employees of the pharmaceutical industry' (*APA*, cited in Read 2005: 596).

Meanwhile, mainstream medicine struggled to introduce and apply a more complex and inclusive model that was less reductionist and included psychological and social aspects of health. Ogden (2000: 4–5) describes how developments in health psychology based on Engel's biopsychosocial model inform health practice today. Decades prior to that, this model was officially adopted as a model to guide general practice by the Royal College of General Practitioners in the UK (1972). Its holistic systemic perspective focuses on understanding the biological causes of disease, but also considering the cognitive, emotional and behavioural aspects of health, and the social norms, values, expectations and demographics of health that influence outcomes. In practice this translates as practitioners listening to their patients and trying to understand the social and psychological context of illness. This also translates as a more intrusive 'medical gaze' than ever before and, although it can be interpreted as benign, it warrants greater authority to intervene in people's lives. In practice though, if you are a time pressed health practitioner, who needs to provide treatment based on reductionist 'evidence-based' physiological medicine as well as weighing up the relevance of psychosocial concerns and contributory factors, the biopsychosocial model is far from easy to apply or compatible with workloads. In one example of cardiac care in the US, Herman (cited in Soltile 2005: 401) observed the 'physician's lament about feeling either inadequately prepared or time-deprived to provide competent psychosocial care'. He noted that physicians admitted not applying the biopsychosocial model to all of the patients who consulted them at a clinic and observed that referrals to multidisciplinary rehabilitation teams was only between 10 and 20% across the US, with girls, women and older people less likely to be referred (Soltile 2005: 400). These matters prompted Soltile to ask the question; how far had medicine been successful in integrating the psychosocial into the biomedical model? This question was echoed in an article by Biderman et al. (2005) in the same year. Simultaneously, according to Read (2005: 596–567) psychiatrists have embraced a 'bio-bio-bio model' retreating into the arms of the pharmaceutical industry. He wondered 'what happened to the 'psycho' and the 'social' in explanations of mental illness.' Perhaps, he pointed out, 'the supposed integration of perspectives implied by the term 'bio-psycho-social' model since the 1970s is more illusion than reality'. Not integration at all, he claims, but 'a colonisation of the psychological and the social by the biological' in a way that reduces social and environmental influences to mere triggers 'of an underlying genetic time bomb'. This, he contends, fails to deal with the wider contextual impacts on health.

Shaping the Meaning of Medical Conditions

The two models of medicine described above, the biomedical and the biopsychosocial, are both theoretical frameworks for explaining phenomena and they shape the meanings of medical conditions; both facts and treatments are derived from within these theoretical frameworks. Even at the level of laboratory science, we note Woolgar's and Gilbert and Mulkay's contentions that the representations of natural scientists are not as objective as some might think. Scientists in laboratories construct their discoveries using the language, discourse and current understandings of their time and place and in the specific ideological discourse of an objective positivist science (Gilbert and Mulkay 1984). Atkinson (1995: 61), for example, demonstrated that 'there is no agreement as to a stable world of phenomena' but medical students are taught to 'see' and interpret what is under the microscope in laboratory training. Even the apparently solid entities seen under microscopes have no independent meaning outside the interpretative frameworks used to define them.

As studies arising from SSK have demonstrated, science is as much a socio-political activity as anything else. A wide range of knowledge disciplines, including the social and health sciences have now adopted a broadly social constructionist approach that is based on the philosophical ideas of Berger and Luckmann (1966/1971). Should these be seen as mere philosophical wrangles and esoteric concerns or do they have a relevance to the everyday lives of health professionals, and people who are affected by conditions such as ADHD? We contend that mental health categories such as ADHD are constructed and understood through the lens of shared culture and through the state of current taken for granted forms of knowledge about science, medicine and what it is to be human. This knowledge can be seen as true, for all intents and purposes, for the present, but constantly in a process of construction, contestation and flux. Since the dynamic forces of construction and process are less visible to us than the finished product of the 'ship in the bottle', we have set our investigation of perspectives on ADHD within that fluid and ever changing context of socially constructed ideas, theories, facts, explanatory discourses and assumptions about human beings, in order to make these more visible.

The aim of this book is to examine how ADHD was, and continues to be, constructed as a category and how discourse about it circulates in knowledge networks in the form of 'translations' (Latour 1989). This does not imply that we are sceptical about the existence and significance of ADHD as a category, or that we are sceptical about the existence of science knowledge or reality for that matter. Current knowledge, what is true for now, is the reality that impacts upon our lives after all. The fact that ADHD is a recognised mental health category within our current systems of classification is *precisely* the phenomenon of interest and we want to see how this 'ship in a bottle' was built and how it is now a fact (albeit a dynamic and controversial one) that affects the lives of many.

Our Approach

To unpick the threads of discourse from a variety of contexts, we will examine both historical and current perspectives on ADHD. We begin by looking at how science, medicine and psychiatry have defined ADHD as a mental health category (in Chapter 2) and then move on to describe how alternative ideas have been taken up by the media, how they are represented and debated (in Chapter 3). We will unpack the matters arising from ADHD discourse produced in the media and how that positions parents, children and adults with ADHD. The parents' perspective is an important aspect of this, so we describe their experiences of having children with ADHD and see how they take up different meanings and resist stereotypes (in Chapters 4 and 5). Finally, but not least important, we consider the personal experience of ADHD through studies of childhood, adolescence and transitions to adulthood, including the voices of women as a more 'invisible' group in relation to ADHD (in Chapter 6). Our chapters draw on a range of original research that we have undertaken and we discuss a range of literature that represents the history, the media debate, parents' viewpoints and personal experience.

Our approach is language based and informed by social constructionist philosophy about the constructed nature of knowledge and the sociology of scientific knowledge (as discussed above), the genealogical approach of Michel Foucault and topics in social psychology such as categorisation, social identities and gendering. Using an analytic approach that focuses on both the detail of interaction and the wider context of discourse, we apply a critical discursive psychology rationale to examine the role that discourse has played and continues to play in constructing our everyday knowledge of ADHD, how individuals are identified and positioned within that discourse and how they respond to that. In this way, we aim to unpack issues and concerns of participants in the discourse of ADHD and map some of the matters arising and social consequences.

We will argue that the category of ADHD, as with all mental health categories, is not a neutral or independent label which has been consistently applied to a pre-existing disorder (see also Rafalovich 2004/2008). Mental health categories have been produced alongside 'cultural and historical practices that shaped the very meaning of mental health' (O'Reilly and Lester 2016: 5). Although our focus is on ADHD, this social constructionist perspective is also applicable to a wider range of general and mental health conditions, although the process of construction might appear more obvious for those with a history of controversy, such as ME or ADHD (Horton-Salway 1998, 2011, 2012). Controversial histories provide a window on the discourse of medical categories especially where the status of both expert and experiential knowledge is much debated (Horton-Salway 2001, 2002, 2004). These discourses have a bearing on social identities, perspectives on normality and pathology, definitions of mental and physical illness, disease and cultural understandings of mind, body and disability. An analysis of such discourses is a way to unpack the constructive processes that have produced ADHD and how this has impacted upon the lives and selves of people who are the subjects of this discourse. We focus on how the facts of ADHD are constructed in theory, media and lay discourse and how a mental health category such as ADHD can rely on various forms of cultural representation for its meaning, such as the construction of social identities and forms of gendering that can be both obvious and subtle.

Social Constructionism and Mental Health Categories

This book contributes to a growing body of work which adopts a broadly social constructionist approach to mental health (see O'Reilly and Lester 2015, 2016; Harper 1995, 2013). ADHD is recognised as a mental health category by the *Diagnostic and Statistical Manual of Mental Disorders* (APA 2013). However, the social constructionist approach takes the view that mental health categories do not have an objective, independent, prior existence. As discussed above, this is a relativist perspective on reality that takes the view that facts are embedded in the historical contexts and discursive practices within which they are produced (Berger and Luckmann 1966/1971). Four assumptions of this perspective were identified by Kenneth Gergen (cited in O'Reilly and Lester 2015: xiv) and are summarised here:

1. That we should take up a position of scepticism in relation to forms of knowledge.
2. That knowledge is situated in cultural, social and historical contexts.
3. That knowledge is produced and sustained by social processes.
4. Descriptions of phenomena are never neutral, but are examples of social action which constitute certain ways of being.

Why Discourse Analysis?

The turn to the study of language and discourse in social science is underpinned by changes in philosophical thought, including a turn to pragmatics in linguistics and social constructionism. In linguistics this was a move towards language as a form of social action rather than treating language as simply reflecting reality (Austin 1962). All forms of discourse analysis share the assumption that discourse is a form of social action and assume that when we describe the world, we also constitute and construct its meaning. Some focus on identifying the broadly defined 'discourses' or explanatory 'repertoires' that are used to make meaning whilst others focus on normative features of conversation and social interactions to see how meanings are negotiated in those contexts (Burr 2003; Edwards and Potter 1992; Potter and Wetherell 1987; Willig 2013). Foucault used the term 'discourse' to refer to all forms of signification, representation, meaning-making, cultural ideas and social practices. Social practices, such as day-to-day interactions, the processes of scientific classification, institutional activities, all social phenomena, theoretical ideas and (medical) categories, are seen as constructed. Knowledge systems in current or historical time and place are regarded as 'regimes of truth' (Foucault 2006). Those who live within their meaning systems are captured by them because dominant forms of truth are largely taken for granted and embedded in the institutional forms of governance that are in place at the time and also because they recognise themselves as the subjects of discourse. This is largely consensual, as are the forms of 'self-governance' that induce the take up of cultural and moral imperatives or self-improvement technologies. These ideas about how discourse functions are some of the influences that underpin the turn to language and discourse in the social sciences and they inform our analytic approach in this book. However they have been relatively 'underexplored' within mental health contexts (O'Reilly and Lester 2015: xiii) although they are especially suitable for the study of lay discourse about mental health (Smith 1978) and also for the study of discourse in mental health contexts (Harper 1995).

A discursive form of psychology is also highly relevant to understanding how social identities are constructed alongside the discourse of ADHD. Rather than taking psychological and social processes as causal factors that contribute to ADHD, discursive psychology is concerned with how the meaning of 'psychological' and 'social' categories are constructed in discourse about ADHD and how they are drawn on to build explanatory accounts. The reasons for this will be apparent in the later chapters of this book as we analyse how biological, psychological and social forms of reasoning contribute to producing the category of ADHD as an epiphenomenon.

Background on Discursive Psychology

Discursive psychology emerged in the mid-to-late 1980s as a critique of cognitivism (Edwards 1997; Edwards and Potter 1992; Wetherell 2007). Cognitivism is a mainstream version of psychology that has its focus on the psychology of internal mental processes, treating language as representing inner thoughts, ideas, attributions and emotions, or reflecting an external reality that pre-exists our description of it. Discursive psychology has an alternative focus on the actions performed by discourse about such categories such as memory, personality, perception or emotion (Edwards 1997). Key figures in discursive psychology's challenge to the cognitivist perspective included Potter and Wetherell (1987), who applied discourse analysis to social psychology topics such as social identities and Edwards and Potter (1992, 1993), who applied discourse methods to a variety of topics in cognitive psychology such as memory, causal attribution and fact constructing. Antaki and Widdicombe (1998) and Billig (1996) also analysed how people reason and argue and Billig et al. (1988) examined the kinds of ideological dilemmas that people encounter when they are using discourse and how they work to resolve them, maintaining their version as credible.

Rather than studying internal cognitions or mental states discursive psychology is concerned with *how* constructions of mental states are produced in talk. We are interested in *how* people describe themselves, others and events, how they attribute cause or blame, how they account for their actions and how they defend themselves or argue points of view. It is in the context of using language and discourse that individuals negotiate and formulate social and psychological concerns like mental states, beliefs, social identities, social categorisation and attribution of causes (Widdicombe and Wooffitt 1995). The construction of social identity is taken to be discursive and language use is thoroughly implicated in the construction of moral psychological selves. Speakers, for example, are concerned to present a 'credible and creditable moral position' (Burr 2003: 135) so as a consequence their management of personal accountability and identity is embedded in their descriptions of actions and events (Potter 1996; Hepburn and Wiggins 2007; Burr 2003; Horton-Salway 2001; Widdicombe and Wooffitt 1995; Edwards and Potter 1992). This is why discursive psychology is a relevant and useful approach to explore the way individuals negotiate their understanding of ADHD. As discussed above, ADHD is a somewhat controversial category that has historically been subject to a range of critical attention. Therefore there is much at stake for science, medical practice, the media and the people who are personally affected by ADHD.

Discursive psychology is influenced by theories located within disciplines including sociology (Berger and Luckmann 1966; Garfinkel 1967; Goffman 1959, 1961, 1963), semiology (Barthes 1964), anthropology (Geertz 1973), linguistics (Austin 1962) and philosophy (Wittgenstein 1980). This multi-various background accounts for a range of different perspectives within discursive psychology that have their emphasis on micro or macro contexts or a blend of the two. Micro approaches to discourse, which include ethnomethodology and conversation analysis originate in the work of Garfinkel (1967) and Harvey Sacks (1995) and they both focus on the 'nuts and bolts' of social interactions, how people make sense of one another's talk in such contexts. This has its focus on the organisation of talk (Heritage 1984; Widdicombe and Wooffitt 1995; Potter and Wetherell 1987) and studies how meaning is accomplished through the sequence of conversational turns, as, for example, in 'troubles-talk' (Jefferson 1988). This is a data driven method focusing on what participants make of their turn by turn interactions and it has been used to explore (among others) the process of mental health encounters between professionals and patients to examine how diagnoses are done and how mental health problems are constructed in the process (see Parker and O'Reilly 2012; Kiyimba 2015; Thompson and McCabe 2016).

Taking a wider focus, the 'macro approach' in discursive psychology, focuses on the discourse of wider cultural and historical contexts. This is influenced by the post-structuralist perspective with its focus on culture, social practices, social relations and institutionalised practices. According to relativist philosophy, discourses and practices within any historical period regulate what can be meaningfully said or known. For example, mental health disorders were produced by dominant institutions such as the church, the law and, most recently, medicine (see Foucault 2003, 2006). Mental illness was variously 'known' within different regimes of truth as evil spirits, a failure of morality, within a psychological discourse as poor maternal attachment and within a biomedical discourse as biochemical imbalance (Lemma 1996). A Foucauldian understanding is that discourse constructs historically and culturally specific forms of knowledge such as science, medicine and psychiatry and these invite individuals to think about themselves and others in particular ways as subjects. As both Willig (2013) and Burr (2003) indicate, within medical discourse, the subject positions of 'patient' and 'medical practitioner' become available, and are legitimate leading to medical treatment that is regulatory but benign. In the study of mental health, the Foucauldian approach draws attention to the circulation of dominant discourses: Medical categories are embedded in 'regimes of truth' and subjects are discursively 'captured' by them (Strong and Sesma-Vazquez 2015; Bailey 2014).

An understanding of the historicising discourses around ADHD is the aim of Chapter 2 of this book, shedding light on how individuals are positioned within certain discourses and how, these both legitimise and de-legitimise the regulatory practices in medicine and psychiatry. This also identifies the discursive resources that people draw upon in talking about ADHD, in taking up social identities as subject positions in discourse, and also in some cases, by attempting to avoid 'discursive capture' by resisting negative positioning (Strong and Sesma-Vazquez 2015: xxiii).

A Blended Approach

We adopt a blended approach to the discourses surrounding ADHD that incorporates both micro and macro analysis. This approach was promoted by Wetherell (1998, 2007) and is a growing approach used in critical discursive psychology analyses of mental health (Brownlow and Lamont-Mills 2015; Davies and Horton-Salway 2016;

Horton-Salway and Davies 2015). We also refer to a developing area of mental health research which shifts the emphasis away from biomedical models of explaining mental conditions to one which emphasises the constitutive effect of interpersonal and socio-cultural practices. However, the biomedical and biopsychosocial models of medicine, discussed above, are both part of the meaning-making phenomena that have given rise to ADHD as a medical category and they have also both contributed to its controversial status. Therefore we retain a position of agnosticism in relation to theorisations of ADHD. We do, however, regard biomedical reasoning and biopsychosocial reasoning as discourse practices rather than guiding models (see also Alvarez et al. 2012). In other words, we are interested in how biological, psychological and social explanations are used in defining and explaining categories like ADHD (Horton-Salway 2002) and how these categories are also drawn on by both professional and lay people (Horton-Salway 2004).

Key Analytic Concepts

Bringing together the wider (macro) and narrower (micro) approaches to discourse analysis allows us to examine the historicising discourses that have defined dominant ideas and truths and also to identify the subjects that have been produced by these discourses. However, our analysis also allows for a narrower lens to examine how individuals construct facts and credible identities for themselves and others. They do so by drawing on available social and cultural meanings therefore we refer to the combined theoretical underpinnings described above, and specifically to some key analytic concepts derived from Foucault's genealogical approach and from critical discursive psychology.

Foucault placed his emphasis on the term 'discourse' to include all forms of signification that represent and construct reality and he was concerned with the relationship between such discourse, the production of knowledge and power. In discursive psychology, however, we also use the term 'interpretative repertoire' to describe how people actively engage with the stock of shared cultural understandings and forms of language, expression, terms, metaphors, ways of explaining and representing reality that have common social currency and circulate (cf. Gilbert and Mulkay 1984; Potter and Wetherell 1987). Foucauldian and critical discursive psychology approaches each draw on the idea that individuals are defined by discourse and social practices. For Foucault this happens when we are recognised or recognise ourselves within a discourse and by this process we literally become subject to it. For discursive psychology it is also the case that people actively take up or resist subject positions or they attribute such positions to other people in the process of their interactions or textual representations. This is an active process of negotiation and contestation and we are particularly interested in how resistance is accomplished in their use of repertoires and subject positions.

We begin our analysis by examining the historicising discourse of science on ADHD (Chapter 2), and then we turn to the representations of ADHD in the media (Chapter 3), the representations of parents who have children with ADHD (Chapters 4 and 5) and the accounts of individuals who have personal experience of ADHD (Chapter 6). We pay attention to the discourse resources they use (for example what kind of interpretative repertoires and subject positions are drawn on) and also discourse practices (how they use interpretative repertoires and subject positions). The former permits an understanding of *what kind of representation of reality is constructed* and the latter permits an understanding of *to what effect*.

Our approach is underpinned by the assumption that individuals are not only produced by discourse but they are also producers of discourse (Burr 2003; Potter and Wetherell 1987). In this sense, individuals are acknowledged to have agency despite the powerful nature of dominant discourses and knowledge forms such as science, medicine and psychiatry; or indeed the discourses that circulate in the media, including social media. We acknowledge the active role taken by individuals in taking up or resisting the defining and positioning effects of dominant discourses. We aim to explore the often taken-for-granted discursive practices that have constructed ADHD as a 'ship in a bottle' and to uncover some of the ways that science, the media, and members of the public have contributed to the different versions of ADHD that circulate (Fig. 1.1).

The themes and issues of this book are picked up as threads that weave through the discourse of ADHD. These are taken up in a discussion of chapter topics that focus on different perspectives on ADHD. Themes are:

1. The socially and discursively constructed nature of ADHD
2. The social identities embedded in different representations of ADHD
3. Gendering as an integral part of the way that ADHD is understood
4. Resistance as a response to negative stereotypes

Fig. 1.1 Key themes of the book

The Structure of the Book

We tell the story of ADHD through our analysis of discourse in the areas of science, the popular media, the family, and from the point of view of personal experience. This volume is by no means comprehensive and does not, for example, represent the perspectives of health or education practitioners. These are addressed elsewhere, for example in Rafalovich (2004/2008) who provided an account of clinicians as mediators of ADHD and how ADHD is framed by teachers in the classroom; Bailey (2014) also studied ADHD in an educational context and Bradley and Butler (2015), examined the detailed interactions of a cognitive behavioural therapy programme for children with a diagnosis of ADHD. O'Reilly et al. (2017) have also used conversation analysis to examine the practitioner-family interactions in an initial assessment for autism spectrum disorder indicating the ways that mental health pathologies are constituted in a medical context.

Chapter 2: Alison Davies charts the historical development of ADHD as a category and considers how changing and competing scientific, psychological and socio-environmental explanations have contributed to its controversial legacy. By adopting a historical framework, Davies shows that understandings of ADHD as a disorder have been imbued with a moral discourse that continues to inform current discourse. She identifies some of the key issues and debates that have emerged from this historical background and considers how the identities of individuals affected by ADHD are morally positioned within alternative explanations of ADHD that are biological, psychological or social. Davies returns to the themes of the book and the debates arising from the historical perspective in this chapter, indicating how the key concepts of discursive psychology, interpretative repertoires and subject positions, can be applied to analyse the historicised discourse of ADHD.

Chapter 3: Mary Horton-Salway discusses the role of media discourse in representing ADHD and maps out some relevant research on ADHD in the media. The chapter discusses how the media frame the ADHD debate as a polemic, how representations of ADHD are produced and how they are gendered to produce stereotypes. The public engage with this material as both consumers and through feedback loops as producers of discourse on ADHD. Of particular interest is the increase in public consumption of science knowledge and healthcare information via print, audio-visual and digital media. From this mass of information, how can the public tell what is accurate? This is discussed in relation to the 'newsworthiness' of stories, the reporting of 'breakthrough science' and the decline in the authority of science and medicine.

Chapter 4: This chapter turns to the discourse of parents as both consumers and producers ADHD discourse. Alison Davies examines first the perspective of mothers examining how they are positioned by dominant discourses of ADHD and parenting. She presents her original research on the experiences of mothers who have a child with ADHD to show how they make sense of ADHD when they talk about their children and family lives. In the family context, the identities of children, mothers and fathers (and sometimes extended family members and ancestors) are at stake when talking about the experience of ADHD. Davies describes how mothers manage and resist negative stereotypes of their children and of themselves as parents. The chapter is situated within wider debates about parenting, such as those addressing issues of maternal responsibility and gendered caregiving. The tensions between discourses constituting 'mother-blame' or mothers as the 'expert parent' responsible for child-care and health are explored in this chapter.

Chapter 5: This chapter turns to the experience of fathers who appear far less frequently within parenting literature and are marginalised by much of the literature relating to ADHD. Davies examines how fathers are positioned differently within the discourses of parenting and ADHD and how they represent themselves as good fathers in a supportive role. The theme of gendering continues through this chapter in the way that fathers construct their own identities in relation to their sons with ADHD in terms of masculinity. The discussions in this chapter present a novel analysis of a father's point of view that is rarely acknowledged in ADHD discourse.

Chapter 6: This chapter begins from the standpoint that personal experience accounts of mental health issues are important. For those who have personal experience of ADHD it is important that their voices are heard. Since ADHD has emerged as a mental health category that affects both children and adults, Mary Horton-Salway examines research on children, adolescents and adults with ADHD. The theme of gendering is elaborated further in this chapter because it has important consequences for children and adults in recognition and diagnosis of ADHD. The discourse of ADHD and cultural understandings shapes how individuals experience and interpret their lives, how others see them and how they see themselves. Horton-Salway examines the idea of narrative as a situated context for troubles-telling, positive talk and the transformation of selves. The chapter examines forms of resistance to pathologised versions of lives and spoiled identities and how accounts of personal experience are produced in response to the micro-politics of a social interaction, the context of troubles-telling and the wider context of ADHD discourse.

Chapter 7: Mary Horton-Salway draws together the key points arising from the different perspectives on ADHD, arguing that the meaning of ADHD is socially constructed in history and in the different 'translations' that are produced in public discourse and in people's accounts of their own experience. The chapter summarises how 'battles over truth' have produced ADHD as the epiphenomenal product of science, media, professional and lay discourse. Construction, resistance and contestation are important aspects of how ADHD and other mental health categories are defined and understood and these social processes are discussed in relation to stigma, the decline of public trust in expert forms of knowledge and public take up of health knowledge as both consumers and producers. The issue of 'resistance' is also discussed in relation to the discourse of neurodiversity and the cultural politics of impairment in categories such as autism or ADHD. We conclude by considering the relevance of a social constructionist and discourse analytic approach to inform educational and clinical practice in mental health care contexts.

An analysis of the discourse of ADHD is not complete without acknowledging the personal perspectives of health professionals and educationalists. There are some illuminating research studies that have examined those contexts in detail elsewhere but we suggest that further qualitative research on clinical contexts and the perspectives of health professionals and educators would be useful to maintain a productive dialogue about ADHD and other forms of mental health category.

References

Alvarez, A. S., Pagani, M., & Meucci, P. (2012). The clinical application of the biopsychosocial model in mental health: A research critique. *American Journal of Physical Medicine and Rehabilitation, 91*(2), 173–180.

American Psychiatric Association. (2013). *Attention Deficit and Hyperactivity Disorder.* Available at http://www.dsm5.org/documents/adhd%20fact%20sheet.pdf (Accessed 15 May 2016).

Antaki, C., & Widdicombe, S. (Eds.). (1998). *Identities in Talk.* London: Sage.

Atkinson, P. (1995). *Medical Talk and Medical Work: The Liturgy of the Clinic.* London: Sage.

Austin, J. L. (1962). *How to Do Things with Words.* Oxford: Clarendon Press.

Bailey, S. (2014). *Exploring ADHD: An Ethnography of Disorder in Early Childhood.* Routledge: Abingdon.

Barthes, R. (1964). *Elements of Semiology.* New York: Hill and Wang.

Berger, P. L., & Luckmann, T. (1966). *The Social Construction of Reality.* Garden City, NY: Doubleday.

Berger, P. L., & Luckmann, T. (1966/1971). *The Social Construction of Reality*. Harmondsworth: Penguin.
Biderman, A., Yeheskel, A., & Herman, J. (2005). The biopsychosocial model-have we made any progress since 1977? *Families, Systems and Health, 23*(4), 379–386.
Billig, M. (1996). *Arguing and Thinking: A Rhetorical Approach to Social Psychology*. Cambridge: Cambridge University Press.
Billig, M., Condor, S., Edwards, D., Gane, M., Middleton, D., & Radley, A. (1988). *Ideological Dilemmas: A Social Psychology of Everyday Thinking*. London: Sage.
Bradley, L., & Butler, C. W. (2015). Managing and normalising emotions and behaviour: A conversation analytic study of ADHD coaching. In M. O'Reilly & J. N. Lester (Eds.), *The Palgrave Handbook of Child Mental Health* (pp. 480–499). Basingstoke, UK: Palgrave Macmillan.
Brownlow, C., & Lamont-Mills, A. (2015). The production of the 'normal child': Exploring co-constructions of parents, children, and therapists. In M. O'Reilly & J. N. Lester (Eds.), *The Palgrave Handbook of Child Mental Health* (pp. 233–251). Basingstoke, UK: Palgrave Macmillan.
Burr, V. (2003). *Social Constructionism* (2nd ed.). Hove: Routledge.
Collins, H. M. (1985). *Changing Order: Replication and Induction in Scientific Practice*. London: Sage.
Davies, A., & Horton-Salway, M. (2016). The construction of adult ADHD: Anna's story. In M. O'Reilly & J. N. Lester (Eds.), *The Palgrave Handbook of Adult Mental Health* (pp. 117–133). Basingstoke, UK: Palgrave Macmillan.
Edwards, D. (1997). *Discourse and Cognition*. London: Sage.
Edwards, D., & Potter, J. (1992). *Discursive Psychology*. London: Sage.
Edwards, D., & Potter, J. (1993). Language and causation: A discursive action model of description and attribution. *Psychological Review, 100*(1), 23–41.
Engel, G. L. (1977). The need for a new medical model: A challenge for biomedicine. *Science, 196*, 129–136.
Engel, G. L. (1980). The clinical application of the biopsychosocial model. *American Journal of Psychiatry, 137*, 535–544.
Foucault, M. (1973/2006). *The Birth of the Clinic*. London: Tavistock.
Foucault, M. (2003). *The Birth of the Clinic*. Abingdon: Routledge Classics.
Foucault, M. (2006). *The History of Madness*. Abingdon: Routledge.
Garfinkel, H. (1967). *Studies in Ethnomethodology*. Englewood Cliffs, NJ: Prentice-Hall.
Geertz, C. (1973). *The Interpretation of Cultures*. New York: Basic Books.

Gilbert, G. N., & Mulkay, M. (1984). *Opening Pandora's Box: A Sociological Analysis of Scientists' Discourse*. Cambridge: Cambridge University Press.
Goffman, E. (1959). *The Presentation of Self in Everyday Life*. Harmondsworth: Penguin.
Goffman, E. (1961). *Asylums*. Harmondsworth: Penguin.
Goffman, E. (1963). *Stigma: Notes on the Management of Spoiled Identity*. Englewood Cliffs, NJ: Prentice-Hall.
Harper, D. J. (1995). Discourse analysis and 'mental health'. *Journal of Mental Health, 4*(4), 347–358.
Harper, D. J. (2013). On the persistence of psychiatric diagnosis: Moving beyond a zombie classification system. *Feminism and Psychology, 23*(1), 78–85.
Hepburn, A., & Wiggins, S. (Eds.). (2007). *Discursive Research in Practice: New Approaches to Psychology and Interaction*. Cambridge, UK: Cambridge University Press.
Heritage, J. C. (1984). *Garfinkel and Ethnomethodology*. Cambridge: Polity.
Horton-Salway, M. (1998). *Mind and body in the discursive construction of ME: A struggle for authorship of an illness* (Doctoral thesis, Loughborough University).
Horton-Salway, M. (2001). Narrative identities and the management of personal accountability in talk about M.E.: A discursive approach to illness narrative. *Journal of Health Psychology, 6*(2), 261–273.
Horton-Salway, M. (2002). Bio-psycho-social reasoning in GPs' case narratives: The discursive construction of M.E. patients' identities. *Health: An Interdisciplinary Journal for the Study of Health, Illness and Medicine, 6*(4), 401–421.
Horton-Salway, M. (2004). Expertise and experience: The local production of knowledge and identities in ME support group talk. *Health: An Interdisciplinary Journal for the Study of Health, Illness and Medicine, 8*(3), 351–371.
Horton-Salway, M. (2011). Repertoires of ADHD in UK newspaper media. *Health (London), 15*(5), 533–549.
Horton-Salway, M. (2012). Gendering attention deficit hyperactivity disorder: A discursive analysis of UK newspaper stories. *Journal of Health Psychology, 18*(8), 1085–1099. Published online before print 1 October 2012. https://doi.org/10.1177/1359105312456326.
Horton-Salway, M., & Davies, A. (2015). Moral evaluations in repertoires of ADHD. In M. O'Reilly & J. N. Lester (Eds.), *The Palgrave Handbook of Child Mental Health* (pp. 158–174). Basingstoke, UK: Palgrave Macmillan.

Jefferson, G. (1988). On the sequential organization of troubles-talk in ordinary conversation. *Social Problems, 35*(4), 418–437.
Kiyimba, N. (2015). The value of discourse analysis: A clinical psychologist's view. In M. O'Reilly & J. N. Lester (Eds.), *The Palgrave Handbook of Child Mental Health* (pp. 42–58). Basingstoke, UK: Palgrave Macmillan.
Kuhn, T. S. (1962/1970). *The Structure of Scientific Revolutions* (2nd ed.). Chicago: University of Chicago Press.
Latour, B. (1989). Cloaking the naked truth. In H. Lawson & L. Appignanesi (Eds.), *Dismantling Truth: Reality in the Post-modern World* (pp. 101–126). London: Weidenfeld and Nicolson.
Lemma, A. (1996). *Introduction to Psychopathology*. London: Sage.
Merleau-Ponty, M. (1945/1962). *The Phenomenology of Perception* (C. Smith, Trans.). New York: Humanities Press.
National Institute of Clinical Excellence. (2009). *Attention Deficit Hyperactivity Disorder: Diagnosis and Management of ADHD in Children, Young People and Adults*. London: National Institute for Health and Clinical Excellence. Available at http://www.nice.org.uk/Guidance/CG72 (Accessed 14 September 2017).
Ogden, J. (2000). *Health Psychology: A Textbook*. Buckingham: Open University Press.
O'Reilly, M., & Lester, J. N. (2015). *The Palgrave Handbook of Child Mental Health* (M. O'Reilly and J. N. Lester, Eds.). Basingstoke, UK: Palgrave Macmillan.
O'Reilly, M., & Lester, J. N. (2016). *The Palgrave Handbook of Adult Mental Health* (M. O'Reilly and J. N. Lester, Eds.). Basingstoke, UK: Palgrave Macmillan.
O'Reilly, M., Lester, J. N., Muskett, T., & Karim, K. (2017). How parents build a case for autism spectrum disorder during initial assessments: 'We're fighting a losing battle'. *Discourse Studies, 19*(1), 69–83.
Parker, N., & O'Reilly, M. (2012). 'Gossiping' as a social action in family therapy: The pseudo-absence and pseudo-presence of children. *Discourse Studies, 14*(4), 457–475.
Potter, J. (1996). *Representing Reality: Discourse, Rhetoric and Social Construction*. London: Sage.
Potter, J., & Wetherell, M. (1987). *Discourse and Social Psychology: Beyond Attitudes and Behaviour*. London: Sage.
Radley, A. (1994). *Making Sense of Illness: The Social Psychology of Health and Disease*. London: Sage.

Rafalovich, A. (2004/2008). *Framing ADHD Children: A Critical Examination of the History, Discourse and Everyday Experience of Attention Deficit/Hyperactivity Disorder*. Plymouth: Lexington Books.

Read, J. (2005). The bio-bio-bio model of madness. *The Psychologist, 8*(10), 596–597.

Royal College of General Practitioners (RCGP). (1972). *The Future General Practitioner: Learning and Teaching.* Exeter: British Medical Journal.

Sacks, H. (1995). *Lectures on Conversation.* Oxford: Blackwell.

Smith, D. E. (1978). 'K is mentally ill': The anatomy of a factual account. *Sociology, 12*(1), 23–53.

Soltile, W. M. (2005). Biopsychosocial care of heart patients: Are we practicing what we preach? *Families, Systems and Health, 23*(4), 400–403.

Strong, T., & Sesma-Vazquez, M. (2015). Discourses in children's mental health: A critical review. In M. O'Reilly & J. N. Lester (Eds.), *The Palgrave Handbook of Child Mental Health* (pp. 99–117). Basingstoke: Palgrave Macmillan.

Thompson, L., & McCabe, R. (2016). 'Good' communication in schizophrenia: A conversation analytic definition. In M. O'Reilly & J. N. Lester (Eds.), *The Palgrave Handbook of Adult Mental Health* (pp. 394–418). Basingstoke, UK: Palgrave Macmillan.

Wetherell, M. (1998). Positioning and interpretative repertoires: Conversation analysis and post-structuralism in dialogue. *Discourse and Society, 9*(3), 387–412.

Wetherell, M. (2007). A step too far: Discursive psychology, linguistic ethnography and questions of identity. *Journal of Sociolinguistics, 11*(5), 661–681.

Widdicombe, S., & Wooffitt, R. (1995). *The Language of Youth Subcultures: Social Identity in Action*. London: Harvester Wheatsheaf.

Willig, C. (2013). *Introducing Qualitative Research in Psychology* (3rd ed.). Maidenhead: Open University Press/McGraw-Hill Education.

Wittgenstein, L. (1980). *Remarks on the Philosophy of Psychology* (Vols. 1–2). Oxford: Basil Blackwell.

Woolgar, S. (1988). *Science: The Very Idea.* Chichester: Ellis Horwood and London: Tavistock.

2

Mapping the Discourses of ADHD: The Historical Legacy

Alison Davies

This chapter examines how ADHD has been constructed in historical discourse and how that has influenced contemporary understandings, specifically, how it has become scientifically theorised as a biological/ neurological disorder. Our aim is to provide an overview of historical and current representations of ADHD, drawing attention to the constitutive effect of these discourses and the consequences for those affected by the disorder. We are sympathetic to the Foucauldian view of discourse as constructive of meanings (Foucault 1991, 2003, 2006) and how discourse and regimes of truth define what is knowable, how we should behave and the kinds of identities we can take up. These processes are largely consensual, as Foucault's metaphor of the panopticon prison tower suggests. A central guard tower represents the possibility of surveillance, inducing prisoners to be compliant. Foucault used this idea to describe the way that governance works in contemporary society. People come to monitor, regulate and discipline their own, and others' behaviour as if they were being observed by an external force.

Self-regulation and self-monitoring, however, require a common understanding and consent and thus, governance is linked to dominant ideas about what are acceptable norms and standards of behaviour.

M. Horton-Salway and A. Davies, *The Discourse of ADHD*,
The Language of Mental Health, https://doi.org/10.1007/978-3-319-76026-1_2

Much of this knowledge and understanding is taken for granted as common sense within any given regime of truth. Developments in knowledge and ideas place new responsibilities and rights upon individuals and enable new forms of self-regulation, at the same time, shaping our understanding of 'normal' behaviour. A very pertinent example of this (and one we return to later) can be seen in the developing role of the 'psy' disciplines during the twentieth century. The 'psy' disciplines is a term coined by Nikolas Rose (1996, 1999) to refer to the developing influence of knowledge that arose from within the disciplines of psychology, psychiatry and psychotherapy. This emerging knowledge came to shape new understandings of children and family life in the UK at that time, and families came increasingly under the clinical gaze of 'psy' experts. As Rose indicated:

> an adjusted child was the natural outcome of a normal family....the normal family could now be specified in psychological terms, and the normal, adapted child construed as its project ....maladjustment, from bed-wetting to delinquency, had become a sign of something wrong in the emotional economy of the family. (Rose 1999: 159)

This developing 'psy' knowledge established new requirements of families to self-monitor and manage their children in appropriate ways in order to produce 'healthy' and 'normal' outcomes. The dissemination of 'expert' knowledge is key to establishing new forms of self-regulation. The psychological knowledge described above, for example, would be disseminated via sites and institutions such as schools and clinics, as well as via media and broadcasting channels.

> In the clinic the troubles of childhood would be diagnosed, norms of adjustment and maladjustment would be produced and refined, and normalisation would be undertaken. [These] would be disseminated from the clinics back to the institutional and family life. (Rose 1999: 158)

These examples indicate how knowledge and power are entwined. The knowledge that circulates within these sites, and society in general, produces the kind of families and children the social context requires them to be. At the same time, this knowledge (or discourse) becomes dominant and established over time as taken-for-granted 'truth'. Foucault's use of the term 'regimes of truth' describes the way that knowledge and power work together to produce new subjects and ways of being. Power is an intrinsic aspect of discourse because it is not possible for individuals to escape the effects of knowledge by stepping outside the social and historical context in which it is produced.

Of course, new values about what is normal, right or acceptable change according to the social and historical context. Ideas about what constitutes mental distress has varied according to the historicising discourses of the time, and these inevitably shape the way that individuals come to understand themselves and others. The dominant common sense knowledge at any given time is rather like the 'ship in a bottle' described in Chapter 1 (Collins 1985). It can be difficult for us to see how it was constructed. What interests us is how these values are taken as truths, and how these work to both constrain and enable particular understandings and identities. Human sense-making is, however, a dynamic and active process. Bodies of knowledge are historically produced, but do not disappear as new knowledge emerges; instead, they linger, providing alternative, sometimes conflicting ways of 'knowing'. Discourses are, therefore, complex and potentially contradictory, providing opportunities for creativity and variation.

In this chapter, we examine the competing bodies of knowledge, or discourses, which have defined the meaning of ADHD for over a century. Broadly, these discourses can be categorised as biological, psychological and sociological and it is towards these we now turn.

Biological Explanations

The extent to which biological factors such as physiology, biochemistry and neurology are drawn upon to explain categories such as ADHD depends on the extent to which biomedicine is used as an explanatory model of mental distress. The focus of biomedical accounts is on disease, classification and treatment, and in accordance with the methods of natural science, emphasis is placed on identifying physically observable cause and effect relationships. The term 'disease' refers to somatic and pathological changes in the body, which can be diagnosed and treated, and can be distinguished from the terms 'illness' and 'sickness', which, respectively, refer to individual experience and social understandings (see Radley 1994: 3 for further discussion). Biomedical explanations for disease are confined to physical and biological causes and, therefore, rest 'upon a dualism of mind and body, privileging the latter through reducing all problems to its pathologies, which are understood as disease' (Radley 1994: 9). As Chapter 1 described, mainstream medicine has adopted, with varying degrees of success, psychological and social explanations in their understanding of disease. Psychiatry, on the other hand, has sometimes been criticised for its affiliation with biological explanations and medicalised solutions (Engel 1977; Read 2005; Doward 2013).

Biological psychiatric explanations provide one, very prevalent, way of 'knowing' ADHD and its subjects. The biomedical understanding of ADHD is one that is represented within prevalent classification systems relating to mental disorders, principally, the American Psychiatric Association's (APA) DSM-5 (2013) (Fig. 2.1). The DSM-5 represents the latest version of ADHD as specified by the APA since it first appeared as Attention Deficit Disorder (ADD) within the DMS-III in 1980, although Hyperkinetic Impulse Disorder was a classification contained within the DSM-II (APA 1968). Psychiatric classifications such as those provided by the APA can obscure the often long and complicated history of reconceptualization to which mental health categories are subject.

Tracing the History of ADHD

A historic perspective of psychiatric categorisation shows how medical and psychiatric explanations have been used to account for human behaviour which transgresses social norms since the late nineteenth century. For example, the medical concept of imbecility took root during the later nineteenth century and came to be applied to behaviours deemed to be socially deviant, such as alcoholism and drug use, forging

ADHD diagnosis is based on a psychiatric assessment of impairments, such as hyperactivity, impulsivity and attention problems using a behavioural checklist provided by the DSM- 5. The DSM-5 organises eighteen diagnostic criteria into two categories that relate to 'inattention' (nine criteria) and 'hyperactivity' (nine criteria). For a diagnosis to be made children must demonstrate at least six of these criteria from both or either of these categories in two or more settings while adolescents or adults (over 17 years) must have five of these symptoms. Several of these symptoms must have been present before 12 years. Many of the criteria refer to behaviour that is problematic within the classroom such as getting out of one's seat, wandering around the classroom, failure to pay attention to details or making careless mistakes in schoolwork. However, DSM-5 now includes developmental criteria appropriate to older adolescents and also adults in the workplace.

A less used, but still quite prevalent, classification system is the World Health Organisation's (WHO) International Classification of Diseases – 10 (ICD-10, 1992).

Fig. 2.1 Summary of DSM-5: ADHD diagnostic criteria

an alignment between the discourses of medicine with discourses of morality. Imbecility was a particularly useful concept for 'medicalising conditions that resided in that netherworld between severe mental incapacitation and relative mental normalcy' (Rafalovich 2015: 84). In the later nineteenth and early twentieth centuries, developing medical knowledge continued to produce new ways of conceptualising, and regulating human behaviour, which brought ever increasing categories of people under the surveillance of the 'medical gaze'. The development of medical classifications in relation to children was implicated with the advent of mass education. In the early nineteenth century, the concept of 'imbecility' was applied to children within institutional sites such as schools. Institutions provided an opportunity for the observation and surveillance of childhood behaviour and this developed into measurement, assessment and normalisation and the interventions of medical, psychiatric, psychological and social experts.

The emergence of the category of the 'moral imbecile' to describe children with hyperactive behaviour (Still 1902) linked organic and neurological causes with 'wayward' social behaviours such as dishonesty and lawlessness (see also, Timimi and Timimi 2015). Causal relationships between biology and 'moral' conduct defined restlessness, fidgetiness and poor attention as indicators of poor moral control in children. Some aspects of this account continue to resonate with contemporary understandings of ADHD, and Still's classification is often referred to as a precursor of the ADHD category (Timimi and Timimi 2015) (Fig. 2.2).

Problematic and persistent presentations of symptoms similar to hyperactivity, restlessness and inattention have since been subject to at least twenty category label changes (Mayes and Rafalovich 2007). Those which are informed by biomedicine include Tredgold's category of 'feeble-mindedness' (see Hall 2008) and post *encephalitis lethargica* (or 'sleepy sickness'). An association between children who had survived an epidemic of *encephalitis lethargica* in the 1920s and inattention and restlessness was identified, and this was attributed to defective neurological impulses, brought on by the condition. Both classifications identified symptoms of irritability, obstinancy, inattention, and general hyperactivity as indicative of moral difficulty in childhood and both explained maladaptive behaviour as physiological pathology (Rafalovich 2008).

The historical discourse of 'moral defects' resonates with a body of research focusing on the association of ADHD with criminality; for example, the effects of medication on criminality (Lichtenstein, Halldner, Zetterqvist, 2013), the impact of ADHD on adult criminality (Mordre, Groholt, Kjelsberg, Standstad, Myhre, 2011), and the predictive risk factors for children with ADHD and criminal behaviour (De Sanctis, Nomura, Newcorn, Halperin, 2012). Such studies are focused mainly on boys and men.

Fig. 2.2 ADHD and criminality

As with Still's 'moral imbecile', the identification of these 'disorders' in children took place within schools where the behaviour was considered inappropriate and problematic. As Rafalovich (2001: 110) states: 'The diagnosis of encephalitis lethargica provided a physiological explanation for unconventional, antiinstitutional child behavior'.

Developing knowledge of *encephalitis lethargica* was underpinned by neurological and psychiatric claims about brain function and its effect on behaviour, bringing children, who displayed 'impaired concentration.... incessant restlessness ....[and] incorrigible impulsiveness' (Foley 2011), under the psychiatric gaze, a gaze which continues to the present day. The focus on physiological causes for children's anti-social behaviour highlights Engel's critique (1977) of the biomedical model adopted by psychiatry and its (then, at least) sidelining of psychological and social factors. As Rafalovich (2001) suggests, the changing classifications of mental health disorders can obscure other possible variables such as environmental factors influencing the manifestation of postencephalitic behaviour in children who had previously been institutionalised. Drawing upon Goffman's looping effect (1961), Rafalovich questions whether psychiatrists may have interpreted children's resistance to their institutional environment as symptomatic of mental disorder.

The involvement of psychiatry in interpreting and classifying problematic childhood behaviour persisted in the following decades. Underpinning psychiatric classification is biomedicine's concern with producing knowledge which can be used in the treatment of disease or mental distress. This became evident during the 1930s, when children, typically 'deviant' and institutionalised boys, became subject to increasing interest in the effects of medication on their behaviour. For example, Charles Bradley (1937) examined the effect of stimulant medication (Benzedrine) on a group of hospitalised boys with a variety of mental health disorders. The stimulant medication produced a significantly positive impact on the motivation and performance of these boys at school, and on their social skills. Of interest to the scientific community, however, was the more surprising subduing effect of the drug on some, but not all, of the boys, 'Bradley hypothesised that children who exhibited such a paradoxical effect may have a more fundamental physiological condition in the brain that the drug was affecting'

(Rafalovich 2015: 87). The 'serendipitous observation' (National Institute for Health and Care Excellence [NICE] 2009: 231) that stimulant medication was effective for hyperactivity in children could, however, only be scientifically meaningful if hyperactivity was already defined as pathological. Educational, medical and psychiatric knowledge had already linked hyperactivity and restlessness with childhood pathology. In a tautological relationship, the discovery of medication that modifies such behaviour becomes evidence that the behaviour had physiological roots. In this way, stimulant medication became a medicalised way to regulate 'pathological' hyperactivity.

Similar to any scientific discovery, the emergence of ADHD as a biological/psychiatric phenomenon was reified through scientific processes of representation, fact construction and reconstruction (see Chapter 1). Bradley's 'discovery' would lead to new avenues of scientific/biological exploration and interest in the effects of medication that continued into the following decades. When Ritalin was first tested on children (in the 50s), according to the psychiatric and medical community, the positive response of the children to the medication provided evidence of the organic/biological roots of the disorder (Mayes and Rafalovich 2007; Singh 2002a).

The 1950s also saw the emergence in 1959 of Knobloch and Pasamanick's concept of 'minimal brain damage' (Lange et al. 2010), which suggested that hyperactivity in children might be caused by lesions to the brain. Lack of evidence of organic lesions on the brain resulted in a subsequent shift in labelling and conceptualisation, leading to the introduction of the label 'minimal brain dysfunction' by The Oxford International Study Group of Child Neurology in the 1960s (Timimi and Timimi 2015). Aside from theorising hyperkinetic disorder in terms of brain dysfunction (rather than damage), the category minimal brain dysfunction (MBD) provided a much broader definition of symptomology, incorporating learning, behavioural and cognitive problems (see Timimi and Timimi 2015). The growing medical acceptance in the 1960s that hyperactivity could not be attributed to brain damage resulted in a shift from 'aetiologically based definitions towards behaviourally based ones' (Timimi and Timimi 2015: 143); hyperactivity was conceptualised as behaviour that 'could arise from organic pathology, but could also occur in its absence' (Timimi and Timimi 2015: 143). In 1968, the category 'hyperkinetic reaction of childhood' replaced MBD in the DSM-II, perhaps introducing 'a degree of psychiatric legitimacy into the discussion of childhood hyperactivity and impulsivity' (Mayes and Rafalovich 2007: 437). Since 1968, there have been five subsequent versions of the DSM (APA 1980, 1987, 1994, 2000, 2013), and five subsequent definitions of ADHD to reflect changing conceptualisations of the relationship between attention/impulse control and hyperactivity (see Timimi and Timimi 2015).

A historic overview of ADHD reveals more recent biologically informed explanations within the areas of cognition, neurobiology and genetics. Cognitive dysfunctions are understood to have an underlying neurobiological basis and include a malfunction of the central nervous system (Kean 2005) and a dysfunction in the dopamine transmitter system, which interferes with concentration and attention (Singh 2008a). Recent interest in neuroimaging has implicated the involvement of fronto-striatal abnormalities in the manifestation of ADHD type behaviour (Weyandt et al. 2013). The language and focus of neuroscientific research constructs neurobiological difference in terms of deficit and this contributes to the neuro-pathology discourse of ADHD. Current scientific research is also interested in establishing a genetic basis to ADHD (Dillon and Craven 2014). Arguments for this are grounded in observations of a greater incidence of ADHD in identical twins than in non-identical twins, and among children and parents who are biologically related, than between children and parents who are not biologically related (Cooper 2001, 2008; Remschmidt 2005).

Problematising Medical Knowledge as Objective and Value-Free

Sociological analyses of the discourses and practices used by scientists have indicated that natural science environments are not necessarily value free and objective (see Gilbert and Mulkay 1984). Regarding the importance of cultural representation in scientific 'discovery', Hawthorne (2010) points out how social values are already embedded within psychiatric classifications.

Hawthorne argues, for example, that ADHD diagnostic criteria, such as 'losing things necessary for tasks' and 'sitting not still at your desk' are essentially a list of behaviours that challenge socially valued norms. Hawthorne also highlights 'the dichotomy between facts and values' in the way that socially valued concepts become infused with the language of science (Hawthorne 2010: 25). With regards to ADHD, this emerges in the process of converting scientific observation of inhibitory control into generalised descriptions of the findings. The neutral language of the original observation notes that inhibitory control is 'slow' in the targeted population of ADHD-diagnosed children. Hawthorne notes, however, that the authors provide a 'slide in usage' from the factual term 'slow' to the evaluative term 'poor'. The term 'poor' is imbued with a socially normative evaluation that faster is better. Similarly, she suggests a further 'slide in usage', as results indicating slowness in the neutral mechanism 'inhibitory control' slide into the socially value-laden characteristic of 'impulsivity'.

This 'slide in usage' from the neutral, objective descriptions of scientific observation into the value-laden justifications of scientific endeavour is subtly embedded within scientific discourse. As Gilbert and Mulkay (1984) indicate, the empiricist discourse of science transforms socially constructed facts into absolute truths. Such rhetorical devices are also used within the discipline of psychiatry (Harper 2013). In accordance with Woolgar's (1988) analysis of scientific knowledge, the reification of scientific facts is supported through the use of 'objectified reliable and valid' methodological tools (Visser and Jehan 2009), which in the case of ADHD involves the increasing use of neuroimaging, MRI and PET scans (Visser and Jehan 2009) in the pursuit of increased scientific knowledge about the disorder. Harper (2013) identifies these practices as the rhetoric of psychiatry, which work to not only legitimise knowledge, but also to legitimise the discipline itself and other institutions. For example, ADHD is framed within psychiatric discourse, and has been reified into an 'uncomplicated, biomedically based phenomenon' (Visser and Jehan 2009). This provides it with an organic and medical aetiology which permits a treatment 'pathway' and justifies medical and pharmaceutical involvement and investment. Hawthorne (2010) argues that the social uptake of the 'valenced concept' results in a feedback loop that permits 'another round of interest in its implications and support of the science' (p. 21).

Diagnostic classification not only legitimises psychiatry itself, but other institutions and disciplines such as clinical psychology, the health insurance industry, funding institutions, scientific journals, and of course the pharmaceutical industry (see Harper 2013). Despite doubts about the validity and effectiveness of medication coming from alternative discourses, medicalised treatment is presented, within the biomedical model, as the 'unproblematic' solution. Stimulant medication such as methylphenidate and dexamfetamine is typically used to treat ADHD and it is officially recommended by the UK National Institution of Clinical Excellence as the first line of treatment for adult ADHD (Moncrieff and Timimi 2013). Doubts about the validity of stimulant medication have been raised since its 'serendipitous' discovery in the 1930s. Contemporary debate includes questions around interpretations of the impact of medication (see Rafalovich 2015) including observations that stimulant medication would have an effect on the concentration and energy levels of any child, not only those with ADHD (Graham 2008; Singh 2005; Timimi and Taylor 2004). Additionally, concern around the potential physical harm caused by taking stimulant medication is well-documented in the literature (Frankel 2010; Graham 2008; Rafalovich 2008). The possible side effects identified include psychotic reactions, the development of tics, an increased tendency to self-harm and a suppression of appetite leading to reduced growth rates. However, effectiveness of treatment is defended rigorously by many psychiatrists (Rafalovich 2015). Moncrieff and Timimi's (2013) also point out how NICE ignore the absence of longitudinal studies into the effectiveness of medication:

> the guideline identified that drug trials have shown no long-term benefit in ADHD, but still recommended treatment with stimulant drugs for children with severe symptoms and for all adults claiming consensus for this position… [The guideline] demonstrates how contradictory data are managed so as not to jeopardise the currently predominant view that ADHD… [is a] valid and un-contentious medical… [condition] that should be treated with drugs. (Moncrieff and Timimi 2013: 59)

Resistance

Although Foucault's explanation of compliance points to the constraining effects of discourse within a regime of truth, individuals are by no means passive subjects: 'being socially constrained does not preclude being creative. Where there is power, there is also, inevitably, resistance' (Goodley and Rapley 2001: 230). Individuals might be constrained by dominant discourse or institutional and social practices, but they are also able to take up or resist subject positions. An example of this can be seen in relation to autism where 'a competing discourse of neurodiversity has emerged as reaction to a medicalised neurological discourse' (O'Dell et al. 2016: 172). The neurodiversity movement rejects the stigmatising effects of impairment discourse and has become an increasing force for activism and resistance. As O'Dell et al. (2016) comment:

> Neurodiversity discourse enables a challenge to dominant understandings of autism as a neurological deficit, instead focusing on autism as neurological difference. It also offers a way of naming non-autism and rendering visible power structures that naturalise an NT [Neurotypical] world [….]. For neurodiversity activists, the power of neuroscience serves to legitimise autism as a positive state rather than a deficit and provides a powerful mechanism for securing social rights and gaining political recognition. (O'Dell et al. 2016: 172)

One constraining, yet enabling effect of knowledge can be seen in the take up of stimulant medication to manage ADHD. Recent years have witnessed a dramatic global increase in the prescription rates of these stimulants and NICE (2009: 28) indicates that between the late 1970s and the late 1990s global prescription rates rose from 0.5 per 1000 children to more than 3 per 1000 in the late 1990s (Horton-Salway 2012). With regards to the UK, NICE (2009) reports a marked increase in prescription rates since the 1990s. Frankel (2010) suggests prescriptions rose from 6000 in 1994 to 461,000 in 2007. UK media reported 50% increase in Ritalin prescription between 2007 and 2012 from 420,000 to 657,000 prescriptions (Donnelly 2013; Meredith 2013; Saul 2013).

However, alongside this willingness to take up medication as a way of regulating behaviour, there are indications of resistance to this. For example, uncertainty around long-term medication of children is suggested by reports of clinicians' ambivalence, and the 'perceived risk of harming children' is managed through talk of 'medication holidays' (Rafalovich 2005: 316). Similarly, parents also reveal an uncertainty around medication, particularly, at weekends and holidays (Singh 2004) and they, too, talk of medication breaks (Neophytou and Webber 2005; Singh 2005) and 'fine-tuning' of their child's medication (Taylor et al. 2006; Litt 2004). This resistance to the 'complete' medical 'package' may be indication of incomplete medicalisation, which occurs when there is medical uncertainty or only partial recognition (Gray Brunton et al. 2014; Malacrida 2004), and this may be linked to the existence of other competing discourses such as the psychological and the social, which we turn to next.

Psychological Explanations

Although we have separated the three discourses of bio, psycho and social, there is much overlap and blurring between the boundaries of these fields of professional expertise. Graham (2007: 13), as cited in Bailey (2014: 101), talks of the 'awkward alliance' between the different medical and mental health discourses within prevalent understandings of ADHD. As Bailey indicates, although the definition of ADHD was first circumscribed within psychiatric discourse by the APA, it is a term used by a range of professionals from across the medical, psychology and social care professions. A distinction that can be made between the discourses of psychiatry and the discourses of psychology is that the former is concerned with biological developmental accounts while the latter is concerned with cognitive, psychosocial or environmental factors to explain developmental difference (see Bailey 2014: 101). Note, however, Harper's observation (2013: 80) that the availability of a moral discourse 'as an alternative to a discourse of psychiatric diagnosis hints at its powerful social functions'.

The 'awkward alliance' between psychiatry and psychology can be traced historically. In the early days of the discipline, between the two world wars, psychologists were 'handmaidens' (Rose 1999: 236) to medicine, required to carry out assessments to support psychiatric diagnosis. However, psychology, in the 1950s, came to occupy a distinct professional position from psychiatry, one primarily informed by behaviourism. As Rose says:

> Neurotic disorders, personality disorders, and many types of criminal conduct were not 'illnesses' but problems of behaviour acquired in large part by the processes of learning, unlearning, or failure to learn. Psychiatry was inappropriate to treat such problems, for the processes involved were outside the scope of medical training and did not require the sophisticated and expensive clinical skills of the doctor. (Rose 1999: 237)

Biological explanations do not always, or entirely, remove responsibility for pathological symptoms from individuals. Recent developments in genetics implicate parents in passing on the ADHD gene, and mothers are often implicated in biological-development accounts of ADHD (see Bailey 2014). However, psychology's focus on psychosocial and environmental factors, implicates individuals and society with ADHD in additional ways. While biomedical explanations situate individuals within a relatively blame free account of 'pathological inheritance' (Bailey 2014: 98), psychological explanations place focus on the individual or family environment.

Despite this difference in emphasis, much of psychological knowledge does not, necessarily, represent a challenge to medical knowledge, but can be understood as an extension of it (Radley 1994). Psychology works alongside medicine to provide alternative, but often, complementary knowledge and explanations of pathology. Mainstream psychology's close association with the medical model of disease is apparent in its methods, informed by the natural sciences to discover cause and effect relationships between cognitive behavioural risk factors and the development of disease or pathology.

While psychological interventions are predominantly aligned with the practice of medicine, with resident clinical psychologists embedded within hospitals and clinics, the psychological technologies for self-improvement and regulation permeate all institutional contexts and fields of human experience, such as schools (educational psychologists), in organisations (organisational psychologists), therapeutic and social work contexts (psychotherapists) and even popular forms of self help. As Rose (1999) argues, popular culture is saturated with psychological knowledge and, therefore, infuses all forms of human experience. The 'giving away' of psychological expertise is a good example of how the practices of governance and self regulation work by inviting individuals to take up methods of self improvement in order to become 'better' citizens. The ever expanding reach of psychological knowledge into different institutional sites and contexts can be seen in the history of ADHD.

The Family and the Psy Disciplines

Of particular relevance to ADHD, are the discourses of developmental psychology, embedded within the differentiating logic of the school and clinic, and psychotherapy. The category of ADHD has, until the most recent DSM (DSM-5, APA 2013), been predominantly identified as a disorder of childhood. The identification of 'disorder' in children is very much tied to the development of the 'psy disciplines' and the emerging science of developmental psychology. This coincided with the emergence of psychoanalysis, originally located within the field of medicine, and its interpretations of childhood behaviours. Both psychology and psychotherapy produce theories which construct normalising notions of childhood and healthy development as well as normative assumptions about what constitutes appropriate parenting. Responsibility for identification, prevention and management of irregular behaviours has been situated within schools and the family.

With mass education came the opportunity for the observation and normalisation of childhood behaviour with the 'psy' professions drawing on the statistical concept of the 'normal distribution' to describe human variability. Developmental psychology, in particular, has established a particularly powerful framework of physical, social and emotional developmental norms for children to be measured against, 'enabling "appropriate" action to be taken by expert psychologists for any individuals falling outside of the "normal range"' (O'Dell and Brownlow 2015: 297). The discursive practices around 'appropriate' developmental stages appear within healthcare and clinical practice, in educational settings and within policy, media and literature directed towards the family. Families are implicated in the successful developmental outcomes of their children, and the idea of normative development is a way of regulating not only children but also their parents, and mothers in particular (see Burman 2008; O'Dell and Brownlow 2015). Within this discourse, ADHD is positioned as a developmental problem to be treated within the context of the family.

Parents are similarly implicated within psychoanalytic discourses, especially in relation to their children's social and emotional development. Psychoanalysis very much focuses on the dynamic relations within families. At the same time as biomedical explanations of children's 'anti-social' behaviour were being proposed, psychodynamic explanations also located these problems within the context of dysfunctional family dynamics (see Rafalovich 2015). In particular, this discourse focused on mother and child relations and was concerned with the effect of mothering styles on children's emotional and psychological outcomes. The 'refrigerator mother' (Bettelheim 1959) became a well-known concept within popular discourse, aligning responsibility for children's atypical development with maternal deficit. The emphasis on mother and child relationships runs through psychoanalytic and psychodynamic discourses, with a particular focus on mothers and emotionally disturbed sons. As we noted in Chapter 1, however, the practice of psychoanalysis had been regarded as 'a hodgepodge of unscientific opinions, assorted philosophies and "schools of thought"...' (cited in Engel 1977: 589) and this critique had led to the subsequent alliance of psychiatry with the biomedical model. Bradley's (1937) work with institutionalised boys, for example, had combined psychoanalytic thinking with his biomedical exploration of stimulant medication to account for, and to treat, the behaviour of emotionally disturbed boys. Singh points out that 'throughout this period of experimentation with Benzedrine the possibility of mother's toxicity and the necessity for separating mother and child went unchallenged in published articles' (Singh 2002a: 590). Maternal accountability for children's developmental outcomes extended beyond their attachment styles to the appropriate management of their children's problems. For example, the problem of 'emotional disturbance' was used in the 1950s to define hyperactivity, inattention, moodiness, delinquency and impulsiveness (Singh 2002a). Although a particularly vague term, the consensus was that emotional disturbance was a secondary symptom of an underlying disorder. This was thought to lead to 'disturbed' behaviour without appropriate intervention and mothers were accountable to be vigilant and alert to their children's underlying difficulties and, so, manage them appropriately.

The influence of psycho-social (or environmental) factors on children's disordered behaviours was a powerful idea within popular culture. According to Singh (2002a), while medical terms such as MBD were more prevalent in scientific literature, the term 'emotional disturbance' was used more in popular literature. MBD was understood to be caused by organic factors and 'emotional disturbance' by anxiety and conflict. However, despite these distinct understandings, they became closely entwined with one another. This convergence of discourses is reflected in the language used by the DSM-II (APA 1968), in which all childhood disorders were described as 'reactions' to childhood (Mayes and Rafalovich 2007), and, specifically, the ancestor of today's ADHD classification was the label 'hyperkinetic reaction of children'.

Although psychoanalytic concepts such as the 'refrigerator mother' are largely discredited today, the legacy of this discourse can be seen within psychological discourse of the early twenty-first century with, for example, a particular group of psychologists classifying ADHD as 'attachment-deficit-hyper-reactivity disorder', a consequence of the impact of post-natal depression on children's behaviour (Halasz et al. 2002, see Bailey 2014: 101). Mothers are similarly implicated by recent psychological studies aligning ADHD with factors such as maternal mood (Vander Ploeg Booth et al. 2010) and mothers' parenting style (Tancred and Greeff 2015; Moghaddam et al. 2013). The focus on mothers and their sons remains a notable feature of the contemporary discourse of ADHD, and it is replicated across a range of contexts that we have explored in this book, through the use of psychosocial explanations of ADHD.

Psychosocial explanations of ADHD are linked with different kinds of interventions from biomedical ones. Psychological knowledge, in the form of cognitive behavioural therapy or parenting classes, informs interventions currently offered for individuals or families affected by ADHD. NICE guidelines (2016) suggest that for pre-school children 'Healthcare professionals should offer parents or carers of pre-school children with ADHD a referral to a parent-training/education programme as the first-line treatment', while for school-age children with moderate impairment 'Group-based parent-training/education programmes are usually the first-line treatment for parents and carers of children and young people of school age with ADHD and moderate impairment' (NICE 2016).

The emphasis in psychological discourse on the role of the family in regulating their child's behaviour is also (re)produced within prevalent neoliberal ideology, which situates responsibility for social problems with the individual, and the family. Francis (2012) argues that essentialist notions of motherhood position mothers as particularly responsible for the 'outcomes' of their families and children. Neoliberal ideology, therefore, provides a context for the convergence of the medical discourse around ADHD with other discourses around parenting and maternal blame. Science, and psychological discourse about ADHD and best parenting practices, has also entered the domestic space in the form of popular magazines, public health information and, in recent years, parenting groups. Parents (and mothers specifically) are implicated within political discourse as well as psychological discourse with their children's disorder, and medicalization of 'disordered' childhood behaviour provides a release from condemnation and stigma (Conrad 2006) as the understanding of the deviant behaviour shifts from one of 'badness' to one of 'illness'. As Conrad (2006: 5) states, 'with badness the deviant was considered responsible, with sickness he [sic] is not'. From this sociological, social constructionist view, a turn to biomedicine exonerates parents, particularly mothers, from blame for childhood deviance and misbehaviour.

Sociological Explanations

Sociological explanations of ADHD relate to social norms, values and expectations and how these have come to shape our definitions and understanding. A sociological viewpoint would consider the practices of medicine and medical expertise alongside the social activities and social context of the patient (see Radley 1994: 12). In this way,

> the actions of the doctors – how they classify disease, how they treat patients, how they admit individuals to the sick role – also become subjects for sociological study. Medical knowledge can be treated as something that does not merely reflect states of the body; it is also a means for doctors to exercise authority over their clients. (Radley 1994: 12)

However, sociological social constructionist critiques of the medical model include the argument that scientific classification is not a value-free scientific endeavour, but produced within particular relational and social contexts and regimes of truth. Diagnosis is located within the fluctuating historical understandings of 'disordered' behaviour and pathology (see Kirschner 2013; Foucault 1991, 2003, 2006) and is also dependent on the subjective basis of clinical judgement.

The subjective basis of judgement is a concern that the *British Psychological Society* raised in relation to DSM-5, particularly in relation to the vagueness of some of its diagnostic categories (BPS 2012). Diagnostic descriptions of mental health disorders are imbued with evaluative terms that require subjective judgement. In relation to ADHD, Whitely (2015) points out that in DSM-IV (APA 2000),

> all 18 behavioural diagnostic criteria include the word 'often'. How often a child 'fidgets or squirms in their seat' or 'interrupts' or 'avoids homework' or 'fails to remain seated when remaining seated is expected' or 'is distracted by external stimuli', etc., so that they exhibit 'some impairment' is not defined in DSM-IV. (Whitely 2015: 498)

The terms used to describe the diagnostic criteria of ADHD include '*some* impairment' (what is meant by some?), 'fails' and 'has difficulty'.

These terms are evaluative and require a degree of subjective judgement about the 'quality' of performance of a task. As Lemma (1996: 4) states, 'everyone performs actions that do not correspond with our definitions of normal behaviour but that only in certain circumstances do they receive a stigmatising label'. Critical approaches to psychiatry argue that ADHD symptoms are barely distinguishable from normal childhood behaviours (Whitely 2015; Timimi and Taylor 2004; Timimi and Timimi 2015).

As Conrad put it, the emergence of ADHD as a psychiatric category is an example of the medicalisation of social problems, particularly the 'deviant' behaviour of young boys (see Rafalovich 2015; Conrad 1975, 2006). This increasing tendency to interpret deviance in medical terms has been identified as significant in the pathologisation of childhood difficulties (Rafalovich 2015). As Conrad and Potter (2006) write:

> Medical diagnostic categories, perhaps especially psychiatric categories are often fluid and subject to expansion or contraction. The extension of established diagnoses is especially interesting for it can occur almost unnoticed as part of regular medical practice and, at the same time, expand the realm of medicalisation in significant ways. (Conrad and Potter 2006: 103)

The fluidity of the ADHD category according to changing DSM classifications is well documented, but in DSM-5 (APA 2013), the category is expanded to incorporate adults as well as widening the inclusionary criteria for children. One way of interpreting this is to suppose that medical knowledge becomes more sophisticated and discovers 'better truths' about its subject matter. Another interpretation, however, is that this is an example of 'bracket creep' (Kirschner 2013), a term used to describe the expansion of both psychiatric diagnostic categories and the number of people who are captured within these categories. The expansion of psychiatric categories or 'bracket creep' becomes accepted and assimilated into diagnostic practice and everyday knowledge. Rafalovich (2015) points out the impact of medicalisation on school-age children, highlighting the quite significantly high numbers of school-age boys taking stimulant medication for behavioural problems.

> it is clear that at the extra-discursive level the discourses of medicine which have realised themselves through medical practices of individuals and clinicians in response to the discursive field of ADHD demonstrate a widespread subscription to the legitimacy of the neurological argument - ADHD is a bona fide brain impairment that requires long-term (if not permanent) medical intervention in the form of stimulant medications. (Rafalovich 2015: 89)

This cumulative process of scientific classification produces categories such as ADHD, and the progression of DSM through its different versions shows how ADHD came to be understood as a discrete condition with recognisable and specific aetiologies and treatment pathways. The legitimacy of the scientific/medical label for ADHD is one that has been taken up globally and is now the most commonly diagnosed psychiatric childhood condition in the world (Bailey 2014). For Rafalovich (2015) and many other critics this is a point of concern. Had diagnoses of health conditions such as cancer or heart disease risen at the same rate as those of ADHD, he suggests, there would no doubt have been widespread public debate and enquiry about the reasons why. Such interrogation, he argues, is not directed towards the 'ADHD industry' (see Rafalovich 2015: 89). In Chapter 3, we will explore how ADHD is represented to the public in an analysis of media discourse.

Medicalisation and the Pharmaceutical Industry

The biomedical, neurocentric perspective of ADHD (see Bailey 2014: 11) constructs, what Rose (2007) identifies as neurochemical citizenship, and for those caught up in its discursive net, this confers particular ways of being and making sense of oneself. This is enabled through 'legitimate forms of knowledge and the correct institutional arrangements' (Bailey 2014: 11), which, in a looping effect, reconfirm the neurocentric view of pathology and normality. A legitimate, and acceptable, way to manage ADHD within this perspective is pharmacological intervention in the form of stimulant medication. It is argued by sociologists (Conrad 2006) that the 'pharmaceutical revolution' that has taken place since the mid-twentieth century has significantly impacted on the increase and diagnosis of childhood disorders such as ADHD. As the DSM expands its diagnostic criteria, there is a parallel expansion in the market for stimulants (Whitely 2015).

Doubts around stimulant medication in the treatment of ADHD describe a symbiotic relationship between pharmacology and psychiatry (Harper 2013) and a critique of the role played by the pharmaceutical industry in promoting medicalization of certain childhood behaviours. Critics also indicate the involvement and financial support of the pharmaceutical companies with some parent support groups (Graham 2008; Conrad 2006, 2007; Lloyd and Norris 1999; Billington and Pomerantz 2004) and they claim this indicates mutual benefit to both the drug companies and the parenting groups. Conrad (2007) has expressed a further concern that redefining ADHD as a lifetime disorder could lead to children and adults being on medication indefinitely.

Variation in Prevalence Rates

The variation in prevalence rates, even within countries, and the increases in diagnosis across the globe are cited as evidence by sociological critiques of medicalisation (Timimi and Timimi 2015). This is particularly so in relation to cultural and gendered differences in diagnostic rates. The British Psychological Society (2012) expressed concern that 'the differential diagnosis rates for the existing condition between the U.S. and the U.K. of 8% to 1.5% are in themselves evidence of the potential risk for overdiagnosis.' In addition to differences in prevalence rates, Timimi and Timimi (2015) point out that diagnosis in these two countries is associated with different social groups. In the UK, diagnosis is more prevalent in boys from lower socio economic groups, who exhibit behavioural problems whereas in the U.S., the disorder is more often associated with low academic achievement in boys from middle socio economic backgrounds.

Variation in prevalence rates across the world is reported in several studies (Polanczyk et al. 2007, 2014). According to Willcutt (2009), worldwide prevalence rates in children and adolescents ranged between 5.9 and 7.1%. At the same time, a UK study claimed ADHD affected

3–5% of children (McCarthy et al. 2009). More current figures put prevalence rates at between 2 and 5% of UK school children (National Health Service 2012). Variation in prevalence occurs within countries as much as it does between countries. Morrow et al. (2012) found that children born at the end of the school year were more likely to have a diagnosis than children born in the earlier part of the year. Such variations in diagnostic rates of ADHD might also indicate the arbitrary nature of diagnosis and raise questions about the cultural and subjective interpretation of behaviour.

However, Singh (2008a) cautions against dismissing ADHD as a mythical scientific category simply because of the discrepancies in prevalence rates and, instead, distinguishes between the causes of ADHD and the causes of over and under diagnosis. Contributory factors to diagnosis include the influence from pharmaceutical companies and contemporary educational practices in western cultures. For example, in the UK, the steepest increase in the number of methylphenidate prescriptions (a rise of over 2000% between 1991 and 1996) coincided with the appearance of Cuba-Geigy, the largest provider of methylphenidate, in the UK (Norris and Lloyd 2000). Problems at school are an important driver for the process of diagnosis and many of the criteria necessary for an ADHD diagnosis are related specifically to an educational context (Bailey 2014; Conrad 1975; Singh 2008b). Adams (2008) suggests that children's compliance and their increased performance in exams has become the prime focus of education in neo-liberal societies. Educational policy and targets combined with reductions in funding can leave teachers struggling to manage contradictory policies of increased attainment along with the inclusion of pupils with special needs (Adams 2008; Graham 2008). Teachers, under pressure to achieve certain targets, in the absence of funded teacher assistants, may be more likely to seek a medical explanation or solution for a child whose behaviour is difficult to control within the classroom. These are possible contributory factors to increased diagnostic rates in such contexts. The availability of a medicalised discourse enables an explanation for low academic achievement other than in terms of school failure and also provides a solution to behavioural problems in the form of medication. The power of such discourse has created new ways of 'knowing' the schoolchild. As Graham (2006: 20) suggests the 'diagnostic vernacular has permeated social and educational discourses to the point that it is hard to describe or conceptualize children's classroom mis/behaviour'.

Sociological approaches to the study of medical categories regard a cross-cultural perspective as useful to illuminate the role of social context in shaping our understanding of disease and disorder. Although the profile for ADHD is changing, with countries such as Brazil reporting similar prevalence rates to the rest of the world (Arruda et al. 2015), ADHD had predominately been confined to Anglophone nations (Mchoul and Rapley 2005), and, specifically located within schools. Behaviour, which might be interpreted as ADHD within a UK classroom is likely to be framed in terms of poor classroom management in Korea (Hong 2008) or within the child's environment in Denmark (Holst 2008). The diverse cultural approaches to ADHD suggest that what is considered deviant behaviour in one culture may be more acceptable in another (Einarsdottir 2008) or it might be attributed in different ways according to the dominant theories in those countries.

However, although it is tempting to adopt a strongly relativist position in relation to these diverse cross cultural interpretations of ADHD, as Singh (2008b: 348) indicates, there is also cross cultural consensus that 'there exists a group of children whose impulsive and hyperactive behaviours are qualitatively different, and more severe, than other groups of children'. Indeed, there is debate around whether cross cultural or geographical variability is truly significant. Despite variances in understandings of ADHD, Polanczyk et al. (2007) argue that, with the exception of significant variability in diagnostic rates between North America and both Africa and the Middle East, variability has been overemphasised in the literature and can be explained by the methodological characteristics of studies. Nevertheless, it is clear that the meaning of ADHD is located within cultural and historical contexts.

ADHD and Gender

Variations in prevalence rates also occur between boys and girls, and men and women. The ADHD diagnosis is far more likely to be applied to boys than to girls (Horton-Salway 2011, 2012; Ohan and Visser

2009; Lloyd and Norris 1999). The DSM-5 (APA 2013) suggests that the prevalence rate of ADHD is 5% of schoolchildren and the ratio of boys to girls diagnosed with the disorder ranges is 2:1. According to the US Centre of Disease Control and Prevention (2014), in 2013, only 5.6% of girls were diagnosed with the disorder compared to 13.2% of boys (Rafalovich 2015). This gender imbalance in rates of diagnosis is not accounted for by neurobiological explanations (Bailey 2010).

One line of argument is that boys have more overt symptoms of ADHD than girls (Quinn 2005). In particular, an ADHD diagnosis for a boy is more likely to have a high co-morbidity with conditions such as conduct disorder or oppositional defiant disorder. In contrast, it is claimed that girls with an ADHD diagnosis are more likely to develop internalising symptoms (Quinn 2005) such as anxiety and depression. The externalising disruptive behaviour displayed by boys is more problematic for teachers and, so, they are more likely to be referred for diagnosis (Horton-Salway 2012; Ohan and Visser 2009). A second line of argument suggests that the disproportionate diagnosis of boys is a result of a perception by parents and teachers that intervention, specifically in relation to learning support within schools, is of more benefit to boys than it is to girls, perhaps reflecting a cultural bias towards education being of higher importance to boys than to girls (Ohan and Visser 2009). A third suggestion is that research into ADHD is disproportionately skewed in favour of boys, and that, consequently, clinician, parental and teacher knowledge of ADHD is constructed through texts in which boys' behaviour becomes visible, whilst girls' behaviour is rendered invisible (Bailey 2009). Bailey suggests this is the legacy of a historic propensity to study problematic male populations. Certainly, the early 'history' of ADHD would support this: from Still's (1902) (boy) moral imbeciles, identified as 'backward' within the context of their school environment, to the identification of *encephalitis lethargica* in the 1920s in the post war male population (specifically within schools and institutions consisting of boys), through to Bradley's (1937) experimental testing of Benzedrine on young, hospitalised boys. As Bailey says (2009: 172), 'each advance in medical perspectives was based on the availability of a male problem population upon which to drive the *natural* science'.

The propensity of research into problem male populations is matched by an equally biased focus towards mothers. Studies can be seen to focus on mothers and, in so doing, to (re)produce the socio-cultural/historic repertoires of mother-blame (Bennett 2007; Blum 2007). It is within this context of mother-blame that diagnosis is sought mostly by women, who are the 'primary instigators of a diagnosis' (Singh 2008b: 356). However, we do note that maternal calls for diagnosis varied across socio-cultural contexts. For example, an earlier study by Malacrida (2001) found that in Canada, which has a higher rate of diagnosis than the UK, mothers were much more likely to resist classification of their sons' behaviour, whereas in the UK, mothers were much more likely to seek out a diagnosis of ADHD, often in opposition to professional opinion. Fathers, on the other hand, appear far less in the literature relating to ADHD (Davies 2014; Horton-Salway 2012; Gray 2008). In addition, fathers are typically presented as being less likely to seek diagnosis (Singh 2003).

The controversy around prevalence rates is intensified by statistics which indicate that, in childhood, ADHD is a condition more commonly diagnosed in boys than girls. In adulthood, however, the male to female prevalence ratio narrows to 2:1 (Williamson and Johnston 2015) which is supported by claims that women represent the highest growth rate in diagnosis (Vingilis et al. 2015; Henry and Jones 2011; Castle et al. 2007). This increase in diagnostic rates amongst women may partially be explained by revision to the DSM-5 (APA 2013), which now includes more adult inclusive criteria (Winter et al. 2015). It could simply be the case that women, whose ADHD was overlooked in childhood, are now 'catching up' in adulthood. It could also be another example of 'bracket creep' discussed earlier. Critical studies of adult ADHD in women also interrogate mental health categories in relation to modern discourses of femininity (Winter et al. 2015; see also Metzl and Angel 2004) which we discuss further in Chapter 6.

Social Explanations

Social explanations for ADHD that provide a powerful complementary discourse to the one provided by the biomedical model are not exclusively put forward by sociologists. Timimi, a child psychiatrist, in dialogue with Taylor, a child psychiatrist who holds different views, queries whether ADHD is a cultural construct rather than a medical reality (Timimi and Taylor 2004). He cites the absence of a medical test for ADHD, cultural differences in prevalence rates, high levels of co-morbidity of the disorder, and the relatively small sample sizes used in neuroimaging studies as reasons to doubt the veracity of ADHD as a biomedical entity. Rather, he considers external factors such as family breakdown, frenetic family life, school pressure, the breakdown of moral authority within the family, and even the competitive nature of the market economy as being detrimental to children's mental health (Timimi and Taylor 2004).

Since the 1940s and 1950s there has been scepticism towards the neurological approach to ADHD. As well as the social factors considered by Timimi, other social explanations offered as a way of understanding the causes of ADHD include the over stimulation of modern life and the bombardment of children with fast and often frenetic visual and sensory information through television and gaming (Rafalovich 2008; DeGrandpre 2000). Since the 1970s, literature linking behaviour and diet has received popular attention. In particular, reactions to artificial food additives (Rafalovich 2008; Feingold 1974) are said to produce hyperactivity in children.

Sociological and social constructionist explanations provide one possible way of interpreting cultural and gendered variations in diagnostic rates of ADHD and in providing alternative explanations for ADHD like behaviours. Sociological knowledge produces a distinctly different discourse from that produced by biological and psychological knowledge. However, these three approaches are combined within the biopsychosocial model.

The Biopsychosocial Approach

Current medical, psychiatric and academic literature acknowledges the 'complex interplay between genetic susceptibility and environmental risk' (Tarver et al. 2014; Vander Ploeg Booth et al. 2010). This interplay is identified in various ways: psychosocial (Bailey 2014; Furnham and

Sarwar 2011), bio-social (Gillies et al. 2016), bio-psycho-social (Gray Brunton et al. 2014), depending on the focus of the study. A biopsychosocial approach brings together biological and psychosocial explanations, and calls for a parallel consideration of biological, psychological and social factors in understanding ADHD. The implication of such an approach is that change in any one of these areas would be associated with change in the other two. The call for a biopsychosocial approach has been made by many ADHD researchers critical of an entirely biological explanation for behavioural symptoms (Cooper 2001, 2008; Gray 2008; Sonuga-Barke 2005; Singh 2002b; Colley 2010). This implies a multimodal approach to treatment incorporating medication with other forms of intervention such as behavioural or family therapy. This is the approach advocated by current UK health policy frameworks (see NICE 2009).

A biopsychosocial approach mediates between the dichotomous viewpoints of ADHD as a biologically produced medical disorder and ADHD as a psychologically/socially produced disorder. The emphasis is on finding and understanding the aetiological or epiphenomenal roots of ADHD, seeking evidence of association between psychological and social factors and biological impairment. This approach, however, does not interrogate the historically situated meanings that produce these perspectives and shape our understanding of the category (Comstock 2011). In this way, the biopsychosocial model does not offer a conceptual challenge to the biological 'truth' of ADHD, and so, the psychiatric category remains robust. For example, biopsychosocial explanations do not challenge how psychiatric knowledge is imbued with social values, defining behaviours such as slow inhibitory control and lack of focus in terms of impairment as in the case of ADHD. Hawthorne (2010) argues that social interests provide support for scientific investigation of ADHD because the classification implicates the socially valued characteristics of control, focus, individual responsibility and productivity. Scientific data collection, she argues, is thus driven by discovering and revealing dysfunction in these areas, so that these problematic behaviours can be managed and appropriate intervention can be identified. Implicated in this largely invisible process of selection and interpretation of data are the pharmaceutical companies, which endorse and financially support research into the effects of stimulation medication on the brain's dopaminergic system (Hawthorne 2010). Despite increasing calls for a multimodal approach, pharmacotherapy is favoured as a treatment approach. At the time of writing, the most recent UK National Health Service fact sheet on treatment of ADHD had foregrounded medication before other therapies (NHS 2014). This can perhaps be understood by considering that treatments used in health are situated within a research, policy and practice context that values and privileges evidence based medicine (EBM). Karim (2015) describes EBM as 'a system which in research terms is dominated by the randomised control trial study [which] is a mechanism used to test the efficacy of a particular treatment' (Karim 2015: 31). Karim goes on to describe how EBM produces 'hierarchies of evidence' which privilege positivist, quantitative research methods (see Karim 2015: 33). EBM regards mental health treatment 'as a series of discrete interventions targeted at specific malfunctions in our biological or psychological make-up' (Thomas et al. 2012: 296). This does not offer the 'whole picture' (Thomas et al. 2012) and sidelines the significance of culture and meaning in mental distress and mental health practice.

Neurobiological Development and Parent Accountability

A biopsychosocial approach understands the social context of the child to potentially impact on the development of ADHD, implicating families in the production and treatment of ADHD. Causal relationships between social and biological variables are increasingly being sought to account for neurobiological development. For example, biological developmental accounts of ADHD reference the potentially adverse effects of mothers' (pre-natal) drinking and smoking on neurological development (see Bailey 2014). Similarly, maternal stress levels and subsequent levels of excess cortisol are implicated in children's neurological development in general (see Gillies et al. 2016) and as a potential risk factor in the development of ADHD symptomology, in particular (Vander Ploeg Booth et al. 2010). This focus on early developmental stages is both enabled by and enabling of neuroscientific and genetic applications. Examples of contemporary research activity include interest in the association between brain plasticity and early childhood experience (see Gillies et al. 2016; Rose 2013) and identifying bio-markers as predictive indicators of psychiatric disorders, including ADHD (Slaby 2010; Singh and Rose 2009). In their paper, Singh and Rose (2009) argue that there is inadequate evidence that bio-markers, alone, can predict the inevitability of a psychiatric disorder. However, if incorporated with social and environmental risk factors, such as poverty, abuse or alcohol, then 'biomarkers could be powerful predictors that a disorder will develop' (Singh and Rose 2009: 203). Whilst many commentators welcome a turn towards the social in biological discourses, others are more cautious, raising concerns that within the neuroscientific lab, the 'social' becomes reduced to interpersonal primary caregiver relations (Gillies et al. 2016; Rose and Abi-Rached 2013) rather than wider social problems such as poverty and inequality. As Gillies et al. (2016) argue, 'maternal behaviour is commonly positioned at the interface of the social and biological, reflecting not only gendered assumptions but also a set of late modern contentions about parenting as profoundly formative of individual life chances' (2016: 223). They argue that biosocial investigation is constructed and understood to be a 'natural, apolitical space' but, in fact, it is guided by normative assumptions about child-rearing and maternal responsibility for children's outcomes.

Developing neuroscientific knowledge produces particular ways of knowing ADHD and legitimises particular maternal practices and identities, shaping mothers' experiences and regulation of family life. Slaby (2010) considers how, on the one hand, neuroscientific discourse plays down personal responsibility for psychiatric disorders through the language of 'hard-wired connections and rigid mechanisms', while, on the other hand, the growing emphasis on plasticity and adaptability to environmental factors seems 'to lead back to quite specific forms of personal responsibility' (p. 406). These resonate with the parent as the responsible subject of neoliberal discourse. The association of neuroscientific knowledge with child development is strengthened through governmental agendas and policies and disseminated to the clinic, the classroom and the family through 'early years intervention', which targets parents and particularly mothers about how best to raise their children (Gillies et al. 2016). One, very common, intervention approach recommended for pre-school children with ADHD is group-based parenting programmes (Smith et al. 2014). Neuroscientifically informed parenting interventions target so called 'impairments' in neuropsychological functioning. Tarver et al. (2014) describe specific parenting interventions which might impact positively on executive functioning deficits, reward processing deficits, temporal processing deficits and academic functioning. These 'good parenting' obligations highlight how parenting 'has moved away from something 'natural' towards something that 'has to be learned and can be perfected or at least improved' (Bailey 2014). Furthermore, such biological accounts force parents 'into a project of parenting according to medically conceived truths of behavioural disorder' (Bailey 2014: 98), and in this way, encourage parents' dependence on specialist knowledge.

Once a child has a diagnosis, parents are required to make informed decisions about medication. Discourses around childhood, parenting and psychiatric diagnosis converge around the issue of medication. Children, within contemporary neoliberal Western societies, are represented as vulnerable, innocent and in need of protection, and their parents are required to assume prime responsibility for their care, protection and well-being. This presents conflicting choices for parents. On the one hand, there are strong arguments against medication for ADHD including side physical side-effects, possible addiction, issues around stigma, autonomy and dependence (see Singh 2005, 2008a; Rafalovich 2005). Billington and Pomerantz (2004) suggest that medication reduces opportunities for children to practise the skills necessary for the development of self-control, responsibility and self-regulation. These are characteristics valued in neoliberal societies and expected to be developed within responsible self-regulating families. On the other hand, there are strong cultural imperatives for parents to seek treatment for their children if they are 'sick'. Hawthorne (2010) argues that social expectations are threaded through the DSM, not only within the value-laden criteria of underlying disorders, but also through compassionate values of care, which include diagnosis and treatment. This may explain why, despite calls for a biopsychosocial approach, medication remains a significant method in the treatment of ADHD.

The Persistence of a Bio-Bio-Bio Approach

It would seem that in relation to ADHD, psychiatry still lies very much within the framework of the biomedical model of medicine supporting Read's view (2005) that the psychological and the social are treated as 'mere triggers' of underlying genetic pre-dispositions. Certainly, this chimes with reservations raised by the BPS about the newly revised DSM-5 (APA 2013) and its failure to address how relationship and social factors might be implicated in the process of classification: 'We consider that, as it stands, the revised DSM-5 would lead to an ongoing risk of pathologising individuals while obscuring well-established social and relationship causal factors' (BPS 2012). Similar concern is expressed by critical psychiatrists, who, whilst not challenging the legitimacy of a biomedical approach in relation to mental distress, draw attention to the turn towards depicting distress in medicalised, and, increasingly, neurobiological terms (Kirschner 2013). Such critical psychiatrists interrogate and resist the 'purely medical framing' of such phenomena (Bracken and Thomas 2010: 223).

Concluding Comments

This chapter highlights the constitutive power of historicised and more recent theorisations of ADHD, showing how ADHD has arisen from a history of biological, psychological and social theories. Moral evaluations are threaded through these shifting understandings and categorisations such that children and parents (particularly mothers) have been positioned as the subjects of a range of discourses and debates. These include ideas about impairment, child-rearing practices and the social conduct of children, academic performance, the increase in medication and a range of other issues arising from the discourse of ADHD.

The meaning of ADHD has been partly defined by the historicised discourse described in this chapter and is partly defined by contemporary discourse. Despite the complexity of the more recent biopsychosocial model arising from theory and medical practice, the polarised explanations of earlier theories continue to circulate and these are available discourses that can be drawn on by professional or lay people to account for behaviour, to explain, describe, define and attribute cause, to offer moral evaluations and to construct identities for children, their parents and also for adults with ADHD. In the later chapters of this volume, we focus on the nature of ADHD representations in relation to the wider cultural and social context, including the moral work that they do.

In the next chapter, Mary Horton-Salway explores how the media represent ADHD to the public and how this might translate in the public imagination.

References

Adams, P. (2008). Positioning behaviour: Attention deficit/hyperactivity disorder in the post welfare educational era. *International Journal of Inclusive Education, 12*(2), 113–125.

American Psychiatric Association. (1968). *Diagnostic and Statistical Manual of Mental Disorders (DSM-II)* (2nd ed.). Washington, DC: Author.

American Psychiatric Association. (1980). *Diagnostic and Statistical Manual of Mental Disorders (DSM-III)* (3rd ed.). Washington, DC: Author.

American Psychiatric Association. (1987). *Diagnostic and Statistical Manual of Mental Disorders (DSM-III)* (3rd ed., revised). Washington, DC: Author.

American Psychiatric Association. (1994). *Diagnostic and Statistical Manual of Mental Disorders (DSM-IV)* (4th ed.). Washington, DC: Author.

American Psychiatric Association (2000). *Diagnostic and Statistical Manual of Mental Disorders (DSM-IV)* (Text Revision). Washington, DC: APA.

American Psychiatric Association. (2013). *Diagnostic and statistical manual of mental disorders (DSM-5)* (5th ed.). Washington, DC: APA.

Arruda, M. A., Querido, C. N., Bigal, M. E., & Polanczyk, G. V. (2015). ADHD and mental health status in Brazilian school-age children. *Journal of Attention Disorders, 19*(1), 11–17.

Bailey, S. (2009). *Producing ADHD: An ethnographic study of behavioural discourses of early childhood* (Ph.D. thesis, University of Nottingham).

Bailey, S. (2010). The DSM and the dangerous school child. *International Journal of Inclusive Education, 14*(6), 581–592.

Bailey, S. (2014). *Exploring ADHD: An Ethnography of Disorder in Early Childhood*. Abingdon: Routledge.

Bennett, J. (2007). (Dis)ordering motherhood: Mothering a child with attention deficit hyperactivity disorder. *Body Society, 13*(4), 97–110.

Bettelheim, B. (1959). Feral children and autistic children. *American Journal of Sociology, 64*(5), 455–467.

Billington, T., & Pomerantz, M. (2004). Resisting social exclusion. In T. Billington & M. Pomerantz (Eds.), *Children at the Margins: Supporting Children, Supporting Schools* (pp. 1–14). Stoke on Trent: Trentham Books.

Blum, L. (2007). Mother-blame in the Prozac nation: Raising kids with invisible disabilities. *Gender and Society, 21*(2), 202–226.

BPS (The British Psychological Society). (2012). *Response to the American Psychiatric Association: DSM The Future of Psychiatric Diagnosis (Final Consultation)*. Retrieved from http://apps.bps.org.uk/_publicationfiles/consultation-responses/DSM-5%202012%20-%20BPS%20response.pdf.

Bracken, P., & Thomas, P. (2010). From Szasz to Foucault: On the role of critical psychiatry. *Philosophy, Psychiatry, and Psychology, 17*(3), 219–228.

Bradley, C. (1937). The behaviour of children receiving benzedrine. *American Journal of Psychiatry, 94*, 577–581.

Burman, E. (2008). *Deconstructing Developmental Psychology* (2nd ed.). London: Routledge.

Castle, L., Aubert, R., Verbrugge, R., & Khalid, M. (2007). Trends in medication treatment for ADHD. *Journal of Attention Disorders, 10*(4), 335–342.

Colley, B. (2010). ADHD, science and the common man. *Emotional and Behavioural Difficulties, 15*(2), 83–94.

Collins, H. M. (1985). *Changing Order: Replication and Induction in Scientific Practice*. London: Sage.

Comstock, E. J. (2011). The end of drugging children: Toward the genealogy of the ADHD subject. *Journal of the History of the Behavioral Sciences, 47*(1), 44–69.

Conrad, P. (1975). The discovery of hyperkinesis: Notes on the medicalisation of deviant behaviour. *Social Problems, 23*, 12–21.

Conrad, P. (2006). *Identifying Hyperactive Children: The Medicalisation of Deviant Behaviour*. Aldershot: Ashgate Publishing Ltd.

Conrad, P. (2007). *The Medicalisation of Society on the Transformation of Human Conditions into Treatable Disorders*. Baltimore: The Johns Hopkins University Press.

Conrad, P., & Potter, D. (2006). From hyperactive children to ADHD adults: Observations on the expansion of medical categories. In *Identifying Hyperactive Children: The Medicalisation of Deviant Behaviour* (Expanded edition., pp. 101–126). Aldershot: Ashgate Publishing.

Cooper, P. (2001). Understanding AD/HD: A brief critical review of the literature. *Children and Society, 15*(5), 387–395.

Cooper, P. (2008). Like alligators bobbing for poodles? A critical discussion of education, ADHD and the biopsychosocial perspective. *Journal of Philosophy of Education, 42*(3–4), 457–474.

Davies, A. (2014). *It's a problem with the brain: A discursive analysis of parents' constructions of ADHD* (Unpublished Ph.D. thesis). The Open University, Milton Keynes.

DeGrandpre, R. J. (2000). *Ritalin Nation*. New York: W.W. Norton.

Dillon, A., & Craven, R. G. (2014). Examining the genetic contribution to ADHD. *Ethical Human Psychology and Psychiatry, 16*(1), 20–28. https://doi.org/10.1891/1559-4343.16.1.20.

Donnelly, L. (2013, August 13). Students taking 'smart drugs' may be behind soaring Ritalin use. *The Telegraph*. Available at http://www.telegraph.co.uk/health/healthnews/10238660/Students-taking-smart-drugs-may-be-behind-soaring-Ritalin-use.html (Accessed 21 November 2013).

Doward, J. (2013, May 12). Psychiatrists under fire in mental health battle. *The Guardian*. Available at https://www.theguardian.com/society/2013/may/12/psychiatrists-under-fire-mental-health (Accessed 20 May 2017).

Einarsdottir, J. (2008). Teaching children with ADHD: Icelandic early childhood teachers' perspectives. *Early Child Development and Care, 178*(4), 375–397.

Engel, G. L. (1977). The need for a new medical model: A challenge for biomedicine. *Science, 196*, 129–136.

Feingold, B. F. (1974). *Why Your Child Is Hyperactive*. New York: Random House.

Foley, P. (2011). A viral infection of the mind? The curious case of encephalitis lethargica. *The Conversation*. Available at http://theconversation.com/a-viral-infection-of-the-mind-the-curious-case-of-encephalitis-lethargica-660 (Accessed 21 May 2017).

Foucault, M. (1991). *Discipline and Punish: The Birth of the Prison*. London: Penguin Books.

Foucault, M. (2003). *The Birth of the Clinic*. Abingdon: Routledge Classics.

Foucault, M. (2006). *The History of Madness*. Abingdon: Routledge.

Francis, A. (2012). Stigma in an era of medicalisation and anxious parenting: How proximity and culpability shape middle-class parents' experiences of disgrace. *Sociology of Health & Illness, 34*(6), 927–942.

Frankel, H. (2010, May 7). Doctors, leave them kids alone. *TES Magazine*. Available at http://www.tes.co.uk/article.aspx?storycode=6043074 (Accessed 20 June 2010).

Furnham, A., & Sarwar, T. (2011). Beliefs about attention-deficit hyperactivity disorder. *Counselling Psychology Quarterly, 24*(4), 301–311.

Gilbert, G. N., & Mulkay, M. (1984). *Opening Pandora's Box: A Sociological Analysis of Scientists' Discourse*. Cambridge: Cambridge University Press.

Gillies, V., Edwards, R., & Horsley, N. (2016). Brave new brains: Sociology, family and the politics of knowledge. *The Sociological Review, 64,* 219–237.

Goffman, E. (1961). *Asylums*. Harmondsworth: Penguin.

Goodley, D., & Rapley, M. (2001). How do you understand 'learning difficulties'? Towards a social theory of impairment. *Mental Retardation, 39*(3), 229–232.

Graham, L. J. (2006). Caught in the net: A Foucaultian interrogation of the incidental effects of limited notions of 'inclusion'. *International Journal of Inclusive Education, 10*(1), 3–24.

Graham, L. J. (2007). *Schooling attention deficit hyperactivity disorders: Educational systems of formation and the 'behaviourally disordered' school child* (Doctoral thesis, Queensland University of Technology).

Graham, L. J. (2008). Drugs, labels and (p)ill-fitting boxes: ADHD and children who are hard to teach. *Discourse: Studies in the Cultural Politics of Education, 29*(1), 85–106.

Gray, C. A. (2008). *Lay and professional constructions of childhood ADHD (Attention Deficit Hyperactivity Disorder): A discourse analysis* (Ph.D. thesis, Queen Margaret University).

Gray Brunton, C., McVittie, C., Ellison, M., & Willock, J. (2014). Negotiating parental accountability in the face of uncertainty for attention-deficit hyperactivity disorder. *Qualitative Health Research, 24*(2), 242–253.

Halasz, G., Anaf, G., Ellingson, P., Manne, A., & Thomson Salo, F. (2002). *Cries Unheard: A New Look at Attention Deficit Hyperactivity Disorder*. Altona: Common Ground.

Hall, J. (2008). Mental deficiency changing the outlook. *The Psychologist, 21*(11), 1006–1007.

Harper, D. J. (2013). On the persistence of psychiatric diagnosis: Moving beyond a zombie classification system. *Feminism and Psychology, 23*(1), 78–85.

Hawthorne, S. (2010). Embedding values: How science and society jointly valence a concept—The case of ADHD. *Studies in History and Philosophy of Biological and Biomedical Sciences, 41*(1), 21–31.

Henry, E., & Jones, S. H. (2011). Experiences of older adult women diagnosed with attention deficit hyperactivity disorder. *Journal of Women and Aging, 23*(3), 246–262.

Holst, J. (2008). Danish teachers' conception of challenging behaviour and DAMP/ADHD. *Early Child Development and Care, 178*(4), 363–374.

Hong, Y. (2008). Teachers' perceptions of young children with ADHD in Korea. *Early Child Development and Care, 178*(4), 399–414.

Horton-Salway, M. (2011). Repertoires of ADHD in UK newspaper media. *Health (London), 15*(5), 533–549.

Horton-Salway, M. (2012). Gendering attention deficit hyperactivity disorder: A discursive analysis of UK newspaper stories. *Journal of Health Psychology, 18*(8), 1085–1099. Published online before print October 1, 2012. https://doi.org/10.1177/1359105312456326.

Karim, K. (2015). The value of conversation analysis: A child psychiatrist's perspective. In M. O'Reilly & J. N. Lester (Eds.), *The Palgrave Handbook of Child Mental Health* (pp. 25–41). Basingstoke: Palgrave Macmillan.

Kean, B. (2005). The risk society and attention deficit hyperactivity disorder (ADHD): A critical social research analysis concerning the development and social impact of the ADHD diagnosis. *Ethical Human Psychology and Psychiatry, 7*(2), 131–142.

Kirschner, S. (2013). Diagnosis and its discontents: Critical perspectives on psychiatric nosology in the DSM. *Feminism and Psychology, 23*(1), 10–28.

Lange, K. W., Reichl, S., Lange, K. M., Tucha, L., & Tucha, O. (2010). The history of attention deficit hyperactivity disorder. *Attention Deficit and Hyperactivity Disorders, 2*(4), 241–255.

Lemma, A. (1996). *Introduction to Psychopathology*. London: Sage.

Litt, J. (2004). Women's carework in low-income households: The special case of children with attention deficit hyperactivity disorder. *Gender and Society, 18*(5), 625–644.

Lloyd, G., & Norris, C. (1999). Including ADHD? *Disability and Society, 14*(4), 505–517.

Malacrida, C. (2001). Motherhood, resistance and attention deficit disorder: Strategies and limits. *Canadian Review of Sociology and Anthropology, 38*(2), 141–165.

Malacrida, C. (2004). Medicalisation, ambivalence and social control: Mothers' descriptions of educators and ADD/ADHD. *Health: An Interdisciplinary Journal for the Social Study of Health, Illness and Medicine, 8*(61), 61–79.

Mayes, R., & Rafalovich, A. (2007). Suffer the restless children: The evolution of ADHD and paediatric stimulant use, 1900–80. *History of Psychiatry, 18*(4), 435–457.

McCarthy, S., Asherson, P., Coghill, D., Hollis, C., Murray, M., Potts, L., et al. (2009). Attention-deficit hyperactivity disorder: Treatment discontinuation in adolescents and young adults. *The British Journal of Psychiatry, 194*(3), 273–277.

Mchoul, A., & Rapley, M. (2005). A case of attention-deficit hyperactivity disorder diagnosis: Sir Karl and Francis B. Slug it out on the consulting room floor. *Discourse and Society, 16*(3), 419–449.

Meredith, C. (2013, August 13). Ritalin use more than doubles in six years sparking 'smart drug' fears. *The Huffington Post UK.* Available at http://www.huffingtonpost.co.uk/2013/08/13/adhd-ritalin-smart-drugs_n_3747748.html (Accessed 20 November 2013).

Metzl, J., & Angel, J. (2004). Assessing the impact of SSRI antidepressants on popular notions of women's depressive illness. *Social Science and Medicine, 58,* 577–584.

Moghaddam, M. F., Assareh, M., Heidaripoor, A., Rad, R. E., & Pishjoo, M. (2013). The study comparing parenting styles of children with ADHD and normal children. *Archives of Psychiatry and Psychotherapy, 4,* 45–49.

Moncrieff, J., & Timimi, S. (2013). The social and cultural construction of psychiatric knowledge: An analysis of NICE guidelines on depression and ADHD. *Anthropology and Medicine, 20*(1), 59–71.

Morrow, R. L., Garland, E. J., Wright, J. M., Maclure, M., Taylor, S., & Dormuth, C. R. (2012). Influence of relative age on diagnosis and treatment of attention-deficit/hyperactivity disorder in children. *CMAJ: Canadian Medical Association Journal, 184*(7), 755–762.

National Health Service. (2012). *Attention Deficit and Hyperactivity Disorder (ADHD).* Available at www.nhs.uk/Conditions/Attention-deficit-hyperactivity-disorder/Pages/Introduction.aspx (Accessed 14 September 2017).

National Health Service. (2014). *Attention Deficit and Hyperactivity Disorder (ADHD)—Treatment.* Available at http://www.nhs.uk/conditions/attention-deficit-hyperactivity-disorder/Pages/Treatment.aspx (Accessed 14 September 2017).

National Institute for Health and Care Excellence. (2016). *Attention Deficit Hyperactivity Disorder: Diagnosis and Management NICE Guideline (CG72).* Available at https://www.nice.org.uk/guidance/cg72/ifp/chapter/Information-for-parents-of-children-with-ADHD (Accessed 14 September 2017).

National Institute of Clinical Excellence. (2009). *Attention Deficit Hyperactivity Disorder: Diagnosis and Management of ADHD in Children, Young People and Adults.* London: National Institute for Health and Clinical Excellence.

Available at http://www.nice.org.uk/Guidance/CG72 (Accessed 14 September 2017).

Neophytou, K., & Webber, R. (2005). Attention deficit and hyperactivity disorder: The family and social context. *Australian Social Work, 58*(3), 313–325.

Norris, C., & Lloyd, G. (2000). Parents, professionals and ADHD: What the papers say. *European Journal of Special Needs Education, 15*(2), 123–137.

O'Dell, L., & Brownlow, C. (2015). Normative development and the autistic child. In M. O'Reilly & J. N. Lester (Eds.), *The Palgrave Handbook of Child Mental Health* (pp. 296–309). Basingstoke: Palgrave Macmillan.

O'Dell, L., Bertilsdotter Rosqvist, H., Ortega, F., Brownlow, C., & Orsini, M. (2016). Critical autism studies: Exploring epistemic dialogues and intersections, challenging dominant understandings of autism. *Disability and Society, 31*(2), 166–179.

Ohan, J. L., & Visser, T. A. W. (2009). Why is there a gender gap in children presenting for attention deficit hyperactivity disorder services? *Journal of Clinical Child and Adolescent Psychology, 38*(5), 650–660.

Polanczyk, G., Silva de Lima, M., Lessa Horta, B., Biederman, J., & Augusto Rohde, L. (2007). The worldwide prevalence of ADHD: A systematic review and metaregression analysis. *American Journal of Psychiatry, 164*(6), 942–948.

Polanczyk, G. V., Willcutt, E. G., Salum, G. A., Kieling, C., & Rohde, L. A. (2014). ADHD prevalence estimates across three decades: An updated systematic review and meta-regression analysis. *International Journal of Epidemiology, 43*(2), 434–442. https://doi.org/10.1093/ije/dyt261.

Quinn, P. O. (2005). Treating adolescent girls and women with ADHD: Gender-specific issues. *Journal of Clinical Psychology, 61*(5), 579–587.

Radley, A. (1994). *Making Sense of Illness: The Social Psychology of Health and Disease*. London: Sage.

Rafalovich, A. (2001). The conceptual history of attention deficit hyperactivity disorder: Idiocy, imbecility, encephalitis and the child deviant, 1877–1929. *Deviant Behaviour an Interdisciplinary Journal, 22*(2), 93–115.

Rafalovich, A. (2004/2008). *Framing ADHD Children: A Critical Examination of the History, Discourse and Everyday Experience of Attention Deficit/Hyperactivity Disorder*. Plymouth: Lexington Books.

Rafalovich, A. (2005). Exploring clinician uncertainty in the diagnosis and treatment of attention deficit hyperactivity disorder. *Sociology of Health Illness, 27*(3), 305–323.

Rafalovich, A. (2015). ADHD: Three competing discourses. In M. O'Reilly & N. Lester (Eds.), *The Palgrave Handbook of Child Mental Health* (pp. 79–99). Basingstoke: Palgrave Macmillan.

Read, J. (2005). The bio-bio-bio model of madness. *The Psychologist, 8*(10), 596–597.

Remschmidt, H. (2005). Global consensus on ADHD/HKD. *European Child and Adolescent Psychiatry, 14*(3), 127–137.

Rose, N. (1996). *Inventing Our Selves: Psychology, Power, and Personhood.* Cambridge: Cambridge University Press.

Rose, N. (1999). *Governing the Soul: The Shaping of the Private Self.* London: Free Association Books.

Rose, N. (2007). *The Politics of Life Itself: Biomedicine, Power and Subjectivity in the Twenty First Century.* Princeton, NJ: Princeton University Press.

Rose, N. (2013). The human sciences in a biological age. *Theory, Culture and Society, 30*(1), 3–34.

Rose, N., & Abi-Rached, J. M. (2013). *Neuro: The New Brain Sciences and the Management of the Mind.* Princeton, NJ: Princeton University Press.

Saul, H. (2013, August 13). Use of ADHD drugs soars by more than 50% in six years. *The Independent.* Available at http://www.independent.co.uk/news/uk/home-news/use-of-adhd-drugs-soars-by-more-than-50-in-six-years-8758768.html (Accessed 21 November 2013 and 14 September 2017).

Singh, I. (2002a). Bad boys, good mothers, and the miracle of Ritalin. *Science in Context, 15*(4), 577–603.

Singh, I. (2002b). Biology in context: Social and cultural perspectives on ADHD. *Children and Society, 16*(5), 360–367.

Singh, I. (2003). Boys will be boys: Fathers' perspectives on ADHD symptoms, diagnosis and drug treatment. *Harvard Review of Psychiatry, 11*(6), 308–316.

Singh, I. (2004). Doing their jobs: Mothering with Ritalin in a culture of mother-blame. *Social Science and Medicine, 59*(6), 1193–1205.

Singh, I. (2005). Will the 'real boy' please behave: Dosing dilemmas for parents of boys with ADHD. *The American Journal of Bioethics, 5*(3), 34–47.

Singh, I. (2008a). Beyond polemics: Science and ethics of ADHD. *Nature Reviews Neuroscience, 9,* 957–964.

Singh, I. (2008b). ADHD culture and education. *Early Child Development and Care, 178*(4), 339–346.

Singh, I., & Rose, N. (2009). Biomarkers in psychiatry. *Nature, 460,* 202–207.

Slaby, J. (2010). Steps towards a critical neuroscience. *Phenomenology and the Cognitive Sciences, 9,* 397–416.

Smith, E., Koerting, J., Latter, S., Knowles, M. M., McCann, D. C., Thompson, M., & Sonuga-Barke, E. J. (2014). Overcoming barriers to effective early parenting interventions for attention-deficit hyperactivity disorder (ADHD): Parent and practitioner views. *Child: Care, Health and Development, 41*(1), 93–102.

Sonuga-Barke, E. J. S. (2005). Causal models of attention-deficit/hyperactivity disorder: From common simple deficits to multiple developmental pathways. *Biological Psychiatry, 57*(11), 1231–1238.

Still, G. F. (1902). Some abnormal psychiatric conditions in children. *Lancet, 1,* 1008–1012, 1077–1082, 1163–1168.

Tancred, E.-M., & Greeff, A. P. (2015). Mothers' parenting styles and the association with family coping strategies and family adaptation in families of children with ADHD. *Clinical Social Work Journal, 43,* 442–451.

Tarver, J., Daley, D., & Sayal, K. (2014). Beyond symptom control for attention-deficit hyperactivity disorder (ADHD): What can parents do to improve outcomes? *Child: Care, Health and Development, 41*(1), 1–14.

Taylor, M., O'Donoghue, T., & Houghton, S. (2006). To medicate or not to medicate? The decision making process of Western Australian parents following their child's diagnosis with an attention deficit hyperactivity disorder. *International Journal of Disability, Development and Education, 53*(1), 111–128.

Thomas, P., Bracken, P., & Timimi, S. (2012). The limits of evidence-based medicine in psychiatry. *Philosophy, Psychiatry and Psychology, 19*(4), 295–308.

Timimi, S., & Taylor, E. (2004). ADHD is best understood as a cultural construct. *The British Journal of Psychiatry, 184,* 8–9.

Timimi, S., & Timimi, S. (2015). The social construction of attention deficit hyperactivity disorder. In M. O'Reilly & N. Lester (Eds.), *The Palgrave Handbook of Child Mental Health* (pp. 139–158). Basingstoke: Palgrave Macmillan.

Vander Ploeg Booth, K., Chronis-Tuscano, A., & Stein, M. A. (2010). ADHD and mood symptoms in mothers of children with ADHD. *CML—Psychiatry, 21*(1), 1–13.

Vingilis, E., Erickson, P. G., Toplak, M., Kolla, N. J., Mann, R. E., Seeley, J., et al. (2015). ADHD symptoms, comorbidities, substance use and social outcomes among men and women in a Canadian sample. *BioMed*

Research International, 2015, Article ID 982072, 8 pages. http://dx.doi.org/10.1155/2015/982072.

Visser, J., & Jehan, Z. (2009). ADHD: A scientific fact or a factual opinion? A critique of the veracity of attention deficit hyperactivity. *Disorder Emotional and Behavioural Difficulties, 14*(2), 127–140.

Weyandt, L., Swentosky, A., & Gudmundsdottir, B. G. (2013). Neuroimaging and ADHD: fMRI, PET, DTI findings, and methodological limitations. *Developmental Neuropsychology, 38*(4), 211–225. https://doi.org/10.1080/87565641.2013.783833.

Whitely, M. (2015). Attention deficit hyperactive disorder diagnosis continues to fail the reliability and validity tests. *Australian and New Zealand Journal of Psychiatry, 49*(6), 497–498.

Willcutt, E. G. (2012). The prevalence of DSM-IV attention-deficit/hyperactivity disorder: A meta-analytic review. *Neurotherapeutics, 9,* 490–499.

Williamson, D., & Johnston, C. (2015). Gender differences in adults with attention-deficit/hyperactivity disorder: A narrative review. *Clinical Psychology Review, 40,* 15–27.

Winter, H., Moncrieff, J., & Speed, E. (2015). "Because you're worth it": A discourse analysis of the gendered rhetoric of the ADHD woman. *Qualitative Research in Psychology, 12*(4), 415–434.

Woolgar, S. (1988). *Science: The Very Idea.* Chichester: Ellis Horwood/London: Tavistock.

World Health Organisation. (1992). *ICD-10 Classifications of Mental and Behavioural Disorder: Clinical Descriptions and Diagnostic Guidelines.* Geneva: World Health Organisation.

3

Media Representations of ADHD

Mary Horton-Salway

The meaning of ADHD was constructed over historical time, competing explanations polarising around biological/genetic causes versus psychosocial influences. These perspectives continue to influence the discourse of ADHD, despite the more complex integrated biopsychosocial understandings that have arisen in more recent years. Historically, biological/genetic explanations arose from research and theory linking neurological difference with developmental impairment, whilst psychosocial explanations have been concerned with the impact of psychological and socio-environmental circumstances on child development and behaviour. These different perspectives on ADHD have been linked to medicalised and psychosocial interventions generating a range of moral evaluations that are threaded through the discourse of ADHD. These influence the public imagination and have social consequences.

A growing concern about medicating children has developed in tandem with these ideas, social constructionist sociologists arguing that the label, ADHD, medicalises what might otherwise be regarded as social problems. Social problems are of course defined according to cultural norms and values. Medicalisation, from this

M. Horton-Salway and A. Davies, *The Discourse of ADHD*,
The Language of Mental Health, https://doi.org/10.1007/978-3-319-76026-1_3

perspective, derives from the conditions of neo-liberal ideology and the powerful influence of the pharmaceutical industry, with its stake in medical research and solutions. The supply of medicines, they argue, is a powerful driver and along these lines, medicalised treatments have been interpreted as a form of social control arising from the needs of neo-liberal societies (Conrad 1975, 2006; Conrad and Potter 2000). Definitions of ADHD and medicalisation are, from this view, linked to cultural values and also gender stereotypes because, in the case of ADHD, this targets boys and conduct issues.

In addition to the gender bias in diagnosis and treatment, social constructionist critiques of ADHD cite variations in its definition and incidence across historical and cross-cultural contexts (see Chapter 2). While we broadly agree with the idea that the meaning of ADHD is a gendered cultural construct that takes its' meaning from socio-cultural ideology, we note that the process of construction and situated meaning is common to all medical, scientific and social categories, even the ones that might be regarded as less controversial (see Chapter 1). This does not imply that such categories are not real, but that their definitions are meaningful within the current terms of cultural reference and scientific knowledge. The phenomena labelled ADHD are more recently understood by science and medicine as the product of biopsychosocial interactions and this contemporary model has a cultural meaning as well as a medical relevance. The biopsychosocial explanation of ADHD, arising from the interrelationship of biological psychological and social factors, is itself a theoretical model that has shaped the meaning of ADHD according to greater complexity, at least in theory. The interpretation, meaning and personal experience of ADHD is, however, a product of discourse and culture; an ongoing dynamic process of feedback informed by the legacy of historical discourse, the current representations of science and research, the interpretations of health professionals, educators, media framing and the discourse of the general public (Fig. 3.1).

The themes of this book are the social construction of ADHD, social identities, gendering and resistance. In this chapter, we explore the following questions in relation to media discourse:

- How do the media represent ADHD?
- What social, gendered or stigmatising identities are captured by these representations?
- What forms of resistance to negative stereotypes might there be in the media?

Fig. 3.1 Representing ADHD in the media: book themes

ADHD, Media Concerns and Media Framing

Social constructionist critiques of 'biomedical control' or the rise in prescription of ADHD medication have lately been some of the more prominent arguments that have been taken up in the UK media and other neo-liberal societies such as the US. Representation of ADHD has been historically variable, however, and ADHD has frequently been framed in the media as a polarised debate, pitting biological explanations against social and psychological ones. There are a greater number of complex representations of ADHD in more recent years (Ponnou and Gonon 2017) although the emphasis differs across cultures.

Psychosocial explanations in the media can translate as parental blame in the public imagination, for example, by association with a psychoanalytic rationale in the French newsprint media (Ponnou and Gonon 2017) or by referring to 'the social, cultural and educational pre-conditions that drive the medicalization of specifically boys' behaviour' in the UK newsprint media (Horton-Salway 2011: 543). In their analysis of Australian newsprint media (1999–2009), Harwood et al. (2017: 7) have also described the way that stories of parental blame are constructed using a metaphor of 'fault' arguing that 'parents were depicted in metaphoric terms of "hands-off parenting" or of not being "on guard".' They also observed,

> a widespread positioning of a rise in rates of "bad" behaviour among children (predominantly boys) as a result of parents (predominantly mothers) focusing their attention on work rather than their children. References to working mothers, busy parents, single-parent families, "hands off parenting" and "poor parenting skills" were littered throughout the newsprint media. (Harwood et al. 2017: 7)

In stories depicting parental blame, the phenomenon of 'mother blame' is a common theme that might derive partly from the legacy of psychoanalytic theories (see Chapter 2). Evidence from Ponnou and Gonan (2017: 1) suggests that '…in France, the biological model of ADHD as a neurological disease has been counteracted by a psychodynamic understanding considering that ADHD symptoms should be seen as a child's response to emotional distress…'. One conclusion they drew from their study of media stories was that 'according to French newspapers, the psychosocial model of ADHD appears to put emphasis on the persons (that is, children and parents) rather than on the society and this might reflect the influence of psychoanalysis in France.' (2017: 8). Feminist writers have also emphasised that the discourse of parenting, family health and child care has an historical focus on mothers as the primary carer, provider of nurturing and parent responsible for healthcare (Blum 2007; Malacrida 2002; see also Chapter 4). Many media stories have taken up the gendered imperatives that arise from these theoretical ideas and the cultural stereotypes that are embedded within them.

Lay discourse about ADHD is likely to be influenced by media representations of ADHD and the stereotypes that they contain. The representation of otherness (us and them) is a popular strategy used by the media to frame concerns about social groups. For example, Olstead described how the media position people with mental illness in hierarchies of difference: 'They are represented as having 'degrees' of difference that radiate from what is constituted as the core, 'normal'…' (2002: 628). The construction of ADHD in the media and its focus on extreme behavioural problems, the social categories of 'naughty boys', 'working mothers' or 'single parents', identified by Harwood's analysis of media stories, are examples of this. In Harwood's example, the category of 'working mother' is evaluated against a normalised 'ideal' of mothers as primary caregivers and, while the term 'single parents' is apparently gender neutral it implies stereotypes that not only define the parents of children with ADHD as other and marginal to the norm of two parent families, but also calls up the more culturally recognisable gendered category of 'single mother' with all of its historical connotations of moral censure. There is a long history of discourse around the category of 'single mother' that implies social problems, irresponsibility, absent fathers and state dependency. For example, Jean Carabine traced how 'lone mothers' have been produced and re-produced in historical discourse as 'undeserving welfare subjects' (Carabine 2001: 286). Even though these historicised discourses are not usually explicitly drawn on by media stories, they are nonetheless hearable in the selection of categories such as 'single parents'. The formula for such stories is the definition of a problem linked to a social group who are marginal and blameworthy. This can be subtle and defined by the selection of descriptive terms, but such stories are common in the media and take many forms, being copied and replicated across many contexts (Valentine 2001). Many representations of ADHD, for example, take the form of cultural narratives that provide a social commentary, function to teach moral lessons, provoke public outrage or generate moral panics. They draw on or imply cultural stereotypes and appear in media news stories as 'a form of modern mythology' that captures the public imagination (Sternadori 2014: 303). Harwood et al. emphasise that the media representation of ADHD is more than a matter of social concern: It is inherently ideological, for example drawing on metaphor and forms of language that depict 'science as fix' but also represents parents as blameworthy (Harwood et al. 2017: 2). Media framing and the forms of language used in stories and science reports are therefore an important aspect of how the public are likely to read and interpret the meaning of ADHD.

One function of the media is to report new knowledge and science information to the public and scientific explanation is a powerful form of discourse implying objective facts. However media debate also feeds upon the reporting of science research findings as a polemic (Colley 2010). While the appearance of balance, neutrality and fact is an important aspect of presenting credible stories and debates, many have argued that complex science can be reduced by the media, to 'a parody of science' (Goldacre 2009: 225). Writing about Australian news media coverage of medication, Robertson et al. (2013: 2) argued that although popular media do indeed provide information on new knowledge and medicines they are also inclined to make 'exaggerated claims of benefits' and 'inadequate coverage of harms'. This has social and medical consequences, since stories about new medicines, they observe, have indeed correlated with 'increased patient requests' (2013: 2).

Despite the circulation of information about ADHD, Furnham and Sarwar (2011) have expressed concern that the public are not at all well informed about causes and consequences. Perhaps families are better informed if they have a personal interest in researching the topic for themselves, as Alison Davies noted in her research on parents' experience (Davies 2014; and Chapters 4 and 5 of this volume). Certainly some sectors of society are deemed to be better informed than others, for example women with a higher level of education are likely to know more about ADHD (McLeod et al. 2007). This is not surprising, since women are usually positioned as the custodians of family health (see Horton-Salway 2012) and those with a better education, resources and more social and cultural capital are likely to have greater skills and access to knowledge networks (Bourdieu 1979). Nevertheless, McLeod et al. have expressed a concern that the general public should be better informed and that 'Future media and educational efforts should seek to provide accurate information about ADHD' (2007: 626). However reasonable this might sound, the question still remains, what constitutes accurate information? This is the challenge faced by the media in presenting ADHD as a controversial category and for the public who try to make sense of it.

Newsworthiness and the Decline of Scientific Authority

Media stories must primarily be newsworthy and they have to make selections about reporting on this basis as well as providing 'factual' information and commentary to the public. However, the selection of newsworthy material is also part of media framing of stories and this constitutes bias (Zhongdang and Kosicki 1993). This happens by 'problem definitions, causal interpretations, moral evaluations, and treatment recommendations as well as key themes, phrases and words.' (Weaver 2007: 43). Stories are framed so that people will understand them as factual drawing on repeated and familiar forms and stereotypical images and identities that appeal to common-sense and cultural knowledge (Sternadori 2014: 303). Balance and complexity can sometimes be sacrificed in favour of formulaic stories using sensational headlines, slogans and even, misleading science reports. Media reports of ADHD might suggest, for example, that 'children are "bad" because they have been brought up to be "bad"…' or that there has been 'a global conspiracy to medicate children' (Colley 2010: 90).

Armon (2015: 3) points out that presenting the facts of science to news media can be problematic since 'journalists and experts differ in what they consider to be newsworthy and relevant'. For example, familiar narratives that are designed to teach moral lessons are one kind of popular construction (cf. Ricoeur 1967). In their study of representations of autism in the UK media, O'Dell and Brownlow (2015) found that stories reporting 'fear of damage' from the MMR vaccine had been given priority over stories presenting scientific explanation. Panics are easily fermented by health scares in the media, especially when parents are trying to protect their children, and this had real consequences expressed in the lower take up of MMR vaccination and the subsequent higher incidence of childhood diseases (see also Kata 2010).

So how do the public know what constitutes accurate scientific knowledge? Science had achieved a somewhat mythical authoritative status during the age of modernity and it is sometimes still the case that science is presented in news reports as 'a grand unveiling of indisputable truth' (Harwood et al. 2017: 5). However, Seale (2003: 522) has pointed out 'a decline in the social and cultural authority of medicine', such that lay people in 'information-rich' post-modern societies are more likely to have access to a variety of knowledge forms and more inclined to question scientific and medical knowledge. The authority of scientists as purveyors of objective truths and medical practitioners as purveyors of evidence based cures have been undermined and the myth of their prior authority called into question. Within the framework of academic and medical tribes, differing viewpoints and critiques of scientific findings have, of course, always been a routine and integral part of the method and progression of science. Science had previously established its claims to be a superior method and form of knowledge, but the underlying processes of scientific claim, critique and counter-claim have become more obvious to the lay public, so also they are more aware of the constructive processes of rhetoric and competing versions of truth. As the public have become consumers of science knowledge and health care information via the media and producers of such information via *The Internet*, the authority of experts has declined (see also, Norris and Lloyd 2000).

Apart from the erosion of scientific and medical authority, the validity and accuracy of media reports on science has been the subject of much criticism. Writing on the coverage of ADHD in the French media, Gonon et al. (2011) claimed that there is frequently a discrepancy between 'neurobiological facts and the firm conclusions stated by the media' (2011: 1). They observed that only one out of the sixty one media articles, in their sample, had been accurate in presenting results and conclusions. They also identified a bias towards reporting on science discoveries published in prominent journals, those that were more likely to have made 'positive biomedical observations' (see also Harwood et al. 2017). Based on a study of French television programs in 2007–2010, Bourdaa et al. (2015: 209) observed that public understanding of ADHD was based on media reports of science that were subsequently refuted or amended but these amendments are rarely reported by the media. As a consequence, media coverage has tended to frame science stories as sensational claims that are constructed using a 'scientific breakthrough metaphor' (Harwood et al. 2017). Along these lines, Partridge et al. (2011: 1) commented on the consequences of 'overly enthusiastic media coverage' of neuroscience, pointing out that this 'can unrealistically raise public expectations about their future impact'. They argued that 'media reporting often misconstrues the scope, feasibility, benefits and risks of new neurotechnologies'.

Clearly, the reporting of 'breakthrough' stories can overlook the incremental changes arising from follow up research that typically defines the normative progression of science. An article entitled *Journalistic*

Deficit Disorder: Reporting Science, appearing in *The Economist* (London) (22 September, 2012: Volume 404, 90–92) agreed with Gonon et al. (2011) that breakthrough stories could be misleading to readers, but also made the point that refutations of original findings are rarely published in the high profile journals that are noticed by journalists. Furthermore, Gonon et al. had also commented on researchers' own 'optimistic extrapolations of preliminary data to "therapeutic prospects"….and their tendency to report 'stronger conclusions than their results warranted' (cited in Partridge et al. 2011: 1). This could also be responsible for inaccuracy or bias in the media and might partly be due to the institutional and stakeholder pressures placed on researchers and scientists to reach a positive outcome that has a practical or therapeutic application. On the other hand it might reflect efforts to be published in a high profile journal, or the media tendency to report sensational stories. Either way, a focus on breakthrough science and exaggerated claims can influence public knowledge of science and this surely contributes to the way that the understanding of ADHD is circulated in the public domain. For example, representations of ADHD as a neurological impairment depicting children as abnormal and in need of medicalised solutions are common and such accounts are often dependent on reports of new science findings on ADHD evidenced by brain scan or gene research (Horton-Salway 2011). Reporting of science varies though, as Ponnou and Gonon's (2017: 8) recent study of French media points out, 'TV programmes showed brain scans on screen and erroneously claimed that brain imaging can reveal ADHD'. However, they also found that 'In contrast, only one article of the general press and none of the specialized press said so'.

There is little doubt that ADHD continues to be newsworthy and controversial, attracting a great deal of attention in the popular media. The topic is reported through the genre of human interest stories, disagreements on science findings and stories that generate 'moral panics' about the behaviour of children and the rise in prescription medication. For example, Schmitz et al. (2003: 384) identified concern about an 'increase of children and adults receiving treatment for ADHD' in the US during the late 1990s. Harwood et al. (2017: 1) identified the decade 1999–2009 as 'a historically significant rise in stimulant prescriptions for Australian children' that had a high profile in the Australian media. In the decade 1985–2008, Ray and Hinnant (2009) identified one metaphor that was used in US magazines, 'comparing Ritalin to insulin'. They observed that this 'contributes to normalizing the disorder, at least in the sense of normalizing taking medication' (2009: 13). Conrad and Bergey (2014) has described corresponding 'large increases in medication usage' across the globe, with the greatest prevalence in the US and European countries especially between the years 1992 and 2006. Like Conrad and Potter (2000) and Conrad (2006), Lloyd and Norris have observed the influence of pharmaceutical companies and the 'aggressive' marketing of diagnosis and prescription drugs for the 'medicalisation' of ADHD (Lloyd and Norris 1999: 511; Norris and Lloyd 2000; see also Harwood et al. 2017). Lloyd and Norris commented on the 'crude biological determinism' reported in the UK media and in 'professional literature for teachers' (1999: 511). They have also noted how UK media stories on ADHD have featured parents as active consumers who feel let down and therefore challenge medical expertise and judgement. Similarly, Harwood et al. have identified a 'struggle metaphor' used by the Australian media to depict how 'the medical profession and parent are engaged in an epic battle of wills' over diagnosis and medication (2017: 6). They noted representations of a 'war between parents and teachers' in which the role of schools in medicalisation is debated (2017: 6). ADHD medication has sometimes been represented by the UK media as a 'chemical cosh' to subdue 'boisterous boys' (Horton-Salway 2011, 2012) or by the Australian media as a 'quick fix' or a means of obtaining school funding or benefits (Harwood et al. 2017). Other media stories have focused on the abuse of medication as 'smart drugs' that enhance cognitive performance (Partridge et al. 2011) or as a 'lubricant for learning' (Harwood et al. 2017: 5) or on the other hand they employ a 'fear of harm' narrative about medication that is reminiscent of health scares such as the MMR vaccine (O'Dell and Brownlow 2015). Referring to the Australian press, Robertson et al. (2013: 5) for example observed 'the discourse for ADHD medicines often related to the dangers of the drug'.

As with Autism (O'Dell and Brownlow 2015) and Chronic Fatigue Syndrome (Horton-Salway 1998), ADHD has been represented in the media as a controversial category that is routinely debated around diagnosis and the interests and opinions of professional and lay people. For example, in their discussion of the role of media discourse and the rise of ADHD in the UK, Lloyd and Norris (1999) and Norris and Lloyd (2000) pointed out a polarisation around 'the voice of parents' and 'the voice of experts'. Parents were sometimes cited as the representatives of organisations with an interest in ADHD while consulted experts were cited as professionals with careers built on ADHD (Lloyd and Norris 1999: 508). They were variably represented as either credible experts or biased by their interests. Schmitz et al. (2003) had found the dominant 'voice' in US print media (between 1988 and 1997) to be that of professionals, while Harwood et al. (2017) more recently identified the 'expert-as-a-parent' to be the most common voice in Australian newsprint media (between 1999 and 2009). It is significant that the 'voices of the children themselves were conspicuously absent and the voices of parents were infrequent and constrained' (2017: 6). In the sample of articles from the French press, Ponnou and Gonon (2017: 3) reported, 'They often gave voice to health professionals (medical doctors, psychologists, psychoanalysts, social workers) and to parents, either as short quotations or full interviews, but not to children'.

Whilst it is reasonable to acknowledge the positive role of the media, in 'mediating information about ADHD' (Lloyd and Norris 1999: 511) or 'in publicising and providing information to parents and to professionals', it is clear that media discourse also necessarily entails 'contributing to the debate as to what ADHD 'is', its origins, characteristics and 'cures' (1999: 511). The media can therefore function to set socio-political agendas with the use of dominant representations (Seale 2003). Many writers have commented on the potential impact that this can have, for example on public knowledge of medical conditions and the understanding of disability and illness (for example, Colley 2010; Harwood et al. 2017; Jones and Harwood 2009; Olstead 2002; Phillips et al. 1991; Wang et al. 2016). For example, the media have depicted children diagnosed with autism as,

> either uncontrollable, aggressive, and even violent, individuals who cause great stress to their families and carers or unhappy and often unloved and poorly treated (both by the system and by their own families). Only in

> very few cases were children, or adults, presented as having any positive characteristics – and these were consistent with the 'stereotype' of people labelled as having autism which has been particularly prevalent in fictional media (for example the movie *Rainman*)- that of the autistic savant who has exceptional talent in a particular area. (Jones and Harwood 2009: 15)

With regard to ADHD, Harwood et al. (2017: 9) have observed that, in the Australian newsprint, 'metaphoric themes had the effect of reinforcing ADHD as a scientific ideology that both medicalizes child behaviour and makes children, parents or teachers problematic'. They identified metaphors of 'breakthrough, struggle and fault' referring respectively to breakthrough science, the struggle of teachers to cope with children in classrooms and the blame attributed to both teachers and parents in pursuing medical solutions. Horton-Salway (2012: 5) identified a range of similar negative stereotypical identities, such as parents who use ADHD as an excuse, those that depict children as 'normal but naughty' and parents who jump on the bandwagon or have no time for their children. Bandwagon representations are something of a meta-narrative in the media and in everyday discourse. They are 'a common feature of the discourse in debates about controversial conditions…' often functioning to differentiate such examples from the genuine case (Horton-Salway 2012: 5). In a more positive media representation of parents they are sometimes represented as a campaigner or struggling hero protecting their victimised child from harm (Lloyd and Norris 1999).

The media's role in reporting on ADHD or disseminating and discussing science can take the form of polarised debates around biological versus psychosocial accounts of ADHD and is productive of stereotypes and social identities (Justman 2015; Danforth and Navarro 2001). However, the emphasis of representations changes over time and varies between cultures. While Horton-Salway (2011) identified the dominant use of psychosocial representations of problem children and their ineffectual parents in UK national newspapers for the years 2000–2009, a decade earlier, Schmitz et al. (2003) had found biological representations of the neurologically impaired child to be more dominant in the US. More recently, Ponnou and Gonon (2017: 7) noted the greater complexity and more subtle representations of ADHD in the French media. They have observed that 'weak biological arguments' are now being overtaken by more 'nuanced' accounts that defend 'a more complex understanding of ADHD etiology and treatment.'

There is clearly a huge variation in how the media have drawn on scientific ideas and what the public make of media discourse on ADHD. As Seale (2003: 514) argues 'we ought to be interested in which stories get told and which are suppressed, and in how members of the media audience (which includes health policy makers and health care providers) respond to mediated health messages'. Since audio, visual and print news media are now usually linked to websites and social media that allow the public to engage with and comment on what has been said or printed, such outlets are an increasingly integral part of how the mass media works with the public. As Seale points out, media consumers are not passive recipients, there are circular feedback loops between media producers, other media producers and in turn the response of consumers so the direction of influence is complex (Seale 2003). Despite the media having played quite a significant role in resisting the medicalisation of ADHD across the globe, according to studies in the UK (Horton-Salway 2011), the US (Leo and Lacasse 2015) in Australia (Robertson et al. 2013) and in Taiwan (Wang et al. 2016), Conrad and Bergey (2014) have pointed out that *The Internet* has been an important vehicle in the globilisation of ADHD.

ADHD Discourse and *'The Internet'*

There is a growing industry on '*The Internet*' that supports and generates discourse about ADHD and many other health matters, controversial or otherwise. Health controversy and use of the internet is a hugely important topic because public engagement with internet sources has all kinds of implications for the authority of science and medicine not to mention other forms of expertise and, indeed, the very processes of information exchange and democracy. These issues go far beyond the scope of this book and have been researched more effectively elsewhere by other writers. However, the influence of the internet is a burgeoning area of research in relation to ADHD (for example, Conrad and Bergey 2014; Felt 2015; Fleischmann and Miller 2013; Foroushani 2008; Kata 2010; Winter et al. 2015). In their paper on the globalisation of ADHD, Conrad and Bergey (2014) identified the Internet as one of the greatest influences affecting how information about ADHD has spread across the globe. Bussing et al. (2012) listed the main sources of information about ADHD for the public as internet, health professionals, newspapers, and television but they identified the internet as the preferred source. Ponnou and Gonon (2017: 8) suggest that television programmes might be the trigger for internet searches and consultations with health professionals.

The internet hosts a plethora of information websites, chat rooms, forums and support groups on ADHD that are open to global public consumption (and production) although, usually, more people in information rich and developed countries have greater access to these sources of information (Conrad and Bergey 2014). It might also be the case that members of the public are inclined to take up information from websites that are in agreement with their own views and experience (Valentine 2001). Parent support groups such as UK based '*ADDers*' and '*ADDiS*' provide easy access to information, support and practical help for the public and many such websites also provide self-diagnostic checklists along with advice about seeking medical or educational help.

Globally, such websites are numerous and they host forums where people can share and discuss their personal experiences. We suppose that the online discourse of parents of children with ADHD is complex and variable, but that they are usually sharing experience with other parents or appealing for information and support. It is therefore important to interpret their accounts in that context. As Olstead (2002: 623) has pointed out, 'media influence is always part of a matrix of other social influences' so that 'meanings are not simply received by a readership, they are mediated in relation to meanings generated and sustained by families and peer groups, and through personal experience.'. Personal experience is used to interpret the ideas that circulate in the popular media and online, as Davies also demonstrates in her analyses of parents' accounts in Chapters 4 and 5. Descriptions of challenging children abound in personal experience stories telling of extreme behaviours and desperate parents who are struggling to cope. Medical websites such as *Netdoctor.co.uk* provide support, information and checklists for the diagnosis of ADHD as do some pharmaceutical companies. Foroushani (2008) claims that these kinds of organisations and institutions have the most dominant presence on the internet and are therefore more likely to promote a medical model of ADHD even if individual medical professionals might personally be critical of this. For example, referring to the French media, Ponnou and Gonon (2017: 9) have found that medical doctors have defended a complex 'nuanced view of the biomedical model in newspapers, but a strictly biological one on TV'.

Conrad and Bergey (2014) point out that checklist tools enabling 'do it yourself diagnosis' have functioned to popularise the criteria for ADHD that are set out in DSM-1V and more recently DSM-5 (summarised in Chapter 2 of this volume). The UK national guidelines on ADHD (NICE 2009) are also a source of information to the public as well as health professionals on diagnosis and best practice. Matching symptoms to diagnostic checklists is therefore easier if people have access to the internet. Hence, perhaps, Stuart Justman's (2015) observation, that the ADHD diagnosis has become a stereotype.

'Counter-Stories'

Stereotypes are a common feature of ADHD representations but resistance to negative stereotypes is also a feature of some media stories that is more commonly identified in parents talk about their children (see Chapters 4 and 5 of this volume) and in adults' accounts of their own personal experience of ADHD (Chapter 6 of this volume). Rodriguez describes how 'counter-stories' are used as 'creative acts of resistance to construct positive identities.' (Rodriguez 2010: 1183). Online discourse is one significant forum where the public contribute to the ADHD debate and they are able to respond with 'counter-stories' so they become producers as well as consumers of media discourse. This is a topic worthy of a whole volume applying to a wide range of topics. We cannot do it proper justice here, but note that resistance to negative stereotyping and stigma is one of the many socio-political activities that people pursue online in relation to disabilities and mental health categories such as autism and ADHD.

The internet hosts research studies that analyse personal experience accounts. Two examples of this are Fleischmann and Miller's (2013) study of the online narratives of adults diagnosed with ADHD and Winter et al.'s (2015) study of women talking about ADHD on *You-Tube*. The narratives in Fleischmann and Miller's study were organised around a description of 'before and after' stories in which experience of life before diagnosis is compared with transformations after. Narratives that pivot around diagnosis are also common in other health conditions (see, for example, Horton-Salway 1998, 2001; Wynne et al. 1992). Many such stories refer to the effect of diagnosis on lives (further discussion of voices of experience in Chapter 6). In the case of ADHD diagnosed in adult life, this can refer to confusion and difficulties experienced prior to diagnosis and the relief that follows medical and social recognition. For example, Fleischmann and Miller (2013: 47) describe the accounts of women who reported 'repeated failures in many aspects of life' and contrasted this with 'a more coherent view of their life and their difficulties' after the diagnosis. These stories feature accounts of adults with ADHD who 'could overcome their challenges.' and who could 'take a more positive view of themselves…and admit to some positive aspects of having ADHD' (2013: 47). Fleischmann and Miller described the way that the conclusions of such narratives told of 'confidence and future expectations' (2013: 55) and improved self-image following diagnosis. These stories are therefore as much about social identities as they are about the events and difficulties of people's lives. Winter et al. (2015: 415) analysed women's accounts on *You-Tube,* arguing that a diagnosis of ADHD is sometimes used by women, burdened by pressures to perform as 'superwomen', to excuse their failings and justify performance enhancing medication. This was not directed as a criticism of the women, but an argument arising from a feminist perspective, that women are 'active consumers' of the ADHD diagnosis' to avoid the stigma of failing to live up to societal expectations about the demands and burdens placed upon them to perform multiple roles. However, we note that the women in this study had also emphasised the positive aspects of having ADHD, such as 'the ability do five things at once' or their 'creativity'. These were also stories of 'unique' and 'successful lives' despite a plethora of problems (Winter et al. 2015). Such accounts construct more positive social identities and echo the transformational stories that appear in newspaper reports in the form of resistance to the more common and stigmatising negative identities that are represented. O'Dell et al. (2016) have identified similar themes in accounts of women's personal experience that will be discussed further in Chapter 6.

Metanarratives and Gendering Identities

Metanarratives are a significant aspect of media discourse: They are overarching story formats that function to shape stories according to familiar forms of cultural common sense or myth and they are populated with recognisable identities. Seale (2003: 521) identified metanarrative in 'contemporary mass media health representations, containing a series of opposed elements, arranged in a way that allows a range of sub-plots, templates, twitches and reversals…'. He summarised these narratives as 'the dangers of modern life; villains and freaks; victimhood; professional heroes; lay heroes'. They are versions of the 'myths of the modern world' that speak to shared cultural common-sense (Barthes 1972; Hartman 2008; Whitt and Perlich 2014): Such stories are often gendered and frequently appear in media discourse in forms such as 'fear of danger' or 'fear of strangers' with variations of stories featuring victims, villains and heroes being used to structure many reports about ADHD in both media and also lay discourse (Horton-Salway 2012).

In UK national newspapers for the years 2009–2011, Horton-Salway (2012) found more emphasis on stories about boys or men as 'delinquent', 'violent' or 'dangerous'. This focus on 'dangerous masculinity' takes up and reproduces a more general and commonly used 'fear of harm' narrative focusing on 'the dangers of modern life' (Seale 2003: 521). This creates sensational headlines and also generates a gendered 'moral panic' about the threat of ADHD to social order. One more general example of how this can function is to link a 'fear of harm' story format with a 'fear of strangers' format to promote the need for greater control of national borders. Both of these ideas draw on cultural archetypes that strike a fearful chord in the public imagination: They function as a means of persuasion, justification and social control.

The theme of 'fear of harm' can either be used to justify medicating boys and men, such as when making a link between deviance or criminality and ADHD, or it can be drawn on to critique the effects of medication as we have seen. Although much of the media coverage of ADHD focuses on boys, 'fear of harm' stories can also be applied as a warning to women about the consequences of pregnancy risks for ADHD, such as the effect of alcohol, drugs, or smoking on the unborn child (Horton-Salway 2012). The linking of ADHD to the wider 'fear of harm' and blame narrative justifies the newsworthiness of such stories and the public surveillance of pregnant mothers. In the case of smoking, drinking or drug taking, even for prescribed drugs such as blood pressure medication, threats to the unborn child warrant the cautioning of maternal behaviour during pregnancy. The headlines are not usually designed to be heard as cautions to health professionals, but as warnings to pregnant women. In a more general sense, narratives such as these are typically drawn on to justify the need for the monitoring and control of women's bodies and their behaviour (Malacrida 2002).

Although these warnings to pregnant mothers derive from biological explanations and the latest scientific research findings on ADHD they differ radically from the biological explanations implicating fathers in the genetic causes of ADHD (Horton-Salway 2012). Mothers are warned about what happens with their bodies during pregnancy, sometimes regardless of whether the harmful substances are prescribed medications or alcohol and harmful substances used in addiction. Conversely, fathers who are referred to in genetic research are not held accountable in the same way. They are not depicted as blameworthy agents in stories about ADHD and genetic research, as mothers might be in pregnancy stories (Horton-Salway 2012). The existence of mother-centred explanations in the media, even when they are biological ones, are more censorial and constructive of 'mother-blame', literally holding mothers to public account for the consequences of their behaviours (see Blum 2007; Malacrida 2002). Blum pointed out that a binary of 'mother-valour' versus 'mother-blame' exists in Western cultures to 'hold mothers responsible for their child outcomes and thus for the health of families, future citizens, and the nation' (2007: 202). Generally fathers are the more invisible parent in health and social care discourse which fails to acknowledge their responsibility and the time that fathers devote to their children (Davies 2014). 'Mother-valour' on the other hand appears in stories of campaigning mothers, such as described by Lloyd and Norris (1999), while 'mother-blame' can be implicit in pregnancy stories and a range of other topics that hold mothers to account for children's upbringing, care and health such as the references to 'working mothers' and 'single parents' in the Australian press (Harwood et al. 2017: 7).

We are not suggesting that mothers ought not to be warned by experts about health risks in pregnancy but rather, that media accounts of ADHD can be gendered by focusing on 'woman-specific' topics in relation to pregnancy, parenting and childcare (see also Sunderland 2006: 504) and also by rendering fathers largely invisible or absent in the ADHD discourse (Davies 2014; Gray-Brunton et al. 2014; Horton-Salway 2011, 2012). The 'blame game' can be quite subtle and embedded in selection of terms, gendered cultural common sense and dominant discourses (Sherriff and Weatherall 2009).

Nonetheless, the 'fear of harm' narrative is generally more often biased towards representations of 'dangerous masculinity' in media discourse and in the case of ADHD this reflects the gendered nature of ADHD with its focus on boys (see Chapter 2). In the media, naughty boys, delinquents and criminal perpetrators have been positioned as the anti-heroes and villains of 'fear of harm' stories about ADHD. The study of US newspaper media between the years 1988 and 1997 by Schmitz et al. (2003) identified a range of genetic/neurobiological, social, environmental and psychological explanations for ADHD. However, the dominant representation identified by this study, for the years 1988–1997, was 'a biological and genetic understanding of cause, an emphasis on symptoms of hyperactivity rather than inattention, and a dominant image of young white boys' (p. 400). This bias towards young boys and deviant conduct was captured by a media example of a fictional character, renowned for his bad behaviour, *Denis the Menace* (cited in Schmitz et al. 2003: 399). Fictional characters such as *Denis the Menace* and *William Brown* have been used in media stories to caricature ADHD in such exaggerated and gendered terms that 'Extreme case formulations construct the behaviour of the 'boisterous boy' as everyone's concern' (cited in Horton-Salway 2011: 543). The gendered stereotype of ADHD, as a dysfunctional condition of boyhood, was identified in many North American magazines in the late 1990s by Schmitz et al. (2003) and also Clarke (2011: 626) who has since described those media stereotypes of 'the dear, if devilish, cartoon character living in the guise of a psychiatric diagnosis' as 'a sort of sexism against boys'.

One of the most common, negative misrepresentations in the popular media draws on the 'fear of harm' narrative in the conflation of mental illness and criminality (Olstead 2002). Ray and Hinnant (2009: 4) argue that 'The most common views of the mentally ill presented in media are that those with mental disorders pose a danger to others and to themselves, with the most prevalent theme as a danger to others…'. With respect to ADHD they studied American magazines (1985–2008) observing that:

> ADD and ADHD behavior was described in terms of acting out, most notably motivated by rage and displaying itself in terms of kicking, hitting, or physically harming others. However, danger to others was also exhibited in the form of inflicting emotional damage on other people. (Ray and Hinnant 2009: 11)

The emphasis on deviance and dangerousness is, they argue, 'because of how media function and judge stories as newsworthy' (2009: 5). For example, extreme representations of ADHD have drawn public attention to research linking ADHD and prison populations, emphasising social conduct issues, violence, and psychotic behaviour (Horton-Salway 2012). The construction of a link between media stories on ADHD and male sex crime has also been noted by Ray and Hinnant (2009). According to Hartman (2008) such examples are commonly used by the media to demonstrate the need to restore order and harmony, to make a point about the need for social concern or they function in discourse to justify an intervention of some kind (Pomerantz 1986). For example, the association of serious mental pathology leading to adult crime has been used to justify medicating young children who have ADHD, particularly boys and young offenders (Horton-Salway 2012). People with mental illnesses are in fact more likely to be the victims of crime than the perpetrators, but media discourse on mental health issues is more likely to report on them as perpetrators rather than victims. The implied victims in crime stories are members of the public who are called upon to imagine the consequences of untreated ADHD, in stories of this kind, holding up the example of delinquents or adult male criminals as an object lesson. By contrast, the less common depictions of girls with ADHD are not typically demonised or focused on the issue of medication (Horton-Salway 2012).

The reporting of victim and perpetrator dichotomies set up by the link between mental illness and criminality is a reversal of the media stories of school exclusion and campaigning parents reported by Lloyd and Norris (1999). For example, the victimhood of children with ADHD has in some stories been framed as a criticism of educational policy and a focus on the effects of educational performance ratings on the school's decision making (Horton-Salway 2012). Such examples depict education regimes that value success rates above the welfare of children with special needs. Typically, stories about schools or colleges that fail to support children and young adults with ADHD or those that give a voice to parents or campaigning interest groups lean towards a representation of ADHD as a learning disability. Rather than demonising boys as a '*Denis the Menace*' type (Schmitz et al. 2003) or emphasising the effects of disruptive or anti-social behaviour in classrooms, media stories about neglectful schools or colleges can construct the child or young adult as a victim of the system: 'The socially excluded, misunderstood or stigmatised boy with ADHD is one of the most common victim stories on ADHD reported in the media' (Horton-Salway 2012: 9).

This format can be effective because, as Seale (2003: 522) points out, 'media producers like to depict victimhood and for this they tend to choose people who represent our selves at our most vulnerable. Thus the most effective victim portrayals in contemporary media are generally of children'.

Contrasting with the demonisation of boys and men with ADHD as potential miscreants and criminals, or the portrayal of children as victims of school exclusion or bullying, there are also valourised representations of people with ADHD appearing as heroes in both the media and in popular fiction. For example, the fictional character, *Percy Jackson* authored by Rick Riordon could be interpreted as a form of resistance against the mainly negative identities that circulate about ADHD (cited in Horton-Salway 2012). When represented in the media, the use of extreme heroic characters constitutes a counter to the more usual stereotypes of naughty boys, excluded victims, or dangerous masculinity. Heroic 'counter-stories' depicting the characteristics of ADHD as an asset of high profile male creative geniuses, athletes, fictional male superheroes or celebrities who have overcome problems valourise difference or they are described in terms of a mythical masculine superhero archetype (Horton-Salway 2012: 11). In this representation, ADHD is constructed as an asset rather than a deficit (Whitt and Perlich 2014) as with *Percy Jackson's* inherited traits for toughness that counter the more usual negative depictions of ADHD and presents them as a more positive asset of boys and men (Horton-Salway 2012: 11). However, the other side of this coin is an 'emphasis on dominance, aggression, extreme self-reliance…' that can also function to reinforce extreme masculine stereotypes (cf. Levant 2011: 765).

The linking of ADHD to success and high performance has also been suggested through media representations of successful high flying public figures, mostly male, such as *Winston Churchill* (Horton-Salway 2012: 11). This example used the metaphor of the battling warrior hero who overcame childhood problems and personal difficulties to become one of the UK's most notable politicians and leaders. Such stories serve a social function (Klapp 1962, 1964) by depicting the hero's journey of self-transformation (Hartman and Zimberoff 2009). As a story this is aspirational, but it also delivers a moral lesson. Strongly positioned against medicating naughty, disruptive boys for ADHD, such stories about successful public figures serve as cautionary tales inviting the public to imagine the loss to the nation if high fliers are subdued by medication. Such stories valourise extreme masculine stereotypes but they also warn of the dangers of dumbing down boisterous boys with ADHD who might become potential heroes or leaders (Horton-Salway 2012). While such stories are undoubtedly entertaining, they by no means represent the experience of most ordinary mortals. Hero representations drawing their rhetorical power from the myth of the male moral hero (Whitt and Perlich 2014) serve a variety of social functions that are both aspirational and moral, providing role models, inspiration and motivation (Hartman 2008: 50).

In Chapter 6, we will further explore how the discourse of transformation, positivity, uniqueness and creativity is drawn on to construct the personal experience narratives of ordinary children, men and women with ADHD. We will discuss further the discursive function of transformative narratives and question whether these are in fact positive forms of resistance and empowerment in the discourse about ADHD or whether such accounts are constrained by cultural and gendered stereotypes and moral imperatives. They might function as a way of applying a moral imperative for people with ADHD to identify with the successful role models and emulate them, or they might equally serve as an object lesson to the public to re-consider the abilities and skills of people with ADHD. The biographical representation of celebrities who have ADHD and other mental health conditions is becoming a burgeoning genre appearing in both print and audio-visual media. One positive aspect of this discourse is that it functions to increase public awareness of personal experiences, and appears as an attempt to overcome the stigma of mental illness and sometimes even to challenge the definitions and meaning of mental health categories.

Concluding Comments

It is clear that science, research knowledge and the media have the power to influence the public imagination about ADHD but also the phenomena of social media and the Internet increasingly engage the public as active participants in the dissemination as well as the consumption of information. The public are far from passive consumers of media discourse so this production and consumption of ideas on mental health and science can be seen as a circular social process that also includes feedback loops between health professionals the public and educators (Seale 2003). We have identified some of the dominant stereotypes and identities that are visible in popular media and commented on how they are gendered in the discourse of ADHD.

Stereotypes about people with ADHD are embedded within different interpretative repertoires that portray ADHD as a biological or psychosocial category. Many of these representations are linked to the stock of media 'metanarratives' that are repeatedly used to frame stories in terms of cultural myths. There are a worrying number of negative identities for children and their parents in stories about ADHD. These stereotypes are likely to generate social consequences, such as stigma, fear, moral outrage and moral panics. That is one reason why there are growing forms of dissatisfaction and resistance to 'spoiled identities' (Goffman 1963). These have burgeoned in online discourse and in support groups to give interested members of the public their own 'voice' and enable them to share experience (Foroushani 2008). However, the consumers of mass mediated messages about health are not only the general public but also the scientists, policy makers and health professionals themselves. In the recent decades of 'knowledge rich' societies, their traditional authority bases have been eroded such that they are increasingly under siege. Neither are professionals passive recipients of this: They react to media stories and public pressures resisting them as well as becoming influenced by them (Seale 2003). For example, health professionals have sometimes expressed concerns when consulted by the media about the rise in demands for ADHD medication. Referring to a US study of clinicians, Rafalovich (2005: 305) observed that 'clinicians do not practice within a vacuum, but are instead largely affected by the marked scepticism that surrounds ADHD' and also 'mental health practitioners harbour varying degrees of ambivalence about the diagnostic criteria, treatment methods, and biological basis of ADHD' (2005: 309). Significantly, he noted 'the difference between academic ADHD forums that continuously seek and debate a crystallised ADHD aetiology and the clinical forum, where the treatment of behaviour may be more important than understanding its origin' (2005: 313).

The historical legacy of ADHD theory (see Chapter 2) and the ongoing discourse of science findings as reported by the media continue to influence how the discourse of ADHD is generated and how the public are able to contribute to that debate as producers and commentators, sometimes resisting the authority of science and medicine with 'counter-stories' or at other times taking up biomedical explanations even when health practitioners are more sceptical. As we have seen, the voices of parents and experts are commonly pitted against each other in UK media coverage of ADHD (Horton-Salway 2011; Lloyd and Norris 1999, 2000) and we note that Harwood et al. (2017) also identified this in Australian print media, while Gray Brunton et al. (2014) and Davies (2014) have observed similar polarised repertoires appearing in parents' interview accounts of their child with ADHD. Gray Brunton et al. (2014) have lamented the lack of research into 'parental constructions of their child's behaviours' pointing out the importance of parent's understandings of ADHD in the process of diagnosis. They, like us, have commented on the issue of gendered representations, such as blameworthy mothers and 'invisible' fathers. They also suggest that there is some evidence that 'fathers' experiences might differ from those of mothers' (Gray Brunton et al., January 2014: 1). They suggest that

> The pathologizing of masculinity in ADHD, implicating boys and their fathers genetically and behaviorally, as suggested by Timimi (2005), warrants further qualitative study, in view of the dominance of feminist research exploring maternal blame only. (Gray Brunton et al. 2014: 6)

These concerns were at the heart of Alison Davies's research on parents' constructions of ADHD (Davies 2014). Her detailed discursive psychology analysis based on this research provides an illuminating view of fathers' as well as mothers' perspectives and the findings inform her contributions to our understanding of ADHD and parents' discourse (see also Chapters 4 and 5). Personal experience is an important aspect of ADHD discourse that can offer valuable insights into the cultural meaning and social consequence of this mental health category. We are most interested in how the parents of children with ADHD experience their parenting and how they talk about this and their relationship with their children. Significant to us, is the way that their narratives might relate to their knowledge of science on ADHD, their take up or criticism of biomedical or psychosocial explanations and how this might relate to the framing of media discourse, the construction of ADHD identities in the media and the stigmatisation of families. It is to these concerns that we now turn.

References

Armon, R. (2015). Expert positions and scientific contexts: Storying research in the news media. *Discourse and Communication, 10*(1), 3–21.

Barthes, R. (1972). *Mythologies*. London: Paladin.

Blum, L. (2007). Mother-blame in the Prozac nation: Raising kids with invisible disabilities. *Gender and Society, 21*(2), 202–226.

Bourdaa, M., Konsman, J. P., Sécail, C., Venturini, T., Veyrat-Masson, I., & Gonon, F. (2015). Does television reflect the evaluation of scientific knowledge? The case of attention-deficit hyperactivity disorder coverage on French television. *Public Understanding of Science, 24*(2), 200–209.

Bourdieu, P. (1979). Symbolic power. *Critique of Anthropology, 4*, 77–85.

Bussing, R., Zima, B. T., Mason, D. M., Meyer, J. M., White, K., & Garvan, C. W. (2012). ADHD knowledge, perceptions, and information sources: Perspectives from a community sample of adolescents and their parents. *Journal of Adolescent Health, 51*(6), 593–600. https://doi.org/10.1016/j.jadohealth.2012.03.004.

Carabine, J. (2001). Unmarried motherhood 1830–1990: A genealogical analysis. In M. Wetherell, S. Taylor, & S. Yates (Eds.), *Discourse as Data: A Guide for Analysis* (pp. 267–310). London: Sage.

Clarke, J. N. (2011). Magazine portrayal of attention deficit/hyperactivity disorder (ADD/ADHD): A post-modern epidemic in a post-trust society. *Health, Risk and Society, 13*(7–8), 621–636.

Colley, B. (2010). ADHD, science and the common man. *Emotional and Behavioural Difficulties, 15*(2), 83–94.

Conrad, P. (1975). The discovery of hyperkinesis: Notes on the medicalisation of deviant behaviour. *Social Problems, 23*, 12–21.

Conrad, P. (2006). From hyperactive children to ADHD adults: Observations on the expansion of medical categories. *Identifying Hyperactive Children:*

The Medicalisation of Deviant Behaviour (Expanded edition, pp. 101–126). Aldershot: Ashgate Publishing.
Conrad, P., & Bergey, M. R. (2014). The impending globilization of ADHD: Notes on the expansion and growth of a medicalized disorder. *Social Science and Medicine, 122*, 31–43.
Conrad, P., & Potter, D. (2000). From hyperactive children to ADHD adults: Observations on the expansion of medical categories. *Social Problems, 47*(4), 559–582.
Danforth, S., & Navarro, V. (2001). Hyper talk: Sampling the social construction of ADHD in everyday language. *Anthropology and Education Quarterly, 32*(2), 167–190.
Davies, A. (2014). *It's a problem with the brain: A discursive analysis of parents' constructions of ADHD* (Unpublished Ph.D. thesis), The Open University, Milton Keynes.
Felt, U. (2015). Sociotechnical imaginaries of "the internet", digital health information and the making of citizen-patients. In S. Hilgartner, C. Miller, & R. Hagendijk (Eds.), *Science and Democracy: Making Knowledge and Making Power in the Biosciences and Beyond* (pp. 176–197). New York: Routledge.
Fleischmann, A., & Miller, E. C. (2013). Online narratives by adults with ADHD who were diagnosed in adulthood. *Learning Disability Quarterly, 36*(1), 47–60.
Foroushani, P. S. (2008). The internet: A place for different voices in health and medicine? A case study of attention deficit hyperactivity disorder. *Mental Health Review Journal, 13*(1), 33–40.
Furnham, A., & Sarwar, T. (2011). Beliefs about attention-deficit hyperactivity disorder. *Counselling Psychology Quarterly, 24*(4), 301–311.
Goffman, E. (1963). *Stigma: Notes on the Management of Spoiled Identity*. Englewood Cliffs, NJ: Prentice-Hall.
Goldacre, B. (2009). *Bad Science*. London: Fourth Estate.
Gonon, F., Bezard, E., & Boraud, T. (2011). Misrepresentation of neuroscience data might give rise misleading conclusions in the media: The case of attention deficit hyperactivity disorder. *PLoS One, 6*(1), e14618. https://doi.org/10.1371/journal.pone.0014618.
Gray Brunton, C., McVittie, C., Ellison, M., & Willock, J. (2014). Negotiating parental accountability in the face of uncertainty for attention-deficit hyperactivity disorder. *Qualitative Health Research, 24*(2), 242–253.

Hartman, K. L. (2008). *The rhetorical myth of the athlete as a moral hero: The implications of steroids in sport and the threatened myth* (Ph.D. thesis, Louisiana State University and Agricultural and Mechanical College).

Hartman, D., & Zimberoff, D. (2009). The hero's journey of self-transformation: Models of higher development from mythology. *Journal of Heart Centered Therapies, 12*(2), 3(91).

Harwood, V., Jones, S., Bonney, A., & McMahon, S. (2017). Heroic struggles, criminals and scientific breakthroughs: ADHD and the medicalization of child behaviour in Australian newsprint media 1999–2009. *International Journal of Qualitative Studies on Health and Well-being, 12,* 1298262. https://doi.org/10.1080/17482631.2017.1298262.

Horton-Salway, M. (1998). *Mind and body in the discursive construction of ME: A struggle for authorship of an illness* (Doctoral Thesis, Loughborough University).

Horton-Salway, M. (2001). Narrative identities and the management of personal accountability in talk about ME: A discursive approach to illness narrative. *Journal of Health Psychology, 6*(2), 261–273.

Horton-Salway, M. (2011). Repertoires of ADHD in UK newspaper media. *Health (London), 15*(5), 533–549.

Horton-Salway, M. (2012). Gendering attention deficit hyperactivity disorder: A discursive analysis of UK newspaper stories. *Journal of Health Psychology, 18*(8), 1085–1099. Published online before print 1 October 2012. https://doi.org/10.1177/1359105312456326.

Jones, S. C., & Harwood, V. (2009). Representations of autism in Australian print media. *Disability & Society, 24*(1), 5–18. https://doi.org/10.1080/09687590802535345.

Justman, S. (2015). Attention deficit/hyperactivity disorder: Diagnosis and stereotypy. *Ethical Human Psychology and Psychiatry, 17*(2), 135–144.

Kata, A. (2010). A postmodern Pandora's box: Anti-vaccination misinformation on the internet. *Vaccine, 28,* 1709–1716.

Klapp, O. E. (1962). *Heroes, Villains, and Fools*. Englewood Cliffs, NJ: Prentice-Hall.

Klapp, O. E. (1964). *Symbolic Leaders: Public Dramas and Public Men.* Chicago: Aldine.

Leo, J., & Lacasse, J. (2015). *The New York Times* and the ADHD epidemic. *Society, 52,* 3–8. Springer Science: Business Media New York.

Levant, R. F. (2011, November). Research in the psychology of men and masculinity using the gender role strain paradigm as a framework. *American Psychologist, 66*(8), 765–776.

Lloyd, G., & Norris, C. (1999). Including ADHD? *Disability and Society, 14*(4), 505–517.

Malacrida, C. (2002). Alternative therapies and attention deficit disorder: Discourses of maternal responsibility and risk. *Gender & Society, 16,* 366–385.

McLeod, J. D., Fettes, D. L., Jensen, P. S., Pescosolido, B. A., & Martin, J. K. (2007, May). Public knowledge, beliefs and treatment preferences concerning attention deficit hyperactivity disorder. *Psychiatric Services, https://Psychiatryonline.org, 58*(5), 626–631.

National Institute of Clinical Excellence. (2009). *Attention Deficit Hyperactivity Disorder: Diagnosis and Management of ADHD in Children, Young People and Adults.* London: National Institute for Health and Clinical Excellence. Available at http://www.nice.org.uk/Guidance/CG72 (Accessed 14 September 2017).

Norris, C., & Lloyd, G. (2000). Parents, professionals and ADHD: What the papers say. *European Journal of Special Needs Education, 15*(2), 123–137.

O'Dell, L. & Brownlow, C. (2015). Normative development and the autistic child. In M. O'Reilly & J. N. Lester (Eds.), *The Palgrave Handbook of Child Mental Health* (pp. 296–309). Basingstoke: Palgrave Macmillan.

O'Dell, L., Stenner, P., Horton-Salway, M., & Davies, A. (2016). *Narratives of ADHD: A qualitative study of women's narrative accounts of living with ADHD.* End of project report to the British Academy.

Olstead, R. (2002). Contesting the text: Canadian media depictions of the conflation of mental illness and criminality. *Sociology of Health & Illness, 4*(5), 621–643.

Partridge, B. J., Bell, S. K., Lucke, J. C., Yeates, S., & Hall, W. D. (2011). Smart drugs "as common as coffee": Media hype about neuroenhancement. *PLoS One, 6*(11), e28416.

Phillips, D. P., Kanter, E. J., & Bednarczyk, B. (1991). Importance of the lay press in the transmission of medical knowledge to the scientific community. *The New England Journal of Medicine, 325,* 1180–1183.

Pomerantz, A. (1986). Extreme case formulations: A way of legitimising claims. *Human Studies, 9,* 219–229.

Ponnou, S., & Gonon, F. (2017). How French media have portrayed ADHD to the lay public and to social workers. *International Journal of Qualitative Studies on Health and Well-being, 12*(Suppl. 1), 1298244. https://doi.org/10.1080/17482631.2017.1298244.

Rafalovich, A. (2005). Exploring clinician uncertainty in the diagnosis and treatment of attention deficit hyperactivity disorder. *Sociology of Health Illness, 27*(3), 305–323.

Ray, L., & Hinnant, A. (2009). Media representation of mental disorders: A study of ADD and ADHD coverage in magazines from 1985 to 2008. *Journal of Magazine & New Media Research, 11*(1), 1–21.

Ricoeur, P. (1967). *The Symbolism of Evil.* New York: Harper and Row.

Robertson, J., Walkham, E. J., Bevan, M. D., & Newby, D. A. (2013). Medicines and the media: News reports of medicines recommended for government reimbursement in Australia. *BMC Public Health, 13,* 489.

Rodriguez, T. L. (2010, January 1). Resisting negative images and stereotypes: One Latina prospective teacher's story. *Brock Education: A Journal of Educational Research and Practice, 19*(2), 1183–1189.

Seale, C. (2003). Health and media: An overview. *Sociology of Health & Illness, 25*(6), 513–531.

Schmitz, M. F., Filippone, P., & Edelman, E. M. (2003). Social representations of attention deficit/hyperactivity disorder, 1988–1997. *Culture & Psychology, 9*(4), 383–406.

Sheriff, M., & Weatherall, A. (2009). A feminist discourse analysis of popular-press accounts of postmodernity. *Feminism & Psychology, 19,* 89–108.

Sternadori, M. (2014). The witch and the warrior. *Feminist Media Studies, 14*(2), 301–317.

Sunderland, J. (2006). 'Parenting' or 'mothering'? The case of modern child-care magazines. *Discourse & Society, 17*(4), 503–527.

The Economist. (2012, September 22). *Journalistic Deficit Disorder: Reporting Science*, 404, 90–92. The Economist Intelligence Unit, N.A. Incorporated (London).

Timimi, S. (2005). *Naughty Boys: Anti-social Behaviour, ADHD and the Role of Culture.* Basingstoke: Palgrave Macmillan.

Valentine, J. (2001). Disabled discourse: Hearing accounts of deafness constructed through Japanese television and film. *Disability and Society, 16*(5), 707–727.

Wang, L. J., et al. (2016). Impact of negative media publicity on attention-deficit/hyperactivity disorder medication in Taiwan. *Pharmacoepidemiology and Drug Safety, 25,* 45–53.

Weaver, D. (2007). Thoughts on agenda setting, framing, and priming. *Journal of Communication, 57,* 142–147.

Whitt, D., & Perlich, J. (Eds.). (2014). *Myth and the Modern World: Essays on the Intersection with Ideology and Culture*. Jefferson, NC: McFarland.

Winter, H., Moncrieff, J., & Speed, E. (2015). "Because you're worth it": A discourse analysis of the gendered rhetoric of the ADHD woman. *Qualitative Research in Psychology, 12*(4), 415–434.

Wynne, L. C., Sheilds, C. G., & Sirkin, M. I. (1992). Illness, family theory, and family therapy: I. Conceptual issues. *Family Process, 31,* 3–18. https://doi.org/10.1111/j.1545-5300.1992.00003.x.

Zhongdang, P., & Kosicki, G. (1993). Framing analysis: An approach to news discourse. *Political Communication, 10*(1), 55–75.

4

'Normal Rules of Parenting Don't Apply': ADHD, Maternal Accountability and Mother Identities

Alison Davies

> It's very confrontational at times too and normal rules of parenting don't apply because they or he will always go to the next level. (Interview with Rachel, cited in Davies 2014: 243)

In this chapter and the next, we turn our attention to the experiences of parents who have a child with ADHD. Chapter 2 indicated how mothers are implicated within historic and contemporary psychological discourses of ADHD, and highlighted a research bias towards mothers and their sons, specifically, problem boys and problematic mothers (see also, Horton-Salway 2012; Singh 2004). Chapter 3 described how distinct gendered identities are implicated within media representations of ADHD, including gendered parent identities. We also noted the focus in media reports on the blameworthy mother through 'women-specific' topics such as pregnancy, or 'fear of harm' narratives linked to boys and men through extreme accounts of 'dangerous' masculinity or even 'heroic' stereotypes.

The next two chapters explore how social and gendered identities are constructed in parents' accounts of their own experiences. Science and media discourse on ADHD is populated with negative

M. Horton-Salway and A. Davies, *The Discourse of ADHD*,
The Language of Mental Health, https://doi.org/10.1007/978-3-319-76026-1_4

representations of children and their parents. Although there are some efforts to construct ADHD in a different way, positive representations are few and they usually refer to extreme examples of sports heroes, fictional superheroes, male geniuses and high achieving celebrities. As Mary Horton-Salway (2012) pointed out in her paper on gendering ADHD, these are not representative of the more mundane lives experienced by ordinary families. However, for parents, it is their own and their children's identities (and sometimes that of extended family members and ancestors) that are at stake when talking about ADHD. The next two chapters focus on how parents draw upon culturally available ideas and discourses about ADHD, and how they manage or resist negative ADHD stereotypes. As ADHD identities are distinctly gendered, this chapter will focus on mothers, and Chapter 5 will focus on fathers (Fig. 4.1).

Unless otherwise stated, the interview extracts cited in Chapters 4 and 5 come from a study by Alison Davies of parents in the UK whose children had an ADHD diagnosis (Davies 2014). Parents were recruited for this study via local ADHD support groups and discourse data was

Keeping in mind the themes of the book, we explore the impact the ADHD debate has on affected families and parents in particular. To do this, we consider the following questions in chapters four and five:

1. How are the social and gendered identities of parents captured by the biological, psychological and social explanations of ADHD, and the wider discourses of parenting in general?
2. How do parents engage with the discourse of ADHD and parenting and to what effect?
3. How do parents resist the negative stereotypes arising from common understandings of ADHD?

Fig. 4.1 ADHD and parenting discourse

collected from discussion groups, interviews with parents on their own (usually mothers) and with mother/father couples. All of the children referred to by the parents in this study were boys. Interview extracts are labelled using pseudonyms plus a page number to identify them to Davies (2014). Any other examples and quotes will appear as references linked to other research studies.

First, it is useful to consider how wider debates about gender and parenting in western societies might impinge on these families and provide a cultural background of assumptions and representations that are drawn upon in discourse. We will discuss how the wider gendered discourses of parenting intersect with those about ADHD to produce a cultural context for the construction of parents' experiences.

Contemporary Parenting Discourses

Contemporary debates about parenting practices in the UK take place within the historical context of neoliberalism, an ideology which advocates a society organised around the principles of the free market, where personal success and failure is the responsibility of the individual alone. Prevailing neoliberal discourses of 'responsibilisation', as theorised by Rose (1999), emphasise 'good' parenting as key to the production of 'good' citizens (Allen and Taylor 2012; Barnes and Power 2012; De Benedictis 2012; Gillies 2005). Parents are, to a greater or lesser extent, held responsible for achieving successful outcomes for their children (Gillies et al. 2016), and, equally, for unsuccessful outcomes too. Harden (2005) identifies a 'parent deficit' stereotype, which holds parents accountable for children who behave in anti-social ways. Similarly, De Benedictis (2012) suggests parents are blamed, demonised and held morally accountable for their children's anti-social behaviour. Parents of children with ADHD are captured within these discourses when their children's actions transgress social norms of acceptable childhood behaviour. For example, parental accountability is invoked in media stories that suggest psychosocial explanations for ADHD.

Of course, parental responsibility for children's outcomes is not a new phenomenon. Ideas about how family life contributed to the healthy development of children came to be widely circulated via clinics, schools and other institutions from the early twentieth century. Knowledge about normal and abnormal childhood came from the psychological sciences, or the 'psy' disciplines (Rose 1999) and gained momentum through the 'benchmarking' of healthy and desirable development, which was associated with 'morally' healthy families. The discourse of normative child development continues to inform current research into ADHD which emphasises associations between parenting behaviours/style and the development of ADHD in children. For example, recent studies have included a focus on the effects of parental involvement on the learning of children with ADHD (Rogers et al. 2009) and the 'qualities' (such as warmth and responsiveness) of parents of boys with hyperactivity (Keown 2011). Studies such as these perpetuate prevailing understandings that there is, at least, an association between parenting behaviour and practices and the outcomes for children affected by ADHD, and, at most, a cause and effect relationship (see Keown 2011; Rogers et al. 2009), which is sometimes reported as linear and unidirectional and can imply blame (Colley 2010). It is via the knowledge produced by such studies that 'good' and successful parenting comes to be described. Expertise, in this case psychological, prescribes the optimum conditions for rearing healthy and developmentally 'normal' children. These 'best parenting practices' can be understood as forms of self governance that parents must take up in compliance with the self regulation of family life (Foucault 1988).

Contemporary (UK) government discourse of 'good' parenting depicts it not as an 'intimate relationship, but as an occupation requiring particular knowledge and skills' (Gillies 2005: 77). Advice and guidance are typically disseminated through parenting books, manuals, television programmes and parenting classes and through governmental 'early years intervention' policies, which target parents/mothers in how best to raise their children (Gillies et al. 2016). Group-based parenting programmes are commonly recommended for parents of pre-school children with ADHD (Smith et al. 2014). As Gillies (2005) points out, interventions are framed within a discourse of parenting support but, in fact, are infused with moral judgement as the emphasis of these interventions is on regulating and controlling the behaviour of families who do not fall within the consensus of what a 'healthy' and 'normal' family should be. The power of these psychological/normative child development discourses is indicated by the way parents engage with them to reflect on their own child's difficulties. For example, Gray Brunton et al. (2014) found that parents of children with ADHD invoked attachment, marital separation and discipline as potential explanations for their child's difficulties.

Although the 'psy' disciplines continue to produce widely disseminated knowledge about optimum parenting practices, in recent years, there has been a growing interest in the association of neuroscientific knowledge with child development. Illustrating the increased professionalization of parenting practice in general (see Bailey 2014), parenting interventions now include strategies underpinned by neuroscientific knowledge such as how to target impairment in neuropsychological functioning (see Tarver et al. 2014). These biomedically informed parenting interventions force parents 'into a project of parenting according to medically conceived truths of behavioural disorder', which encourages their dependence on specialist knowledge (see Bailey 2014: 98).

Current political discourse provides strict formulations of good parenting with an emphasis on marriage, stable family environments and the presence of an authoritative father. However, despite this emphasis on stability, and a 'strong' father presence, it is mothers who are held most responsible for their family's behaviour (Allen and Taylor 2012; Barnes and Power 2012; De Benedictis 2012; Gillies 2005). This positions fathers and mothers differently and renders maternal care-giving to overwhelming scrutiny and accountability, reflected also in media representations.

Gendered Care-Giving and the Blameworthy Mother

The gendered nature of caregiving and responsibility for caregiving is well-documented within sociological and psychological literature (Bennett 2007; Doucet 2006; Gillies 2005; Harden 2005; Litt 2004).

Parenting research often emphasises mothers over fathers because, in the words of Vander Ploeg Booth et al. (2010), mothers have 'a key role in task-related aspects of parenting' (2010: 2). Mothers are held responsible for their children's well-being, and future outcomes (Weusten 2011; Blum 2007; McKeever and Miller 2004). If children deviate from social and/or developmental norms, then mothers can be judged not to be good mothers because they do not have good children (Austin and Carpenter 2008). Mothers of children with an ADHD diagnosis are affected by this discourse of 'mother-blame' as the behaviour of these children can be 'disorderly, disorganised and disruptive' (Austin and Carpenter 2008: 378). Additionally, McKeever and Miller (2004) contend that 'mothers are often implicated in, and considered responsible for, their [children's] disabilities or illnesses' (2004: 1182).

Historically, maternal behaviours have been held up for scrutiny and constructed as a cause for their children's deviance. Constructs such as 'the psychogenic mother' and the 'refrigerator mother' (see Bettelheim 1959) have been blamed for a range of medical conditions or social ills, such as autism and schizophrenia (Weusten 2011; Berman and Wilson 2009; Blum 2007; Singh 2002) and it is within this cultural context of mother-blame (Malacrida 2001) that mothers' care-giving practices are situated. Blame and vilification is attached to 'bad' mothers who are deemed to have 'failed' in some way. A mother is marked as 'failed' for 'an attribute that conveys her devalued (or tainted) status as a mother' (Wigginton and Lafrance 2016: 31), this might include a mother who has failed to produce a 'healthy' child, such as a mother of a child with ADHD. The 'blameworthy mother' is a pervasive feature within the literature relating to mothers of children with ADHD, with a large body of research documenting mothers' feelings and experiences of blame (Gwernan-Jones et al. 2015; Gray Brunton et al. 2014, Broomhead 2013; Austin and Carpenter 2008; Blum 2007; Neophytou and Webber 2005; Litt 2004; Singh 2004; Harborne et al. 2004; Klasen and Goodman 2000).

The 'failure' of mothers to produce 'healthy' children stands out as a stigma: a "mark' of social disgrace, a deeply discrediting attribute, that results in the social devaluation of a person for their 'spoiled' identity' (Wigginton and Lafrance 2016: 31; see also Goffman 1963).

Certainly, stigmatisation and marginalisation appear as themes within studies relating to parenting and ADHD (Gray Brunton et al. 2014; Watson 2011; Harden 2005; McKeever and Miller 2004; Gray 2002a, b). Parents of children with ADHD may be affected by stigma because of the non-normative characteristics of their children's behaviour. Goffman identifies this as 'courtesy stigma' (Goffman 1990), suggesting that individuals, through their association with a 'stigmatised' person (in this case, a child with ADHD), come to share in their stigma and marginalisation. Parents may also be affected by stigma because of their own discredited position within sections of society. 'Public stigma' (see Mueller et al. 2012) refers to the stigma that arises through publicly held attitudes and beliefs towards those individuals and their families who are affected by mental distress. Parents of children with ADHD can be understood to experience public stigma (Mueller et al. 2012) on account of the deficit parenting stereotypes that circulate in society and within the media.

This public stigma can be seen in studies which indicate that mothers become objects of scrutiny in their encounters with medical professionals relating to their children (Watson 2011; Berman and Wilson 2009; Litt 2004; Malacrida 2001). Similarly, parents consistently report how their parenting practices are subject to the 'disciplinary gaze' (Foucault 1991) of teachers (Gwernan-Jones et al. 2015; Honkasilta et al. 2015) as well as other professionals, family and friends (Berman and Wilson 2009; Ryan 2006; Harden 2005; Todd and Jones 2003). As Singh states (2004: 1201), 'to this extent it does not matter whether mothers are actually experiencing this judgement or 'imagining' it. The point is that even their imagination reflects the internalisation of this disciplinary power'. This internalised judgement by others may account for the high number of accounts which describe feelings of isolation and alienation (Honkasilta et al. 2015; Bull and Whelan 2006; Neophytou and Webber 2005; Segal 2001; Klasen and Goodman 2000), withdrawal from social situations (Berman and Wilson 2009) and feelings of low self-worth (Bennett 2007; Singh 2004).

It is interesting to observe how parents engage with the position of the blameworthy, stigmatised mother through their accounts of isolation and victimhood (Davies 2014). Taking a discursive approach, we understand social identities to be constructed as subject positions in a flexible and fluid way depending on the context of interaction and how people are using them. As Zverina et al. (2011) suggest, 'in making accusations, criticising, mitigating, asking questions and positioning each other in talk, people manage their stake in conversation and construct their identities through moment-by-moment enactments'. A victim identity is just one identity that mothers can draw upon to do discursive work. Here, the distressing experiences of victimhood described by the examples below demonstrate how mothers represent themselves as victims and how they draw on cultural resources to do this.

Resisting a Stigmatised Identity

When mothers represent themselves as victims in relation to ADHD, this works to mitigate the stigmatisation and marginalisation they have experienced from other parents. In effect, this turns the focus of criticism away from themselves and back towards those who are victimising them. Scrutiny, or 'felt stigma', as Goffman (1990) terms it, is particularly experienced in public spaces and situations (Ryan 2006; Gray 2002b), where parental competence is most likely to be judged and, where a child's disruptive behaviour challenges the ability of parents 'to affect a presentation of family normality' (Gray 2002b: 740). This may partly explain why several of the mothers' accounts of stigma and marginalisation are located in the school playground:

> and I used to stand in that playground and I'd I'd rather die than sit in that blinkin' playground. (Julie: cited in Davies 2014: 196)
> that's where people are all eyeing themselves up it's a horrific place to go. (Ingrid: ibid.: 196)

Julie's spoiled maternal identity is made clear as she juxtaposes the seemingly mundane and routine maternal activity of collecting her son from school with her dread of entering the hostile environment of the school playground: 'I used to dread, dread I can't tell you how much I used to dread collecting him' (Julie: 197). Her pain and humiliation are poignantly conveyed in this description of her treatment by other parents.

Both victimhood and heroism are common media representations of ADHD, the latter originating in fictional myths and metanarratives. It is with these dominant narratives in mind that we attend to mothers' accounts of stigmatisation and resistance. These familiar media stories of ADHD, populated with victims, villains and heroes, are readily available cultural resources (or interpretative repertories) which parents draw upon to construct particular versions of the world (Horton-Salway 2012). The familiarity of these as a cultural stock of stories means they require little explanation or detail. Because of the culturally shared nature of these story formats, one fragment of the story can be sufficient to imply the rest (see Wetherell 1998). Within such familiar stories, the construction of identities is relational and constitutive (Burr 2003; Shotter 1997). Julie's account of her 'dread' of entering the school represents a stigmatised and marginalised mother who is a victim of hostility. The subject position of victim calls into being that of perpetrator and depicts the victim as morally righteous in relation to the perpetrator. We are invited to imagine the judgements of other parents who are presented as the 'gaze' of societal moral censure, 'people are all eying themselves up it's a horrific place'. As another mother put it:

> they had a petition behind our back to get him out of school the parents the whole school ganged up together [...] and parents came out every single day and I couldn't go to school ground without my friend literally holding my arm I was terrified. (Ingrid: cited in Davies 2014: 208)

The intimidating nature of this social censure is represented as commonplace 'everybody would be saying 'that kid's just a little git" (Paula: cited in Davies 2014: 209). As Stokoe and Edwards (2007) suggest, when a speaker reports that they have been the recipient of an insult this is 'to invite the listener to make inferences about the producer of the [...] language' (p. 353). For example, the moral cowardice and intimidation of other parents are two representations implied in Paula's and Ingrid's accounts of the playground:

> they'd just all stand there and I'd be completely on my own and everybody would be saying 'that kid's just a little git'[...] but they weren't brave enough to come up and say anything. (Paula: cited in Davies 2014: 209)

> every single day some parent would come up to me and say 'your child did this, that, that to my child what you going to do about it?' and I said 'I'm sorry I can't do anything', I said 'I apologise I can't do anything else'. (Ingrid: ibid.: 208)

These are common descriptions of mothers' experiences in relation to their children with ADHD and they use them to describe the difficulty of their situation and also to resist discrediting versions of themselves as failing parents. It is important to note that these are situated accounts of experience rather than fixed enduring identity categories of 'victim' or 'perpetrator' in the sense that they are familiar forms of social identity categories, arising from culturally recognisable ways of describing the world. They are used in social interactions as a flexible, discursive resource. In other places in their account of experience, mothers might describe themselves differently and in more positive terms. A victim identity works to claim the moral high ground which is a way of recruiting support for troubles and resisting condemnation. However, a victim identity is also a risky one to take up as it can reproduce and reaffirm discourses of blame and stigma. As Zverina et al. (2011: 2388) state, 'it is not surprising that identity work [...] involves a delicate balance in which victim identities are both embraced and resisted'. Paula and Ingrid, the mothers who took up a stigmatised, victim identity (above) also took up very positive, pro-active mother identities at other times.

Resisting Discourses of Blame: Turning to the Biomedical Model

The use of biological explanations works to resist the stigma of discrediting parental and child identities, stigma and blame that arise from psychosocial explanations of ADHD (Ghosh et al. 2016). Many studies have observed how this happens in the accounts of mothers of children with ADHD to explain their children's 'disordered' behaviour (Broomhead 2013; Ryan and Runswick-Cole 2008; Bennett 2007). This is a situated form of resistance to the stigmatising representations of children and parents that populate the discourse of ADHD. Furthermore, it is significant that the take up of biomedical explanations and medicalised interventions for ADHD is conflictual for parents as we now demonstrate in relation to mothers' discourse. Mothers draw on biomedical knowledge in certain situations, but they reject it in others.

Similar to Singh's (2004) findings, the mothers' narratives in Davies (2014) tended to be organised around before and after stories of diagnosis, which enabled the 'transformation of blame from mother to brain' (Singh 2004: 1194). The 'before' stories consisted of very raw accounts of trouble, which gave way to less troubled 'after' (post diagnosis) stories. 'Troubles-telling' (see Jefferson 1988) is particularly relevant to accounts of parenting children with ADHD. On the one hand, troubles-telling is a necessary feature of accounting for and seeking validation for ADHD. Without 'troubles', there would be no reason for medical or educational intervention, help or support. Put simply, 'troubles-telling' is a way of conveying to the listener how problematic an event or experience has been. In one example, a mother explained how her decision to seek a diagnosis came after a pre-school visit: 'and he's running about off there and he's pulling it down and he's kicking it and he's pushing in I couldn't it was too much so I did what I could eventually I did get him diagnosed' (Donna: cited in Davies 2014: 144). However, troubles-telling such as this can also suggest a problematic identity. In the case of parents of children with ADHD, this might be indicated by a parent being unable to cope with their 'disruptive' child. Parents have to navigate these tensions in their talk, and as Miller and Silverman (1995) point out, troubles talk in ordinary conversation is 'complex and varied, even disordered' (p. 727). With the variable and situated nature of accounts in mind, we note the pragmatic function of troubles-telling in mothers' accounts of 'before diagnosis'.

The mother-blame/brain-blame binary (see Blum 2007; Singh 2004) describes how the 'medicalization of problematic behaviors in young boys includes an inherent narrative of blame transformation' from mother to brain (Singh 2004: 1193). In Davies (2014), most of the mothers accounted for ADHD by locating the cause within the brain:

> it's a brain…it's a problem with the brain it's something to do with the uhm frontal cortex or something of the brain and the frontal lobes or something not working properly. (Paula: ibid.: 138)

Paula credentials her familiarity and knowledge of ADHD in much the same way as the media might report on science research by drawing on technical terms that demonstrate familiarity with the neuroscience of ADHD. Mothers routinely offer biological explanations for ADHD sometimes suggesting that their children's 'difference' was evident from birth, or even within the womb (Bull and Whelan 2006). For example:

> I knew the minute he could walk there was something I mean I knew there was something wrong when he was tiny […] he used to do some quite bizarre stuff. (Paula: cited in Davies 2014: 180)

Early indicators of 'atypical' behaviour in their children are common in mothers' accounts representing ADHD as something intrinsic to the child, rather than due to the environment or their parenting. In describing these initial concerns about their child's behaviour, even in vague ways, such as 'something wrong', mothers are also depicting themselves as observant, knowledgeable good mothers, who monitor the progress of their children. As Goffman (2006) suggests, vagueness and ambiguity are useful strategies for managing a positive 'face', as they deter challenge and examination (see also Potter 1996; Macmillan and Edwards 1998). The 'pervasiveness of the discourse of normative child development' (O'Dell and Brownlow 2015: 302) is evident in the way that mothers indirectly orient to their children's deviation from 'normative' developmental expectations: 'he didn't like to be touched he didn't like to be picked up and things like that' (Paula: cited in Davies 2014: 180).

The Significance of Diagnosis as a Pivotal Event

The significance of the competing nature of biological and psychosocial explanations of ADHD is made clear in Ingrid's relief at the doctor's diagnosis of her son's ADHD:

> and he said 'you're doing fantastically there's absolutely nothing that you've done wrong' [...] we phoned everybody I phoned my mum I was like [...] like 'this is the happiest day of my life' [...] yeah so relieved and somebody actually told us told us that 'you're doing a great job' he said 'you are fantastic. (Ingrid, in Davies 2014: 178)

This example is typical of parental relief at medical diagnosis of ADHD (see Ghosh et al. 2016; Neophytou and Webber 2005; Singh 2004; Segal 2001; Klasen and Goodman 2000). Ingrid makes clear what is at stake for her (and her partner) with regard to obtaining this diagnosis for their child. The doctor's independent and expert diagnosis is presented through the use of reported speech (see Potter 1996; Widdicombe and Wooffit 1995; Wooffitt 1992), and this provides Ingrid with a vindication of her parenting in his words, 'you're doing fantastically there's absolutely nothing that you've done wrong'. Her use of extreme case formulations (ECFs) (Pomerantz 1986) such as 'phoned everybody' and the 'happiest day of my life', even if understood as non-literal, shows her investment in this explanation for her child's problems. Indeed, we understand this to be a day which makes sense of her parenting experiences and, in her narrative, the diagnosis features as a pivotal event that brings her relief.

Expressing relief about this diagnosis is risky for parents. Parents are often accused of jumping on the ADHD bandwagon in media reports that represent an ADHD diagnosis as an excuse or a way of securing financial support (see Chapter 3; Harwood et al. 2017; Horton-Salway 2012). One way that mothers orient to this is by establishing their own initial reluctance in accepting an ADHD diagnosis. For example:

> and then when he went to primary school the teacher was very worried about his eye contact and they asked us to get him [...] to the GP and get him seen and we thought "they know nothing" [...] it took two years of me saying "no there's nothing"....' (Julie: cited in Davies 2014: 147)

Julie's description of her initial resistance to a medical diagnosis is typical of many mothers' accounts. Her original opposition to the teacher's suggestion, and to medical intervention, "they know nothing", manages the controversial issues arising from the diagnosis of ADHD. Parents can be accused of having their own agenda so the management of stake and interest is an important aspect of constructing a credible account. Stake management is a key feature of establishing lack of motive or bias in every-day discourse (Potter 1996; Edwards and Potter 1993). A parent who had not initially sought this diagnosis is less likely to be heard as jumping on the bandwagon.

Securing a Diagnosis: Taking on the Experts

The full extent of what is at stake, for the mothers of children with ADHD, can also be heard in the descriptions of difficulties they face in obtaining a diagnosis. In contrast to accounts which downplay their initial engagement with the idea of a medical diagnosis there are also accounts which describe how mothers actively work to secure such a diagnosis, even if this means challenging or rejecting the opinion of unsympathetic practitioners. Many of the mothers talked about unsympathetic doctors, quite often GPs. One mother, whose child had a dual diagnosis of autism and ADHD, describes how her son's GP did not know about autism: 'he's got autism spectrum disorder and his GP a senior GP went 'what's that?'' (Linda: cited in Davies 2014: 154). The doctor's status as 'a senior GP' is further called into account by Linda's suggestion that 'anyone on the street' or any 'non-specialist' would recognise that her son is autistic. Querying the expertise of health professionals is one way that lay people respond to lack of recognition for controversial health categories and this also mirrors the undermining of consulted health professionals in the media (Lloyd and Norris 1999) and the decline of medical authority observed by Norris and Lloyd (2000).

Medical practitioners who do not endorse an ADHD diagnosis are described as problematic by parents who are keen to secure recognition for this diagnosis and help for their children. Generally, parents draw on the authority of medical knowledge to support their claims about ADHD. In contrast, unsympathetic medical opinion is formulated as being so because of 'contingencies' such as the doctor's personality, age or unhelpful characteristics, rather than based on scientific knowledge (see also Gilbert and Mulkay 1984):

> he was just up there and he said there's nothing called ADHD it doesn't exist he was a very old doctor. (Ingrid: cited in Davies 2014: 153)
>
> I think he's quite close to retirement. (Linda: ibid.: 154)

In both accounts, the doctors are constructed as old, their views as old-fashioned and, consequently, it is implied that their knowledge is inadequate. These mothers represent ADHD (and autism) as requiring a modern understanding and an up-to-date body of knowledge that some doctors have and others might lack. This allows a criticism of medical practices that does not threaten the status of the medical model (see Chapter 1 discussion of empiricist and contingent repertoires, Gilbert and Mulkay 1984).

As we saw in Chapter 3, the challenge to medical opinion takes place within a culture of increasing 'mediatisation' of medical knowledge (Seale 2003) and take up of media representations along with the definition of health 'consumers' encourages individuals to take up whichever expert opinion matches their own viewpoint (see Valentine 2001). The availability of knowledge about ADHD, especially from medical websites that list diagnostic criteria (Conrad and Bergey 2014; Foroushani 2008), makes everyone a potential expert meaning 'the professional hero is no longer a secure category' (Seale 2003: 523). Parents are able to challenge professional decision making because they now have access to different perspectives on medical knowledge.

On the one hand, it is tempting to interpret mothers' accounts of challenging professional authority as acts of resistance and empowerment. However, these acts take place within a context of a pervasive mother-valour/mother-blame binary (see Blum 2007). Either way, mothers are held accountable for their children's outcomes. This includes becoming experts on ADHD. As one parent put it: 'it's such a hard slog to get actually [...] to get the help we got him the help he obviously needed' (John: 178). Mothers' challenges to professionals can be interpreted as demonstrations of good mothering and maternal fitness, where mothers wield medical and psychological knowledge to gain the best results for their children.

These examples have demonstrated the complexity and variability of accounts relating to diagnosis, indicating what is at stake for mothers when they are talking about diagnosis of their child's medical condition. The mothers interviewed all engaged with a biomedical explanation for ADHD, but accountability and blame are reframed rather than entirely abolished within these accounts (see Bailey 2014; Blum 2007; Singh 2004). So enduring is the spectre of mother-blame, that a biomedical diagnosis of ADHD simply reconstitutes it in a different form (Blum 2007; Singh 2004). Blum (2007) identifies this blame as 'proximate blame', in which mothers, although free from blame for causing their child's condition, are held responsible for the subsequent management and care of their children. This reconstitution of blame can be seen in the way that mothers are held to account over issues relating to medication.

Transformative Accounts of Medication

Concerns and accounts of guilt about medication feature commonly in mothers' accounts. Mothers are caught in a moral dilemma of social condemnation. As one mother put it, 'I feel damned if I do give him the pills and damned if I don't' (Taylor et al. 2006: 120). Seale's (2003) argument that media audiences participate in a dialogue with 'an imagined community of other viewers, people 'like me'' (p. 517) is highly pertinent to the way that mothers negotiate the moral positioning they experience in relation to the circulating discourse of ADHD and medication. Singh (2004) points out, for example, that mother-blame is 'reconstituted' through media discussions of medication, where mothers seeking medical intervention are represented as self-serving. The mother in the following example shows awareness of how she is positioned within the discourse of ADHD:

> the other thing I think parents get with ADHD is uhm I think it's a label you can't win it's a label which is 'there's nothing wrong with them it's just

> the parenting… oh they just drug that child. (Caroline, cited in Davies 2014: 184–185)

She is aware of how the 'imagined community' might interpret her decision to medicate her son: 'there's nothing wrong…they just drug that child'. Stories depicting medication as a 'chemical cosh' or those that link medication with 'fear of harm' invite mothers to recognise themselves as the subjects of this critical discourse (see Chapter 3; also Harwood et al. 2017; Horton-Salway 2011; O'Dell and Brownlow 2015).

As a consequence, mothers' accounts of their decisions to medicate orient to the possibility of public condemnation and are carefully managed. For example, many of them deploy transformative stories to illustrate the beneficial effects of medication for their children:

> he's exhausting I mean physically and mentally exhausting […] we had huge huge meltdowns massive anxiety uhm that I by that stage was pretty skilled and I knew what I was doing so I was able to work with him very intensively to try and you know bring down his anxiety and the other thing I did was […] I went privately to a consultant […]immediately put him on medication and the transformation was unbelievable […] completely changed his life overnight on the first dose within half an hour […] he had transformed. (Caroline: in Davies 2014: 185–186)

In Caroline's example, the contrast between the extreme meltdowns 'before' and the change in his life 'after' pivots around medication such that the account functions as an endorsement of this course of action. However, the dilemma of troubles-telling is clear here. On the one hand, there is an interactional and moral requirement for Caroline to describe the 'troubles' experienced by her son and family in some detail to warrant her decision to seek medical intervention. On the other hand, troubles talk, and the need for medication, positions the child as challenging and Caroline as unable to cope with him. This potential for 'reconstituted blame' is countered by working up her own identity as a skilled mother who was not overwhelmed by the difficulties her son presented or looking for a 'quick fix' to manage her son's behaviour, as suggested by some media stories (Harwood et al. 2017).

A common way that mothers resist 'reconstituted blame' is by linking the use of medication with positive educational outcomes: 'and he was like a different child and suddenly he was able to focus and he could learn' (Caroline: 186). Medication becomes aligned with better school performance; the account of 'troubles' is therefore closed, and 'business as usual' is resumed (see, for example, Jefferson 1988). These examples alert us to the dilemmas that mothers must manage with regards to medication. Within the biological repertoire, medication for the 'sick' child is not only reasonable, but to some extent, expected or a requirement of the educational context. Parents who seek medication for their children are 'doing right by their child', and maximising their potential to achieve at school. From this view a parent who resists diagnosis and medication is neglecting their duty, and risks their child's exclusion from school. Contrary to this are psychosocial explanations in which children are constituted as 'normally' naughty, or so extremely naughty that parenting interventions might be suggested.

The Intensification of Maternal Responsibility

Mothers' care-giving and responsibility for their children comes to the fore around issues of medication. For example, concern about the side-effects of medication is managed by mothers who provide medication 'breaks' for their children (Neophytou and Webber 2005; Singh 2005), thereby assuming responsibility for the monitoring and 'fine-tuning' of their child's medication (Taylor et al. 2006; Litt 2004). By resisting regulated medication of their children, mothers demonstrate both concern for their children and developing expertise in relation to their children's medical condition. For example, Rachel described the decision to medicate based on the medical professional's advice:

> she sort of uhm I was… going to …talk us into but that wasn't the fact at all cos it was entirely our decision but she gave us enough information that took away all the scare and went through all the potential side-effects and the thing that swung it for us was that she said it's not addictive. (Rachel: cited in Davies 2014: 188)

The issue here is not the accuracy of Rachel's account, but the way that she is representing herself as an agent who was required to choose. The tension between (medical) authority and expertise and the neoliberal ideals of individualism, personal autonomy and agency is revealed in talk about decision making relating to medical matters (Bishop and Yardley 2004). Bishop and Yardley argue that because the giving of advice from doctor to patient is socially and institutionally sanctioned, not to take-up medical advice is an accountable action. On the other hand, the contemporary discourse of citizen choice and professional partnerships is also embedded in neoliberal societies, so service users are positioned as responsible partners who take part in decisions about their healthcare. Therefore, when parents in the UK engage with health services they are captured by the cultural imperatives of individual choice, but constrained by the discourses of proper parenting, including taking medical advice. In the above example, the power of the medical expert lies in her authority to present an 'informed' case for medication to a concerned parent. Rachel attends very closely to issues of parental agency, drawing attention to the tension between authority and personal autonomy herself: 'I think she sort of uhm I was…going to…talk us into but that wasn't the fact at all 'cos it was entirely our decision' (p. 188). Clearly though, choice does not necessarily imply power, since Rachel and her husband could not medicate their child without the doctor's sanction.

Nevertheless, the discourse of 'choice' and user involvement in decision-making is part of the contemporary practice of health services and this is implied by Rachel's account. This is not without risk of moral censure because making choices on behalf of children against doctors' advice might be regarded as irresponsible. This is why Rachel is concerned to point out that the doctor had encouraged them to make this choice themselves. In mothers' accounts of decisions to medicate, the responsibility for children's medical welfare shifts between doctor and mother to account for these issues.

Similar to the way mothers might embrace the biomedical explanation of ADHD while also rejecting the views of sceptical practitioners, mothers are contradictory in their take-up and management of medication. They comply with medication, but not always as medical authority directs. Rachel, for example, showed her awareness of some side-effects of medication such as reduced appetite and weight loss, and described how she manages these potentially harmful effects by taking 'medication holidays', or even by 'tweaking' the prescribed dosage of drug. Mothers do not surrender wholly to medical prescription for ADHD as they (perhaps) might with conditions such as diabetes. It is hard to imagine a parent admitting to giving 'insulin holidays' to their children, and easy to imagine the condemnation they would receive if they were to do so. Interpreting ADHD prescription in a flexible way might only become an accountable issue if the outcomes for the child were jeopardised. Otherwise, the management of ADHD medication is a means by which mothers (re)assume their maternal responsibility for their children. According to Singh (2004: 1202), medication lends mothers a 'material authority', providing them with a 'biotechnical tool' with which to perform maternal fitness in line with a reconfigured biological narrative of maternal caregiving.

This ambivalent behaviour towards medication could be an indication of the incomplete medicalisation of UK society (see Gray Brunton et al. 2014; Malacrida 2004), and in this case, linked to the existence of competing and dilemmatic discourses around ADHD and the decline of scientific authority. Mothers' decisions to medicate are held up to scrutiny against this background and might be criticised for being negligent in a number of competing ways. Mothers must navigate a territory that places them at fault whatever they do. Mothers attend to this by demonstrating an awareness of the 'fear of damage' metanarratives around medication (see Wang et al. 2016) and responding to this accordingly. Their accounts of maternal agency around medication represent them as 'good' mothers, who pro-actively assume responsibility for managing their child's illness.

The assumption of responsibility for children's medication is just one example of the extended care-giving practices demanded of mothers once their children have received a diagnosis of ADHD. Post diagnosis, mothers are under an imperative to perform a 'concerted action' of valourised maternal care (Blum 2007). This is accomplished through an 'intensification of 'normal' motherhood' (see Blum 2007: 205) involving intensive carework, advocacy and vigilance to obtain the necessary services and resources for their children.

Resistance and Compliance: The Politics of Parenting

Accounts of caregiving, coping, management and advocacy featured frequently in the accounts of mothers in Alison Davies' study (2014). Mothers reported how their everyday parenting practice was held up to scrutiny, and most indicated there was a common expectation they should attend parenting classes: 'oh yeah I've been to three parenting groups' (Ingrid: 245). Mothers' accounts of parenting classes highlight the unequal power relations between parents and professionals. Power that circulates in the discourse, institutions and practices of experts still has the potential to constrain and dominate (Gwernan-Jones et al. 2015; Honkasilta et al. 2015; Hodge and Runswick-Cole 2008). Resonating with findings from other studies (Gwernan-Jones et al. 2015; Berman and Wilson 2009; Austin and Carpenter 2008; Malacrida 2001), both mothers and fathers demonstrate awareness of a requirement to be deferential and compliant at a parenting class: 'and you know I didn't say I didn't pick anything up because I did you know I I you know you can hear things and you think "oh I can turn that into..."' (Ingrid: Davies 2014: 245). Maternal compliance can, therefore, be understood as a form of 'game playing' (Austin and Carpenter 2008), in which mothers, such as Ingrid, do not want to position themselves as uncooperative. This token compliance may be understood as a form of resistance, with mothers working to validate their own positions within the hierarchical professional/lay relationship at the same time as avoiding being defined as troublesome. The micropolitics of parenting (see Miller and Silverman 1995: 743) are apparent in the complex interplay between compliance and resistance. Parents resist and undermine 'professional' parenting techniques with token compliance while at the same time credentialing their own experiential parenting skills or knowledge gained from personal research.

Parents are positioned within a double bind in relation to parenting classes (see Holt 2010). If they fully engage with the classes, and adopt new parenting strategies to deal with their children, then, clearly, they needed 'training', and their identity as 'deficient' parents was justified. However, if parents refuse to engage, then they could be deemed uncooperative and risk further scrutiny and interference. As Holt (2010) argues, parents need to be seen to engage, while resisting the need to change. Ingrid (cited in Davies 2014) resisted the need to change her parenting practice by drawing on her own experiential knowledge of her child and claiming a 'lack of fit' between the practices put forward by the parenting experts and her own 'extraordinary' familial situation:

> they they'd all talk about the 1 2 3 you know timeout and stuff but they were focusing a lot on that and none of them things worked on L so most of the time I was sitting there going [...] sticker charts [...] but they only worked for a short moment of time because he doesn't have the same you know. (Ingrid: 246)

Ingrid (carefully) resists the strategies offered within the parenting group, 'time out and stuff...sticker charts', the implication being that her son has different requirements, 'he doesn't have the same you know'. This is an example of how mothers challenge professional and expert authority by claiming superior knowledge of their own children. However, resisting taught parenting strategies is a risky business. Parents, to display a positive moral identity, need to show a willingness to assume responsibility for their children (Holt 2010; Ribbens McCarthy et al. 2000). Ingrid tempers her resistance to the taught strategies by conceding that she could learn something, 'I didn't say I didn't pick anything up because I did' (Ingrid: cited in Davies 2014: 245). However, the strategies offered are only useful once she adapts them to the needs of her child, 'oh I can turn that into' (Ingrid: 245). She holds back her criticism so as to avoid a negative judgement of herself as uncooperative, someone not prepared to participate in the classes nor assume responsibility. Such mothers consistently indicate that their children's behaviour requires exceptional parenting that exceeds that of parents of 'normal' children, as Rachel says, 'normal rules of parenting don't apply' (Rachel, in Davies 2014: 243). This resonates with Colley's (2010) contention that the parenting skills required of parents of children with ADHD are counter-intuitive and extraordinary.

Parenting-as-a-Project

As the examples of parenting classes and medication suggest, mothers experience intensification of the disciplinary gaze post-diagnosis and are positioned within powerful authoritative discourses (medical, educational, political), which provide them with little 'natural' authority of their own. The power of the disciplinary gaze is that it is not only directed towards individuals by external and powerful authorities but also exercised by everyone, turning them into both the objects and subjects of discourse. In this way, parents are encouraged to observe themselves and discipline their own actions accordingly. Mothers of children with ADHD respond by displaying an increased vigilance of their children and their children's encounters with the world (see Blum 2007; Singh 2004), working harder to be 'good' mothers and secure the very best for their children.

Parenting classes are a good example of how parenting has become increasingly professionalised. 'Good' parents in need of support are invited to undergo training to learn the optimal strategies for managing their families. Acting as a 'disciplinary mechanism' of governance in the Foucauldian sense, parenting classes establish the necessary knowledge and skills to raise 'good and normal children'. In line with Foucault's ideas about self-governance, parents are also encouraged to discipline themselves and self-regulate, apparently of their own free will. As we see with Ingrid, although she shows some resistance to the preferred discourses of the group, she has tried some of the techniques suggested, and her self-monitoring of parenting has become a conscious endeavour. In this way, she takes up the disciplining authority of the parenting class and to some extent responds to its discourse and practices to work on herself and her family. Parenting strategies are frequently referred to by mothers (Davies 2014). They demonstrate both a familiarity with the performance of 'good' parenting practice, and, at other times, they reject recommended practice in favour of their own superior knowledge.

This is a good example of the variability we commonly see in the discourse of parents, arising as it does from the dilemmatic nature of ADHD, parenting discourse and situated cultural context.

The orientation of so much of the mothers' talk towards parenting practice and skill indicate that mothers are alert to their positioning as proximate causes of their children's difficulties. They treat their parenting identities as reflexive projects in which they have to be made and consciously developed. Mothers demonstrate their concerted 'parenting-as-a-project' in accounts of 'relentless action' and valorised motherhood (Blum 2007: 122). This provides opportunities for mothers to resist the negative stereotypes of deficit parenting discourses. In doing so, they orient to the ways that they 'are policed and police themselves through fear of mother-blame, being judged inadequate, unnatural, or selfish' (Blum 2007: 202).

The Skilled Mother

Through accounts of extreme and 'abnormal' behaviour, mothers can demonstrate the need for exceptional parenting and their own development of skill, expertise and ability to cope with their children (Bull and Whelan 2006; Litt 2004; Segal 2001). The following extended extract is a good example of how one mother manages this:

> like I say to my son "I don't like some of the things that you do but I understand why you do them and it's not your fault that you can't control yourself but what we need to do is think of what you could do instead of doing that" you know "what would be a better solution to feeling like that than doing that like?" When he was little he used to attack me physically [...] but now he doesn't hit me at all [...]I didn't have a clue I just had this child who was really uncontrollable and quite violent and I didn't' know what to do[...]and uhm he hurt me numerous times you know he tried to push me down the stairs he threw scissors at me threw knives at me and I ended up with a broken nose where he headbutted me in the face uhm black eyes you know he was very very violent [...] and it wasn't until I read a bit about ADHD and I thought "I know! I'm going to let him hit, but he's not hitting me anymore we've got to find something else he can hit" and that's when I (unclear) the punchbag and I did that with him [...] he doesn't do it he very very rarely attacks anybody

> he'll throw things and he'll still wreck things in the house if you're not able to intervene quick enough uhm but he wouldn't physically hurt anybody now. (Paula: cited in Davies 2014: 228–229)

This account pivots around Paula's successful interventions as a mother with respect to her son's behaviour. His previously extreme and violent behaviour is pathologised and contrasted with his behaviour after she has developed the skills to manage him. Similar to the transformative narratives identified by Fleischmann and Miller (2013) described in Chapter 3, Paula's account tells of how she overcame the challenge presented by ADHD, and the pivotal event in this transformation is that Paula 'skilled up' by reading about ADHD, gaining invaluable expert insight into how to manage her son's behaviour. Paula, just like other mothers, has developed in-depth subject knowledge of her child's condition to successfully manage him (see Taylor et al. 2006; Segal 2001). This account of 'learned mothering' (see Taylor et al. 2006; Litt 2004; Segal 2001) is another example of how self-governance operates through the discourses of ADHD and parenting. Paula's developing skills and knowledge in relation to her son are an example of a project of 'concerted cultivation' (Lareau 2003; Blum 2007) in which 'good' parents become preoccupied with their children's development.

In 'doing' good mothering, mothers also take up intensified action by claiming authority to speak and act on behalf of their children. Mothers are vigilant in their advocacy role, particularly in managing their children across the educational and health care systems and ensuring their access to appropriate resources (Blum 2007). They 'act as vigilantes seizing authority from legitimate, credentialed professionals on behalf of their children' (Blum 2007: 222). The mothers interviewed by Davies (2014) gave similar accounts of fighting for their children as the following analysis demonstrates.

Fighting for Their Children

Several of the mothers in Davies (2014) described how they must fight to obtain services for their sons with ADHD. Mothers use the language of battle, for example, Paula describes how she has to fight for every bit of support for her son: 'you've conquered one thing, there's always something else' (Paula: 220). At the time of the interview, she was trying to persuade her son's school to provide transport: 'the school he's in now won't give him transport so I'm fighting constantly with them' (Paula: 220–221). Another mother talks about how the process of getting her son statemented was like a 'battleground' and a 'horrible battle' (Caroline: 224). In using 'fighting talk', mothers take up the position of the child's lone supporter defending them against unsympathetic professionals, negatively working against the child's interests.

'Fighting talk' appears throughout the literature relating to mothers' experiences with other parents, teachers and medical professionals (Blum 2007; Harborne et al. 2004; Norris and Lloyd 2000). Mothers of disabled children are reported as starting as 'worriers and becoming warriors' (Ryan and Runswick-Cole 2008: 204), moving from a passive, invisible position into a more assertive, active position (Gwernan-Jones et al. 2015). Caroline describes how she was obliged to take up an assertive role to gain a statement of educational needs for her son (below):

> The school couldn't cope in the end …in the end the school admitted that they couldn't cope he'd stopped talking in school and become a selective mute[…] and the teachers were just shouting at him and uhm he'd just stopped responding so in the end we withdrew him from school […] this battleground really went on up until […]he was fully statemented at that point which was a battleground in itself […] the statementing process was absolutely horrendous because we were not supported in that […]and every possible uhm barrier was put in the way of trying to get him statemented but we fought through that with an awful lot of money and legal help […] and so eventually we did get a statement after a long and arduous and horrible battle…. (Caroline: cited in Davies 2014: 223–224)

This account resonates with some media reports that represent boys with ADHD as the victims of injustice due to 'callous and uncaring' schools (in Horton-Salway 2012: 9). These stories describe valourised mothers who 'take on' the 'Goliath' authorities in defence of their victimised children. Mothers' responsibility for and dedication to their children is conveyed in stories of struggle to gain support and services for their children. Mothers prioritise their children before their own social and medical needs in descriptions of extraordinary care:

> you know why should I have to drive him to school every day? It's 56 miles there [...] do that twice a day and it works out at 56 miles a day that I travel and when you've got chronic fatigue it's hard work to drive [...] I have to I don't have any choice. (Paula: cited in Davies 2014: 221)

Prevalent discourses of normative maternal caregiving deem 'natural' mothering to be selfless, and mothers perform 'good' mothering by demonstrating their willingness (and desire) to take up the fight on behalf of their children, often at substantial cost to themselves. This parallels other literature which indicates that mothers take up a proactive role to demand access to health and educational resources on behalf of their children (Honkasilta et al. 2015; Austin and Carpenter 2008; Taylor et al. 2006; Litt 2004; McKeever and Miller 2004; Todd and Jones 2003). In this way, 'good' mothering becomes aligned with notions of activism, action, resistance and advocacy. The adversarial position that mothers describe is a risky one that can lead to confrontation with professionals. Parents (particularly mothers) are sometimes described as being provocative and conflictual (McKeever and Miller 2004). On the one hand, good mothers are those who agitate and demand for their children and this might in some situations be regarded as difficult or even pathological (Berman and Wilson 2009).

The Professional Mother

One way in which mothers resist this negative positioning is by assuming a professional parent identity. They do so by participating in a professional partnership between themselves and their children's school, for example, Gill (in Davies 2014: 235) explains how she educates the school about strategies that work, 'so whatever phrases or things we use we'll tell the school'. This is a potentially problematic position to take up with a delicate path to be negotiated between a helpful parent, who is engaged with their child's schooling and a parent who is too involved, presuming to advise teachers, or even interfering in their child's school life. Mothers who appear as confrontational or challenging can be considered less deserving of resources and support, and may not invite sympathy or empathy (Malacrida 2001; Berman and Wilson 2009). Mothers have, however, found ways to draw on their own expertise while ensuring that this expertise did not undermine or threaten the 'face' or standing of others. Gill, for example, reports that she is as equally willing to accept advice from teachers as she is to pass advice on to them: 'and if they find things that work they'll say: 'oh by the way we've learned that' (cited in Davies 2014: 235). In this way, Gill can be understood as co-operative and open to advice, mitigating the face-threatening act of advising others (Goffman 2006; Jaworski and Coupland 2006), in this case, teachers. Gill assumes a far from passive role in the professional partnership between her and the school pointing out that:

> I seem to be uhm a project manager and I think you find that a lot with the parents it's...and I felt do you know what he's my son so it's my job to liaise with school and do my own research and do ...find out from psychiatrists and I'm the one who pulls the information together for him. (Gill, cited in Davies 2014: 2235)

Drawing upon professional language in their accounts of interacting with schools and medical experts represents these mothers as being skilled, effective and expert in dealing with their children, but this can also be understood as an appropriation of the professional 'gaze' to which they are subjected. A professional mother identity positions them positively in their claims to maternal entitlement and authority while also complying with the cultural imperatives of 'parenting-as-project'. Certainly, Gill's account positions her as the person in charge of her son. In invoking her 'duty' to her son, she is indicating a privileged status in relation to him vis-à-vis the school, and in so doing establishes her own power entitlement to assume responsibility and participate in decisions about him.

It is tempting to understand such parent/professional dynamics in terms of mothers exercising their power and maternal authority over their children through the use of 'superior knowledge claims' obtained from articles, specialist sites, journals and books (Gwernan-Jones et al. 2015; Malacrida 2001). The powerlessness experienced by mothers (and fathers) within institutional contexts such as the school can be responded to by appropriating specialist discourses and taking up advocacy roles, thus enabling parents to question and resist the knowledge and power of professionals. A less positive interpretation, however, is that mothers' developing specialist expertise about their children works to reinforce 'the child's deficit and the family's dependence on specialist knowledge' (Bailey 2014: 108). The appropriation of expert knowledge by parents is both an act of resistance, but also a form of self-governance as parents monitor and regulate themselves and their families in accordance with cultural institutions.

In line with contemporary UK government discourse, good parenting is less about intimate and intuitive parenting and more about acquiring certain skills and knowledge. Thus, the appropriation of specialist knowledge can be interpreted as an example of how mothers must 'defend their legitimacy to knowledge about their child' (Bailey 2014: 110). As Hodge and Runswick-Cole (2008: 640) suggest in an article on parent–professional partnerships, parents 'cannot be only parents [but]...must be both a parent and a para-professional in the disciplines of medicine and education'. Seemingly, mothers' vigilance of their children has extended to all areas of their child's experience, including teaching and learning. This is experienced both as empowerment and a burden:

> and you're thinking actually I've got enough in my remit [...] as a parent without having education on on the top. (Jane, cited in Davies 2014: 240)

The Authority of Maternal Experience

As we have seen, mothers of children with ADHD are positioned within contradictory, dilemmatic and gendered discourses of 'good mothering' (and 'good parenting'). On the one hand, there is a societal expectation that 'good parents' will take up 'parenting-as-a-project', acquiring the skills and knowledge necessary to manage and parent their children to produce 'good families'. However, on the other hand, there remain strong essentialist discourses about maternal caregiving, which depict mothers as their children's 'saviour':

> well, how much more damaged can you get than you sit in a corner and you try and cut yourself and cut your wrists and then ring mum? ring me, school didn't even realise and he rang me and said "mum I really want to die" at which point I just got in the car and drove down there put him in the car and drove off and said "he's never ever going back there". (Caroline, in Davies 2014: 225)

Such accounts of distress and survival were also identified by Singh (2004: 1198), who contended that 'mothers' desperation to save their sons must be understood as part of an effort to preserve part of their deepest identity as women and mothers'. Studies by Todd and Jones (2003) and Baruch (1981) suggest that mothers provide this kind of harrowing detail as a way of pointing to their own 'essential humanity and to the coldness and separateness of professionals' (Todd and Jones 2003: 232). Maternal care and vigilance is pitted against the uncaring, neglect of the school in Caroline's account and her criticism of the school is grounded in her maternal awareness that her son is not thriving:

> I could see that he wasn't coping [...] I could see recognise the signs that he was in a desperate state and he wasn't coping but I wasn't being listened to again uhm and they again said it was that he needed discipline he needed to be brought into line [...] and they just started to increase discipline and boundaries which is not what he needed and that crashed and burned completely when he started self-harming.... (Caroline, cited in Davies 2014: 224–225)

In this example, maternal hyper-vigilance is emphasised over and above the regulatory strategies of the school. This mother's instinct that her son was not coping was, sadly, accurate.

The prioritising of their maternal experience over professional opinion was a common feature in the talk of mothers and supports the findings of earlier studies (for example, Todd and Jones 2003; Norris and Lloyd 2000). Mothers were often critical of the methods used by teachers with their children:

> but I think because the school don't see the… I mean I would say most of the self-esteem comes out of the anxiety […] and all the teachers are talking about is consolidating learning and I'm thinking "you've missed the point completely"…. (Jane: cited in Davies 2014: 238)

This entitlement to criticise teaching practices is grounded in Jane's position as a mother (see Sacks 1995). This entitles her to make experiential claims about strategies that do and do not work and to claim superior knowledge of what lies at the heart of some of her son's behaviour: 'the whole the key to it all is anxiety' (Jane: 238).

Challenges to professional opinion come from mothers' experience and understanding of their children and from the knowledge they have acquired in doing their own research about ADHD (see also Honkasilta et al. 2015; Segal 2001; Klasen and Goodman 2000). However, despite these claims of superior knowledge and acts of resistance, mothers (and fathers) remain accountable and are relatively disempowered in the unequal relations between parents and professionals (Gwernan-Jones et al. 2015; Honkasilta et al. 2015; Hodge and Runswick-Cole 2008). As one mother said, whenever she challenges her son's teacher about the strategies used in class, this resulted in 'another jibe at your parenting' (Jane: cited in Davies 2014: 240).

In the above examples, mothers have resisted the blame-worthy mother discourse through accounts which demonstrate their expertise and experience as parents. Accounts of parental experience and expertise intersect with accounts of 'trouble' that might, on the one hand, provide opportunity for parents to demonstrate their skills but also have the potential to reinforce the stigma attached to parents of children with ADHD. Family trouble legitimises scrutiny and professional interference, reinforcing parents' sense of a 'spoiled identity' (see Holt 2010; Goffman 1990). Mothers fluctuated from attending to the troubles of their children on the one hand, to resisting this discourse on the other. This was typically achieved through accounts which reinforced the 'ordinariness' of their family lives as well as through positive accounts of their children's skills and creativity.

Resisting Troubled Identities

The biological explanation for ADHD reinforces normative assumptions about child development and so encourages a deficit account of those children affected by it (McVittie et al. 2008). A deficit account of child development might position children and their families in ways which invite sympathy and attention, but they also become the subjects of regulation, scrutiny and intervention. Extraordinary phenomena that transgress moral and social codes need to be accounted for while ordinary, everyday life needs no account. Therefore, 'doing being ordinary' is a common discursive strategy used to perform rhetorical business (see Sacks 1995). Presenting ourselves as ordinary, non-exceptional people allows us to describe 'business as usual' (see Jefferson 1988) without having to account for actions that depart from the norm (Locke and Edwards 2003). Voysey (1972), for example, suggested that minimising the distinctiveness of a child's disability can protect families from scrutiny and professional intrusion. Similarly, Todd and Jones (2003) found that in their dealings with professionals, mothers typically resisted being pathologised along with their children by presenting themselves as caring, 'ordinary' mothers, just like 'any other'. By understating difference, families remain unexceptional and therefore morally robust.

An ordinary family identity is achieved by making light of the extraordinary and any distressing events that occur. Mothers use humour and laughter as a way of signalling their resilience and capacity for not taking the situation too seriously (Jefferson 1984; Edwards

2005). For example, one mother described a distressing incident in which her child soiled himself just before she was about to go into a meeting, 'I have to see it I have to try and say at the moment "this will seem funny later" (laughs)' (Kim: cited in Davies 2014: 254). Similarly, Julie explains:

> we use humour you know to deal with the things that he does cos you have to laugh at some of the things he does cos otherwise the alternative is to cry at them but yeah just try maintain a sense of humour with them. (Julie: 254)

Both of these mothers resist being positioned as not coping by showing an ability to 'laugh off' their troubles. These accounts can also be heard as not complaining or asking for special treatment, which would potentially risk their positioning as sympathetic figures (Edwards 2005). By laughing in the face of adversity, they present themselves as having 'strength of character', and this accords them a moral integrity and worth (see Radley and Billig 1996: 227). Broberg (2011) considers that through emphasising ordinariness, parents assume an active subject position, one permitting them the possibility of 'normality, involvement and mastery' in relation to their parental duty of care.

Mothers minimise the extraordinariness of their situations by describing how their children 'fit' with their families:

> I'm sort of glad he's born into our family cos we're equipped to deal with it. (Kim, cited in Davies 2014: 256)
> 'no we want somebody quite dynamic and spirited and we got that' [...] I'm happy that we got that. (Gill: 256)

The notion of family 'fit' resonates with Broberg's (2011) findings in relation to parents' accounts of their children with intellectual disabilities. Broberg identified a repertoire of belonging in the way parents framed acceptance of their children's difference. This, Broberg (2011) suggests, is a way of resisting the social and cultural expectation that families of 'atypical' children will feel sad and bereaved (see also

Watermeyer 2009; Goodley and Tregaskis 2006). Such families can be positioned within a dominant 'tragedy' narrative that is potentially compounded by their involvement in research interviews where difficulties are described (Swain and French 2000).

Mothers reframe the deficit account of their children's behaviour by providing positive interpretations of characteristics which might otherwise be described in pathological ways:

> I actually find him quite funny, a little comedian and he's really quirky and he's full of beans and he's wild [...] I quite enjoy it he's very spirited he's good fun. (Gill, cited in Davies 2014: 255)

The problematic hyperactivity identified with ADHD is reformulated by this mother in positive terms as a description of any 'ordinary' child. The 'tragic' narrative is also resisted by mothers who predict and imagine positive futures for their sons:

> he's he's going to do great he's going to be brilliant he's going to [...] get a career and whatever he wants. (Gill: 256)

Positive talk such as this enables mothers to resist the stigmatised identities more usually attached to them and their families. We address the function of positive narratives in more detail in Chapter 6, but here we note that such talk, which emphasises difference and diversity, may be understood as a form of resistance to the deficit accounts of impairment discourse (see O'Dell and Brownlow 2015).

The to-ing and fro-ing between accounts of trouble and troubles resistance points to the dilemmas around health, illness and maternal responsibility. One mother describes the complexity of her experience:

> uhm (pause) I don't know uhm I sometimes feel that it... on the whole I feel quite positively about it really because I think we can deal with it uhm so in that way I'm sort of glad he's born into our family [...] in some ways the whole family without meaning to everything revolves around him and he we're sort of lead by him we don't

> do the restaurants much and the coffee shops or anything but because we never did that before him it's not such a.... (Kim, cited in Davies 2014: 257)

The hesitancy of this mother's account, 'uhm (pause) I don't know uhm...' may indicate some of the difficulties mothers have in expressing ambivalence towards their situation. A cultural imperative to think positively (Wilkinson and Kitzinger 2000; Radley and Billig 1996) does not really permit a 'good' mother to express ambivalence about her child or her situation, so this is risky territory.

Positive talk typically came towards the end of mothers' narratives, following accounts detailing trouble and distress and this can be understood as a way of managing the interactional context as well as resisting unwanted social identities. The 'closing down' of troubles-telling (Wilkinson and Kitzinger 2000) through such talk also enables the interaction to finish on an 'upbeat' note and protects both the speaker and the listener from a potentially difficult and awkward interactional moment.

Concluding Comments

This chapter has shown how current understandings of ADHD position mothers in very particular ways. The discourse of ADHD has emerged from historicised theories that polarised around an unhelpful nature/nurture axis that has since become entrenched in commonsense explanations. First, the psychosocial repertoire links children's 'naughty' behaviour with an inadequate environment, provided by ineffective parents, while the biological repertoire represents ADHD as a biological phenomenon, to be treated, medically. These two explanations of ADHD position parents within a highly moralised debate that exists within contemporary neoliberalism, and the concept of 'responsibilisation' and parental accountability for children's outcomes. These ideas are particularly aligned with notions of good mothering and problem boys.

The interview data in the examples from Davies (2014) demonstrated that through the take up of diverse subject positions, mother identities are fluid and flexible in their accounts of ADHD and that this is a situated discursive phenomenon, rather than an expression of fixed attitudes or beliefs. In this chapter, we saw how mothers take up subject positions and attribute them to their children within the shifting demands of the local interaction and in relation to the wider cultural discourse of ADHD. Although mother identities were constructed on and for each occasion, all of their accounts made relevant the good mother subject position in one form or another. The changing ways in which mothers talk about their experiences is indicative of the very complex ways in which mothers 'negotiate and understand their children' (Goodley and Tregaskis 2006).

For example, they have to negotiate the position of the 'blameworthy mother' when they talk about their children and families. Mothers of children with ADHD account for themselves as objects of scrutiny and the subjects of blame (Blum 2007; Singh 2004; Malacrida 2001). Davies (2014) found that they resisted the social censure of other parents in accounts of their victimhood and by drawing on stories of exceptional parenting and biological and medicalised explanations of their child's ADHD. However, mothers demonstrated a complex relationship with medicalised explanations and interventions; sometimes taking up biomedical explanations and at other times rejecting doctors' opinions and the interventions of professionals.

Despite some positive accounts of resistance, agency and expertise in mothers' accounts, they are somewhat constrained by subject positions arising from the discourse of ADHD and they are also subject to the wider gendered discourse of parenting. To manage this, mothers account for themselves and legitimise their parenting using extreme examples to describe their children and provide evidence of extraordinary understanding and exceptional child care practices (Fig 4.2). Reflecting the gendered bias in the historical discourse of ADHD and media accounts, this chapter has focused on mothers as the parent most accountable for childcare. The next chapter turns its attention to how fathers are positioned within contemporary discourses of parenting and ADHD and how they respond to these.

- The diagnosis of ADHD is described as a transformational and 'pivotal event'.
- 'Troubles telling' constructs families and children as pathological, while normalising accounts work to resist this view of family life.
- Mothers take up expert forms of knowledge in relation to parenting-as-a-project.
- Despite this, there are unequal power relations arising between parents and professionals.
- The spectre of mother blame is never far away in mothers' accounts.
- Mothers use 'fighting talk' to resist disempowerment.

Fig. 4.2 Issues arising from the accounts of mothers

References

Allen, K., & Taylor, Y. (2012). Placing parenting, locating unrest: Failed femininities, troubled mothers and riotous subjects. *Studies in the Maternal, 4*(2), 1–25. https://doi.org/10.16995/sim.39.

Austin, H., & Carpenter, L. (2008). Troubled, troublesome, troubling mothers: The dilemma of difference in women's personal motherhood narratives. *Narrative Inquiry, 18*(2), 378–392.

Bailey, S. (2014). *Exploring ADHD: An Ethnography of Disorder in Early Childhood.* Abingdon: Routledge.

Barnes, C., & Power, M. J. (2012). Internalising discourses of parental blame: Voices from the field. *Studies in the Maternal, 4*(2), 1–21. https://doi.org/10.16995/sim.36.

Baruch, G. (1981). Moral tales: Parents' stories of encounters with the health professions. *Sociology of Health & Illness, 3*(3), 275–295.

Bennett, J. (2007). (Dis)ordering motherhood: Mothering a child with attention deficit hyperactivity disorder. *Body Society, 13*(4), 97–110.

Berman, R. C., & Wilson, L. (2009). Pathologising or validating: Intake workers' discursive constructions of mothers. *Qualitative Health Research, 19*(4), 444–453.

Bettelheim, B. (1959). Feral children and autistic children. *American Journal of Sociology, 64*(5), 455–467.

Bishop, F. L., & Yardley, L. (2004). Constructing agency in treatment decisions: Negotiating responsibility in cancer. *Health: An Interdisciplinary Journal for the Social Study of Health Illness and Medicine, 8*(4), 465–482.
Blum, L. (2007). Mother-blame in the Prozac nation: Raising kids with invisible disabilities. *Gender and Society, 21*(2), 202–226.
Broberg, M. (2011). Expectations of and reactions to disability and normality experienced by parents of children with intellectual disability in Sweden. *Child: Care Health and Development, 37*(3), 410–417.
Broomhead, K. (2013). Blame, guilt and the need for "labels"; Insights from parents of children with special educational needs and educational practitioners. *British Journal of Special Education, 40,* 14–21.
Bull, C., & Whelan, T. (2006). Parental schemata in the management of children with ADHD. *Qualitative Health Research, 16*(5), 664–676.
Burr, V. (2003). *Social Constructionism* (2nd ed.). Hove: Routledge.
Colley, B. (2010). ADHD, science and the common man. *Emotional and Behavioural Difficulties, 15*(2), 83–94.
Conrad, P., & Bergey, M. R. (2014). The impending globalization of ADHD: Notes on the expansion and growth of a medicalized disorder. *Social Science and Medicine, 122,* 31–43.
Davies, A. (2014). *It's a problem with the brain: A discursive analysis of parents' constructions of ADHD* (Unpublished Ph.D. thesis). The Open University, Milton Keynes.
De Benedictis, S. (2012). 'Feral' parents: Austerity parenting under neoliberalism. *Studies in the Maternal, 4*(2), 1–21. https://doi.org/10.16995/sim.40.
Doucet, A. (2006). *Do Men Mother?* London: University of Toronto Press.
Edwards, D. (2005). Moaning, whinging and laughing: The subjective side of complaints. *Discourse Studies, 7*(1), 5–29.
Edwards, D., & Potter, J. (1993). Language and causation: A discursive action model of description and attribution. *Psychological Review, 100*(1), 23–41.
Fleischmann, A., & Miller, E. C. (2013). Online narratives by adults with ADHD who were diagnosed in adulthood. *Learning Disability Quarterly, 36*(1), 47–60.
Foroushani, P. S. (2008). The internet: A place for different voices in health and medicine? A case study of attention deficit hyperactivity disorder. *Mental Health Review Journal, 13*(1), 33–40.
Foucault, M. (1988). Technologies of the self. In L. H. Martin, H. Gutman, & P. Hutton (Eds.), *Technologies of the Self: A Seminar with Michel Foucault* (16–49). Amherst, MA: University of Massachusetts Press.

Foucault, M. (1991). *Discipline and Punish: The Birth of the Prison*. London: Penguin Books.

Ghosh, M., Fisher, C., Preen, D. B., D'Arcy, J., & Holma, C. (2016). "It has to be fixed": A qualitative inquiry into perceived ADHD behaviour among affected individuals and parents in Western Australia. *BMC Health Services Research, 16,* 141.

Gilbert, G. N., & Mulkay, M. (1984). *Opening Pandora's Box: A Sociological Analysis of Scientists' Discourse*. Cambridge: Cambridge University Press.

Gillies, V. (2005). Meeting parents' needs? Discourses of 'support' and 'inclusion' in family policy. *Critical Social Policy, 25*(1), 70–90.

Gillies, V., Edwards, R., & Horsley, N. (2016). Brave new brains: Sociology, family and the politics of knowledge. *The Sociological Review, 64,* 219–237.

Goffman, E. (1963). *Stigma: Notes on the Management of Spoiled Identity*. Englewood Cliffs, NJ: Prentice-Hall.

Goffman, E. (1990). *Stigma: Notes on the Management of Spoiled Identity*. London: Penguin Group.

Goffman, E. (2006). On face-work: An analysis of ritual elements in social interaction. In A. Jaworski & N. Coupland (Eds.), *The Discourse Reader* (pp. 299–310). Abingdon, Oxon: Routledge.

Goodley, D., & Tregaskis, C. (2006). Storying disability and impairment: Retrospective accounts of disabled family life. *Qualitative Health Research, 16*(5), 630–646.

Gray, D. E. (2002a). Ten years on: A longitudinal study of families of children with autism. *Journal of Intellectual and Developmental Disability, 27*(3), 215–222.

Gray, D. E. (2002b). 'Everybody just freezes. Everybody is just embarrassed': Felt and enacted stigma among parents of children with high functioning autism. *Sociology of Health and Illness, 24*(6), 734–749.

Gray Brunton, C., McVittie, C., Ellison, M., & Willock, J. (2014). Negotiating parental accountability in the face of uncertainty for attention-deficit hyperactivity disorder. *Qualitative Health Research, 24*(2), 242–253.

Gwernan-Jones, R., Moore, D. A., Garside, R., Richardson, M., Thompson-Coon, J., Rogers, M., et al. (2015). ADHD, parent perspectives and parent–teacher relationships: Grounds for conflict. *British Journal of Special Education, 42*(3), 279–300.

Harborne, A., Wolpert, M., & Clare, L. (2004). Making sense of ADHD: A battle for understanding? Parents' views of their children being diagnosed with ADHD. *Clinical Child Psychology and Psychiatry, 9*(3), 327–339.

Harden, J. (2005). Parenting a young person with mental health problems: Temporal disruption and reconstruction. *Sociology of Health & Illness, 27*(3), 351–371.

Harwood, V., Jones, S., Bonney, A., & McMahon, S. (2017). Heroic struggles, criminals and scientific breakthroughs: ADHD and the medicalization of child behaviour in Australian newsprint media 1999–2009. *International Journal of Qualitative Studies on Health and Well-being, 12,* 1298262. https://doi.org/10.1080/17482631.2017.1298262.

Hodge, N., & Runswick-Cole, K. (2008). Problematising parent–professional partnerships in education. *Disability and Society, 23*(6), 637–647.

Holt, A. (2010). Managing 'spoiled identities': Parents' experiences of compulsory parenting support programmes. *Children and Society, 24*(5), 413–423.

Honkasilta, J., Vehmas, S., & Vehkakoski, T. (2015). Self-pathologizing, self-condemning, self-liberating: Youths' accounts of their ADHD-related behavior. *Social Science and Medicine, 150,* 248–255.

Horton-Salway, M. (2011). Repertoires of ADHD in UK newspaper media. *Health (London), 15*(5), 533–549.

Horton-Salway, M. (2012). Gendering attention deficit hyperactivity disorder: A discursive analysis of UK newspaper stories. *Journal of Health Psychology, 18*(8), 1085–1099. Published online before print 1 October 2012. https://doi.org/10.1177/1359105312456326.

Jaworski, A., & Coupland, N. (2006). Editors' introduction to Part Four. In A. Jaworski & N. Coupland (Eds.), *The Discourse Reader* (pp. 289–298). Abingdon, Oxon: Routledge.

Jefferson, G. (1984). On the organisation of laughter in talk about troubles. In J. M. Atkinson & J. Heritage (Eds.), *Structures of Social Action: Studies in Conversation Analysis* (pp. 346–369). Cambridge: Cambridge University Press.

Jefferson, G. (1988). On the sequential organization of troubles-talk in ordinary conversation. *Social Problems, 35*(4), 418–437.

Keown, L. (2011). Fathering and mothering of preschool boys with hyperactivity. *International Journal of Behavioral Development, 35*(2), 161–168.

Klasen, H., & Goodman, R. (2000). Parents and GPs at cross-purposes over hyperactivity: A qualitative study of possible barriers to treatment. *British Journal of General Practice, 50*(452), 199–202.

Lareau, A. (2003). *Unequal Childhoods.* Berkeley: University of California Press.

Litt, J. (2004). Women's carework in low-income households: The special case of children with attention deficit hyperactivity disorder. *Gender and Society, 18*(5), 625–644.

Lloyd, G., & Norris, C. (1999). Including ADHD? *Disability and Society, 14*(4), 505–517.
Locke, A., & Edwards, D. (2003). Bill and Monica: Memory, emotion and normativity in Clinton's Grand Jury Testimony. *British Journal of Social Psychology, 42*(2), 239–256.
MacMillan, K., & Edwards, D. (1998). 'Designer families': A discourse study of fact and accountability. *Journal of Sociolinguistics, 2*(3), 323–345.
Malacrida, C. (2001). Motherhood, resistance and attention deficit disorder: Strategies and limits. *Canadian Review of Sociology and Anthropology, 38*(2), 141–165.
Malacrida, C. (2004). Medicalisation, ambivalence and social control: Mothers' descriptions of educators and ADD/ADHD. *Health: An Interdisciplinary Journal for the Social Study of Health Illness and Medicine, 8*(61), 61–79.
McKeever, P., & Miller, K. (2004). Mothering children who have disabilities: A Bourdieusian interpretation of maternal practices. *Social Science and Medicine, 59*(6), 1177–1191.
McVittie, C., Goodall, K. E., & McKinlay, A. (2008). Resisting having learning disabilities by managing relative abilities. *British Journal of Learning Disabilities, 36*(4), 256–262.
Miller, G., & Silverman, D. (1995). Troubles talk and counselling discourse: A Comparative Study. *Sociological Quarterly, 36*(4), 725–747.
Mueller, A. K., Fuermaier, A. B. M., & Tucha, L. (2012). Stigma in attention deficit hyperactivity disorder. *Attention Deficit Hyperactivity Disorder, 4*(3), 101–114. Published online 8 July 2012. https://doi.org/10.1007/s12402-012-0085-3.
Neophytou, K., & Webber, R. (2005). Attention deficit and hyperactivity disorder: The family and social context. *Australian Social Work, 58*(3), 313–325.
Norris, C., & Lloyd, G. (2000). Parents, professionals and ADHD: What the papers say. *European Journal of Special Needs Education, 15*(2), 123–137.
O'Dell, L., & Brownlow, C. (2015). Normative development and the autistic child. In M. O'Reilly & J. N. Lester (Eds.), *The Palgrave Handbook of Child Mental Health* (pp. 296–309). Basingstoke, UK: Palgrave Macmillan.
Pomerantz, A. (1986). Extreme case formulations: A way of legitimising claims. *Human Studies, 9,* 219–229.
Potter, J. (1996). *Representing Reality: Discourse Rhetoric and Social Construction*. London: Sage.

Radley, A., & Billig, M. (1996). Accounts of health and illness: Dilemmas and representations. *Sociology of Health & Illness, 18*(2), 220–224.
Ribbens McCarthy, J., Edwards, R., & Gillies, V. (2000). Moral tales of the child and the adult: Narratives of contemporary family lives under changing circumstances. *Sociology, 34,* 785–803.
Rogers, M. A., Wiener, J., Martin, I., & Tannock, R. (2009). Parental involvement in children's learning: Comparing parents of children with and without attention-deficit and hyperactivity disorder (ADHD). *Journal of School Psychology, 47*(3), 167–185.
Rose, N. (1999). *Governing the Soul: The Shaping of the Private Self.* London: Free Association Books.
Ryan, S. (2006). People don't do odd, do they? Mothers making sense of the reactions of others towards their learning disabled children in public places. *Children's Geographies, 3*(3), 291–305.
Ryan, S., & Runswick-Cole, K. (2008). Repositioning mothers: Mothers, disabled children and disability studies. *Disability and Society, 23*(3), 199–210.
Sacks, H. (1995). *Lectures on Conversation.* Oxford: Blackwell.
Seale, C. (2003). Health and media: An overview. *Sociology of Health & Illness, 25*(6), 513–531.
Segal, E. S. (2001). Learned mothering: Raising a child with ADHD child and adolescent. *Social Work Journal, 18*(4), 263–279.
Shotter, J. (1997). The social construction of our inner selves. *Journal of Constructivist Psychology, 10*(1), 7–24.
Singh, I. (2002). Bad boys, good mothers, and the miracle of Ritalin. *Science in Context, 15*(4), 577–603.
Singh, I. (2004). Doing their jobs: Mothering with Ritalin in a culture of mother-blame. *Social Science and Medicine, 59*(6), 1193–1205.
Singh, I. (2005). Will the 'real boy' please behave: Dosing dilemmas for parents of boys with ADHD. *The American Journal of Bioethics, 5*(3), 34–47.
Smith, E., Koerting, J., Latter, S., Knowles, M. M., McCann, D. C., Thompson, M., & Sonuga-Barke, E. J. (2014). Overcoming barriers to effective early parenting interventions for attention-deficit hyperactivity disorder (ADHD): Parent and practitioner views. *Child: Care, Health and Development, 41*(1), 93–102.
Stokoe, E., & Edwards, D. (2007). Black this, black that: Racial insults and reported speech in neighbour complaints and police interrogations. *Discourse Society, 18*(3), 337–372.

Swain, J., & French, S. (2000). Towards an affirmation model of disability. *Disability and Society, 15*(4), 569–582.

Tarver, J., Daley, D., & Sayal, K. (2014). Beyond symptom control for attention-deficit hyperactivity disorder (ADHD): What can parents do to improve outcomes? *Child: Care, Health and Development, 41*(1), 1–14.

Taylor, M., O'Donoghue, T., & Houghton, S. (2006). To medicate or not to medicate? The decision making process of Western Australian parents following their child's diagnosis with an attention deficit hyperactivity disorder. *International Journal of Disability, Development and Education, 53*(1), 111–128.

Todd, S., & Jones, S. (2003). Mum's the word!: Maternal accounts of dealings with the professional world. *Journal of Applied Research in Intellectual Disabilities, 16,* 229–244.

Valentine, J. (2001). Disabled discourse: Hearing accounts of deafness constructed through Japanese television and film. *Disability and Society, 16*(5), 707–727.

Vander Ploeg Booth, K., Chronis-Tuscano, A., & Stein, M. A. (2010). ADHD and mood symptoms in mothers of children with ADHD. *CML—Psychiatry, 21*(1), 1–13.

Voysey, M. (1972). Impression management by parents with disabled children. *Journal of Health and Social Behaviour, 13*(1), 80–89.

Wang, L.-J., Lee, S.-Y., Yuan, S.-S., Yang, C.-J., Yang, K.-C., Lee, T.-L., & Shyu, Y.-C. (2016). Impact of negative media publicity on attention-deficit/hyperactivity disorder medication in Taiwan. *Pharmacoepidemiology and Drug Safety,* 25, 45–53.

Watermeyer, B. (2009). Claiming loss in disability. *Disability and Society, 24*(1), 91–102.

Watson, C. (2011). Home–school partnership and the construction of deviance: Being and becoming the Goldfish family. *Journal of Research in Special Educational Needs, 11*(1), 20–29.

Wetherell, M. (1998). Positioning and interpretative repertoires: Conversation analysis and post-structuralism in dialogue. *Discourse and Society, 9*(3), 387–412.

Weusten, J. (2011). Narrative constructions of motherhood and autism. Reading embodied language beyond binary oppositions. *Journal of Literary Cultural Disability Studies, 5*(1), 53–70.

Widdicombe, S., & Wooffitt, R. (1995). *The Language of Youth Subcultures: Social Identity in Action*. London: Harvester Wheatsheaf.

Wigginton, B., & Lafrance, N. (2016). How do women manage the spoiled identity of a 'pregnant smoker'? An analysis of discursive silencing in women's accounts. *Feminism and Psychology, 26*(1), 30–51.
Wilkinson, S., & Kitzinger, C. (2000). Thinking differently about thinking positive: A discursive approach to cancer patients' talk. *Social Science and Medicine, 50*(6), 797–811.
Wooffitt, R. (1992). *Telling Tales of the Unexpected: The Organisation of Factual Discourse*. Hemel Hempstead: Harvester Wheatsheaf.
Zverina, M., Stam, H. J., & Babins-Wagner, R. (2011). Managing victim status in group therapy for men: A discourse analysis. *Journal of Interpersonal Violence, 26*(14), 2834–2855.

5

'Just an Active Boy': Intersecting Discourses of ADHD, Masculinity and Father Identities

Alison Davies

> My mum would probably have just said I'm just just what does she call it? 'an active boy' […] I'm an active…and maybe that that thirty or forty years ago having an active outdoor boy was good and that was ok I was just active and on the go. (Alan, cited in Davies 2014: 308–309)

Within research, policy and clinical practice in matters relating to family and children, there is a focus on mothers (see Panter-Brick et al. 2014). This also applies to disability discourse, with fathers rarely appearing in the literature (Potter 2016b). The previous chapter described how mothers are positioned as the main caregivers in relation to their children with ADHD, and the more accountable parent in matters of child care and successful outcomes. Fathers on the other hand are identified as 'hard to reach', 'the invisible parent' and the 'peripheral parent' (Carpenter and Towers 2008: 118) such that the stereotype of the absent father has become a common theme in the discourse of ADHD. The focus on mothers in research studies about children with ADHD is likely to be related to the absence of fathers from the ADHD diagnostic process (see Berman and Wilson 2009; Hjorne 2005; Singh 2003). However, this risks overlooking the importance of

M. Horton-Salway and A. Davies, *The Discourse of ADHD*,
The Language of Mental Health, https://doi.org/10.1007/978-3-319-76026-1_5

fathers' distinct contribution to parenting and the 'gendered aspects of engagement' with family life (Potter 2016a: 490).

This chapter explores how fathers talk about their own experience of their child with ADHD and how they represent the fathering role. Due to the negative stereotypes that circulate in public discourse, the identity of the 'good father' is at stake in accounts of fathers and sons. However, there is more than one way to represent the idea of a 'good father' and these variations intersect with discourses of ADHD, ideas about masculinity and father identities.

Contemporary Debates Around Fathering

Gendered division of family responsibilities has, traditionally, positioned mothers as responsible for the private sphere and fathers responsible for relations with 'the outside world' (Boström and Broberg 2014: 811). However, this traditional positioning of fathers as 'public facing' now coexists with a contemporary emphasis on their active involvement in family life. Fathers are encouraged to take up more involved roles within two strong ideological discourses. The first promotes the 'gender neutral dual earner family' through economic and political policy making (Yarwood 2011); the second, indirectly encourages father involvement through discourse which demonises the 'absent father' (see Robb 2004).

The development towards gender equality within dual-income families has created a context, if not a moral imperative, for mothers to work outside the home. This, simultaneously, diminishes the traditional positioning of fathers as 'chief breadwinners' and also positions them inside the home alongside mothers, as much as it positions mothers outside the home alongside fathers. This provides increased scope for fathers to enhance their paternal role (Featherstone 2009). However, the opportunities for enhanced father involvement coexist with powerful discourses of traditional gender role division that dominated previous centuries and are still evident today. These discourses are based on assumptions that mothers are instinctively better at providing the care and emotional needs of their children (Doucet 2006; Harden 2005; Litt 2004; Lupton and Barclay 1997). Doucet has also observed that women can seem reluctant to give up this area of power and expertise (Doucet 2006).

Commenting on gender role divisions within the home, however, Dixon and Wetherell (2004: 175) point out that 'Principles such as "fair shares" or "equity", for example, are moral evaluations that are quite literally *brought to meaning* within day-to-day discourse'. [Italics in original] In contrast to the subject position of 'good mother', the subject position of 'good father' 'appears not to depend to quite the same extent upon demonstrating expertise in and dedication to the care of one's children' (see Lupton and Barclay 1997: 132). Instead, fathers are able to draw on alternative repertoires and subject positions to represent themselves as 'good' fathers. Ideas about providing for and supporting families (Pedersen 2012; Yarwood 2011; Summers et al. 2006; Riley 2003; Ranson 2001) as well as mentoring, teaching, nurturing (Summers et al. 2006) and 'protection' of their vulnerable and dependent children (Lupton and Barclay 1997) are significant for good fathering. This indicates the diverse ways of defining 'good fathering' that can lead to tensions as well as opportunities for fathers, at work and in family life (Ranson 2001). When talking about these topics, 'good fathering' discourses can appear contradictory and result in ideological dilemmas (see Billig et al. 1988; Edley and Wetherell 1999). In other words, fathers have to find ways of resolving the tensions between diverse and sometimes contradictory cultural imperatives about being a 'good father' when they talk about these matters.

The Cultural Context and Two Versions of the 'Good Father'

Ideas about fathers' involvement in family life in the UK arise within the cultural context of neoliberal discourses of the self-sufficient, 'hard-working family' (see Runswick-Cole et al. 2016). This emphasises familial responsibility for family life, and the desired 'stable family' (Allen and Taylor 2012; Barnes and Power 2012; De Benedictis 2012). De Benedictis (2012) argues that neoliberal ideology promotes 'stricter forms of parent subjects' and, consequently, 'stricter formulations of the "good father"... (2012: 6). Stability within the family has been associated with marriage and a 'strong', authoritative, father presence. Such families were traditionally held up as the optimum environment for the production of 'civilised' children and contrasted with negative representations of dysfunctional families with 'absent' or 'dangerous' fathers: that is, fathers who, respectively, either neglect or abuse their child in some way (see Robb 2004; Lupton and Barclay 1997). The ideologically charged 'absent father' subject position has been aligned with notions of a lack of parental authority or responsibility and this stereotype is often related to psychosocial explanations for ADHD in the media (Horton-Salway 2011).

However, contemporary ideas about good fathering challenge more traditional forms and there are now two dominant ways of representing good fathering that intersect with competing ideas about masculinity and the discourse of ADHD. Edley and Wetherell described these as two repertoires that can be drawn on to talk about fathering, the traditional father and the new father. As Edley and Wetherell (1999) suggested, the 'new father':

> departs from the example of his patriarchal predecessor. He not only accompanies his partner during labour, but also sits down with her beforehand to work out their birthplan. He's keen to master the art of nappy changing, enthusiastic when it comes to bottle feeding and burping, and happy to walk around town all afternoon with the child strapped to his chest. (Edley and Wetherell 1999: 182)

The 'new father' contrasts with his traditional counterpart who is represented as strong but less emotionally articulate in line with more traditional notions of masculinity. Ideas about 'traditional fathering' or 'new fathering' are drawn on by the fathers represented in this chapter to make sense of their family lives and their relationships with their sons with ADHD. These representations of fathering are potentially dilemmatic so an analysis of how fathers draw on them when they talk about parenting a child with ADHD will allow us 'to appreciate how men's lives, thoughts and experiences are organized around a particular set of `ideological dilemmas' (Edley and Wetherell 1999: 183). The remainder of this chapter explores how the discourses of father identities, ADHD and masculinity intersect, drawing on examples of data from original research (Fig. 5.1).

> The primary data analysed in this chapter comes from an original study of parents' experiences by Alison Davies, outlined in chapter four of this book (Davies 2014) . The examples and quotations used to illustrate the analysis are taken either from joint interviews with fathers and their partners or they are from the context of parent discussion groups. We are treating accounts of parental experience as discourse data in this chapter, focusing on the ways that fatherhood and father identities are constructed in relation to mother identities. Therefore, the examples will include representations of father identity made by mothers and the subject positions taken up by parents are negotiated between them in the process of talking about ADHD. Accounts of fathering are situated in the interactional context of the research setting and the wider cultural context with all of its normative categories, definitions and stereotypes. This is the background against which father identities are made relevant when talking about their sons with ADHD.

Fig. 5.1 A study of parents' experience by Alison Davies

Traditional Fathers and Lenient Mothers

Declining paternal authority is a wider social and political concern that is identified within sociological literature (Barnes and Power 2012; De Benedicitis 2012; Yarwood 2011; Gillies 2005). The focus on lack of discipline has also been a significant media concern, sometimes represented as a contrast with a golden age of 'old fashioned discipline' administered by fathers in the past (Horton-Salway 2011: 543) while at other times lack of discipline is linked in the media with single parenting and absent fathers (see Chapter 3). Such cultural representations circulate in the public imagination and inform how ideas about fathering might be taken up when parents talk about their experience of family life. There is, for example, significant engagement, by the fathers who participated in Davies' (2014) study, with representations of traditional fathering and ideas about discipline and authority. As with previous research findings (Gray Brunton et al. 2014; Gray 2008), these fathers presented themselves as willing to take up a disciplining and strict role if called upon: 'I'm used as a threat 'right if you don't do that then I'm going to call daddy' (John, cited in Davies 2014: 264).

An authoritative father role is often constructed as relative to the more lenient approach of the mothers. Ingrid, for example, describes her 'difficulty to draw the line' with her son's behaviour, 'sometimes you'll say "ah well I'll let him get away with it because he has ADHD" but then I think "well actually no it's still not acceptable" but it's really difficult [...] I find it very hard to draw the line' (Ingrid: in Davies 2014: 265). This admission risks endorsing the very criticism that is so often directed at parents of children with ADHD, that they are to blame for their behaviour (Horton-Salway 2011). Ingrid's partner resists this positioning, asserting, 'I've got very strict boundaries of behaviour' and he makes it clear that he does not use his son's medical diagnosis as an excuse for 'bad' behaviour:

> I don't care if you've got ADHD ABC or 123 [...] at the end of the day "behave yourself" that's it you know "you push the mark once don't do it again" simple as that. (John: cited in Davies 2014: 265–266)

Ingrid and John explained their different approaches to discipline using traditional gendered positions of the 'stay at home' mother and the 'out at work' father. In her account, Ingrid has said that the son 'definitely pushes a lot more with me' and this is explained partially by the fact that she is at home all day with the children. As her partner explains:

> but then you've got R as well and then you've got the little one on the way as well and I'm at work I don't envy you. (John, cited in Davies 2014: 268)

John acknowledges that Ingrid is a busy mother with her hands full, so it is understandable that she cannot be as firm a parent as he can, but she is represented as a busy but good mother whose leniency is balanced by John's firmness as a father. Being out at work all day is established as an explanation for being able to take on the stricter parent role while the role of 'stay at home mother' is used to mitigate maternal leniency:

> yeah and he still plays us off against each other [....] and it's 'oh well I'll ask mummy cos I always get it mummy's an easier tar [...] cos you let things go more than I do isn't it? Whereas I've probably got a diff... my criteria... cos I'm not there all the time. (Alan: cited in Davies 2014: 268–269)

Supporting findings by Riley (2003) and Lupton and Barclay (1997), the fathers in Davies (2014) represent the traditional female role of 'stay at home' mother as central and important. Traditional fatherhood is relational to motherhood in these examples, with each category drawing meaning from the other (Pedersen 2012). Note, however, Dixon and Wetherell's observation that these are '...evaluations that are quite literally *brought to meaning* within day-to-day discourse...' (2004: 175, Italics in original). The subject positions of authoritarian and more lenient parent are constituted here in relation to each other to showcase an effective parenting team, a theme we will revisit later in the chapter.

Traditional representations of good fathering are drawn on in the above examples to resist the psychosocial explanations of blameworthy parenting that might arise from their remoteness or their partners' more lenient approach to discipline. However, the existence of contradictory discourses of good fathering renders the identity position of traditional father potentially problematic.

Navigating Dilemmatic Discourses of Good Fathering

The association of paternal authority and discipline with ADHD is made relevant within two distinct repertoires. The psychosocial repertoire can link fathers' lack of authoritative presence with their children's ADHD (Horton-Salway 2011). Conversely, studies have identified a link between authoritarian fathering and children's ADHD. These studies emphasise an association between ADHD and intrusive fathering (Keown 2012) and excessively controlling fathering (Keown 2011;

Rogers et al. 2009; Gerdes et al. 2003). Fathers are reported as being 'over reactive' (Keown 2011) while 'negative fathering' and 'aggressive disciplinary practices' (Rogers et al. 2009) are linked with disruptive behaviour in children. Bull and Whelan (2006) also note that mothers typically raise fathers' authority as an issue in their talk of their partners' interactions with their children.

Debates about corporal punishment are similarly conflicted since the use of smacking as a punishment is controversial, with calls from the NSPCC for a total ban (O'Reilly 2008). However public opinion surveys indicate that fear of an increase in crime and moral panic contribute to the attitude that smacking is a necessary punishment for naughty children (O'Reilly 2008). Media stories and research linking ADHD with criminal behaviour also focus on ADHD as a social conduct disorder. Therefore, parents navigate a complicated terrain with respect to a range of conflicting ideas about authoritarian or permissive discipline. As much as it is important for fathers to assert a disciplinary presence, excessive strictness might be considered controversial, especially if a child's troubling behaviour can be accounted for medically.

Dilemmas such as this are managed by showing a willingness and capacity to discipline without the need to actually exercise it:

> it's just the threat of a smack. I'm used as a threat 'right if you don't do that then I'm going to call daddy"… . (John: cited in Davies 2014: 264)

This father represents himself as an authoritative presence and deterrent while avoiding the negative implications of abuse that might be associated with corporal punishment. Parents often resist being positioned as excessively authoritarian by distancing themselves from corporal punishment and they typically associate smacking with an older generation. On the other hand, they do not construct the past as a golden age or a benchmark against which to judge current parenting practices, as do some media representations of societal decline (see Chapter 3 and Horton-Salway 2011). Instead, they describe excessive discipline as inappropriate, ineffective and, distinctly old-fashioned. One father reported how a senior member of his family commented on his son: 'he just needs a good clip round the ear […] a good slap will put him into position' (Mick:

cited in Davies 2014: 156). His partner, Gill, quickly condemned this form of discipline as unhelpful and outdated commenting: 'that slightly older generation [....] they don't know about ADHD' (Gill: 156).

However, contradictory discourses of the past and the present are both drawn on in the context of explanation and argument when fathers are required to account for and justify their decisions about methods of discipline. For example, one father explains why he gave up an authoritarian position:

> because of my background and because of who I am you know... I wanted to be... I thought I was going to be very disciplinarian (smacks hand) you know but that just doesn't work it took a while for me to work that out [...] well the way I th... I always thought I'd bring up children is fairly strict not brutally strict just firm very firm. (Mick: cited in Davies 2014: 270–271)

Mick's prior expectations were that he would be a strict father 'because of my background' but admits that his ideas were challenged by having a child with ADHD 'that just doesn't work'. He positions his current approach to discipline in contrast to his initial ideas of being 'very disciplinarian'. Rather than appearing weak, his account reinforces and protects his identity as a good father who is prepared to adapt to the needs of the child and take a flexible approach to parenting (Lupton and Barclay 1997). Fathers describe how they developed their knowledge about what is best for their children:

> there's not one set of rules it doesn't work that way and uhm and yeah me trying to be this s...strict person [...] wanting to do the best for my children [...] and it wasn't working and I thought 'agh' you know...and he 'why is he being like this why can't he just do as he's told?'[laughs] and he never will. (Mick, cited in Davies 2014: 271)

When Mick parodies his former disciplinarian position as naïve, 'why can't he just do as he's told?' [laughs], his partner agrees: 'you kind of have to be adaptive' (Gill: 271). Adaptive parenting techniques were common in the accounts of fathers in Davies' study, and as Bailey

(2014) puts it, this represents a 'more personalised responsibilisation of the good parent' through projects of 'self-improvement' (Bailey 2014: 112). In describing their relationship with their partner and their family, willingness to adapt and learn different ways of fathering was a significant aspect of many fathers' accounts of parenting a child with ADHD.

Rational-Emotional Talk

The traditional father position is not associated with the ability to articulate emotion since 'emotion talk' is highly gendered. Seymour-Smith and Wetherell (2006) observed that, within heterosexual couples, emotions are typically 'done', or carried, by women (see also Seale 2003). A similar pattern of emotional 'work' is also identified by Doucet (2006), who suggests that worry about children is externalised by mothers and internalised by fathers. This psychological explanation of gendered emotion is a further indication of the gendered nature of the discourse of emotion. In the study by Davies (2014) emotional strength was made relevant by several of the fathers when they talked about how they had managed the difficulties arising from their child's ADHD. Parents accounts of emotional distress in couple interviews illustrate how extraordinary their situations are and how this affects them. John and Ingrid described the difficult period leading up to getting a diagnosis for their son:

John: I'm very sort of stubborn and strong-minded but even for me yeah it did get me down […] and I know for a fact it got Ingrid down because as I said she was in fits of tears

Ingrid: there was times when I just I just burst and I just couldn't uhm

John: couldn't cope with it […] and I can …I can see people out there that it would have destroyed them basically […] honestly I can […] 'cos you know because there are a lot of people out there who aren't that strong and even for me (laughs) I've gone to the borderline with it and you it even broke you and you as you say you're a very strong person I know that but yeah.

(John and Ingrid, adapted from Davies 2014: 274–275)

In this example, John is building an account of his own strong disposition and Ingrid's more emotional one in relation to one another: 'I'm very sort of stubborn and strong-minded but even for me yeah it did get me down'. The phrase 'even for me' indicates the extreme circumstances that they had faced and he describes his own and Ingrid's distress as unusual and untypical rather than dispositional (cf. Edwards 1997). The admission that he has 'gone to the borderline with it' is risky and could imply that he is not coping. However, he manages this by drawing on traditional discourses of paternal (masculine) strength, 'being stubborn and strong minded'. 'Strong minded' implies a rational and mindful position rather than an emotional, 'feeling' disposition and John's representations of himself imply that he has been able to maintain 'reasoned control' in contrast to Ingrid's emotional response that has resulted in tears and 'bursting' (Lupton 1998, cited in Wetherell 2012: 94; see also Edwards 1997). However, the degree of situational difficulty and the dispositional strength of both parents are also being worked up in parallel, as John acknowledges that Ingrid is normally 'a very strong person' but 'it even broke you'. While John clearly demonstrates his understanding of Ingrid's emotional reaction, he is also distancing himself from it. To consolidate this position, he compares himself favourably with 'a lot of people out there who aren't that strong' so this bolsters his identity as an exceptionally strong father who is capable of remaining so in extreme circumstances and it also positions Ingrid and John as better parents than many others who would not cope.

Drawing on traditional discourses of masculinity that are associated with rational dispositions and emotional strength enables fathers to present themselves as supportive of their families, resonating with the 'sturdy oak' representation of masculinity as identified by Pleck (1987). The emotionally resilient and supportive father is a valued identity within a cultural context of moral panic and blame that stigmatises the parents of children with ADHD. In the example above, traditional representations of masculine emotional strength and rationality are drawn on to close down emotional troubles-telling and to illustrate that despite everything this family is coping and managing, perhaps better than many.

The Problem with Boys

As we argue throughout this book, there are gendered stereotypes that intersect with the discourses of ADHD. Historically, scientific enquiry about ADHD has focused on problematic boys and their social conduct (Chapter 2). This association continues in media representations which link ADHD with criminality and a dangerous masculinity (Chapter 3). Alongside this, runs another potentially contradictory media-fuelled moral panic about over-diagnosis and the rise of prescription. According to this viewpoint, 'normal' and benign boyhood behaviours are being over-diagnosed with the implication that the 'mischievous' behaviours of characters such as *Denis the Menace* and *Just William* would, nowadays, be interpreted as ADHD (Chapter 3; Horton-Salway 2012; Schmitz et al. 2003). Support for this argument is garnered through the disproportionate number of males diagnosed compared to females (Rafalovich 2015); the lack of a current neurochemical explanation for this (Bailey 2014) and the sociological view of ADHD medication as social control.

While there are some representations of ADHD that counter the stigmatising discourses linking ADHD and masculine dangerousness, these continue to be gendered as they draw on extreme masculine stereotypes or they illustrate ADHD using examples of successful men who overcame personal difficulties (see Chapter 3). Such representations link extreme or traditional forms of masculinity with ADHD and indicate how such cultural and gendered stereotypes have intersected with the discourse of ADHD. Furthermore, some media summaries of gene research have been framed to suggest a link between ADHD and fathers that is misleading. It is, therefore, interesting to see how fathers have drawn on these culturally available ideas when they talk about their sons with ADHD and their own identities.

Bailey (2014) suggests that the medical category of ADHD captures all that is problematic with moral panics about boys and their failing education. As he argues, the categories of 'bad, sad and stupid' schoolboy are subsumed within the category of ADHD. As one father admits, if he did not know his son had ADHD, he would just think 'he was a bad boy' (Mick, cited in Davies 2014: 169). The cultural categories of 'bad' and 'stupid' map onto Singh et al.'s (2012) contention that children with ADHD occupy one of two ecological niches in school, a conduct niche or a performance niche. In the former, the focus is on social behaviours and being good, while in the latter, ADHD is viewed as a 'disorder of academic performance' (2012: 14). Bailey argues that the '*bad* and the *stupid* talk each other into pedagogical concerns, leaving the *sad* in silence' (Bailey 2014: 81). The latter category refers to inattentive ADHD, which is more likely to be overlooked in school (see Chapter 6 for a discussion of ADHD in girls). As Bailey notes, however, ADHD is most typically defined in terms of hyperactivity, impulsivity and disruptive behaviour, and these behaviours are usually attributed to the *bad* schoolboy who disrupts the school agenda, in Singh's terms, the 'conduct niche' is the most prevalent way of understanding ADHD in the UK. Furthermore, ADHD is frequently correlated with Conduct Disorder and Oppositional Defiant Disorder (Bailey 2014: 79), two other psychiatric categories which are associated with *bad* schoolboy behaviour. Moral panics around excluded or failing schoolboys are characterised by predictions of future delinquency, criminality or violence. This representation chimes with media reports that represent boys and men as a threat to the social order with stories linking ADHD with delinquency, violent crime, prisoners and even psychosis (see Chapter 3).

Normalising and Pathologising Behaviour

The line between normal and pathological can be a fine one and boundaries between normal but naughty and a diagnosable disorder can sometimes appear blurred. These issues arise for Jane and Alan as they respond to the views of other parents who imply that her son is just like any other naughty child:

Jane: 'I'm thinking "well no this is 24 hours a day" and I think that's what most parents find that they may be informed about some areas of it but to the extent of how that stops a child and the family leading a normal life that's where it ends I think [...] "oh mine runs up the curtains and does all this"

Alan: '..."yeah and fixates on lego" and I'm like "yeah but from the moment he gets up to the moment he goes down to sleep to the moment he gets up to the moment he gets to sleep seven days a week" [...] for the past four months that type of intensity? no it's in the first you know or in the intensity of every other question of "can I have it?" "Can I have it?" "Can I have it?" or "I want it" "I want it" "I want it" yeah it's not that level of "oh yes my Johnny wants something now"...'

(Jane and Alan, adapted from Davies 2014: 160–161)

Alan and Jane's account of their son's relentless behaviour conveys that this is an extreme case and cannot be compared with the behaviours of 'normal but naughty' children (cf. Pomerantz 1986). According to Alan and Jane, their child is often interpreted as 'normally naughty' by people who do not identify any difference between him and their own children (or other children they know) 'well my child's like that' (Jane, cited in Davies 2014: 160). The mimicking of other parents' 'voices' (Potter 1996; Wooffitt 1992) parodies their comparisons, 'oh mine runs up the curtains' and 'yeah fixates on lego' and 'oh yes my Johnny wants that now'. The reference to 'my Johnny' also invokes a gendered stereotype of ADHD conflated with ordinary boyish behaviour (Horton-Salway 2012: 5–6). Alan draws on this name to dismiss the way that other parents blur the distinction between ADHD and 'boisterous' behaviour. Alan and Jane continued in this interview to represent ADHD as an inherited family trait by comparing their son's behaviour with Alan's father:

Alan: my dad's near enough identical to J in terms of ADHD and Asberger's [sic]probably a bit more high functioning than

Jane: uhm...behavioural traits are exactly the same he's not he's unable to let anything go so he would rather disrupt everything that's going on to get his own way than walk away even as an adult... we pick up quite a few negatives from him we actually want to change for our own son to ...so that when he does get to that point we want to you know [...]

Jane: he'll need to keep on disrupting and disrupting and disrupting until
Alan: he gets his own way
Jane: his own way
Alan: so then you've got…so we try and limit our exposure to him 'cos two controlling personalities let alone my personality in the mix as well 'cos I've got a bit of the hyperactivity aspects but I don't think I've got any of the other […]
Jane: and I don't think it never crossed my mind about ADHD then until until we'd had …
Alan: well I'd always said he was socially inept because my dad could was just difficult to deal with …
Jane: it was cringeworthy …but I think some things get diluted and other things come out and I guess it depends on you know other factors like your family
Alan: but it's the male gene though isn't it? 'cos … my line is very male
Jane: yes yes much rarer in female

(Alan and Jane, adapted from Davies 2014: 302–304)

This description of Alan's father pathologises his behaviours as difficult and disruptive and compares him with their son. Not only does this draw on the idea of ADHD as a genetic condition passed down through the male line, but it also allows Alan and Jane to represent this as an imagined projection of what their son might become, if not for their own interventions as good parents. Jane indicates that she and Alan 'want to change for our own son' some of the more negative characteristics he shares with his grandfather. Here, ADHD is represented as manageable and possible to control, but this is dependent on the environment. She says, 'I think some things get diluted and other things come out and I guess it depends on you know other factors like your family'. Making relevant the genetic inheritance of ADHD through Alan's side of the family has implications for how Alan and his son are positioned in relation to the disruptive grandfather. Jane manages this contingency by suggesting that the more negative features of ADHD become diluted as they are passed down through the generations, and she also draws on the psychosocial repertoire to explain the beneficial effect of a good parenting environment.

Alan and Jane's account of a genetic basis for ADHD is typical of the majority of parents in this study and common elsewhere (see also, Ghosh et al. 2016). In 'mobilising notions of hereditariness' (Frigerio and Montali 2016: 946), parents' accounts offer support for medicalised explanations for their children's problems and offer some relief from being socially accountable. Nevertheless, as indicated above, accountability is not entirely removed. The hereditability of ADHD is a mainstream theory within neurodevelopmental discourse (see, for example, Thapar and Cooper 2016, Karakas et al. 2015) and ADHD is firmly positioned as a 'familial disorder' of inheritance (Thapar and Cooper 2016: 1242). Simplistic reports of research findings in the media can mislead (see Chapter 3) and might imply that ADHD is transmitted from fathers to sons (see also Horton-Salway 2012: 5) however, scientific studies do not actually report genetic research in this way. According to Karakas et al. (2015: 3604), 'the genetic load is higher in mothers, and mothers have a higher risk than fathers of transmitting ADHD to their children'. Although some mothers trace ADHD through their own families (see Davies and Horton-Salway 2016), genetic accounts in this study were mainly worked up in parents' accounts through the male line, 'it's the male gene though, isn't it?' (Alan: cited in Davies 2014: 304). The tendency for parents to implicate fathers in genetic accounts may be an indication that parents are taking up simplistic accounts of gene research, or that they are orienting to the male gender bias in representations of ADHD and diagnostic rates. Either way, they are taking up the gendered stereotypes that are embedded in the discourse of ADHD.

Resisting the Narratives of Pathology and Impairment: 'Just an Active Boy'

Despite the take up of genetic accounts of ADHD by parents, this calls into being narratives of impairment. These are resisted by fathers who describe their own childhoods in terms of 'normal' boisterous boy behaviours. Alan compares his son with his own childhood behaviour, suggesting that he would have been described as 'just [...] an active boy' (Alan, cited in Davies 2014: 308). In aligning himself with his son's behaviours, he lists some of the characteristics that they might share, 'I'd probably want to get excited about things more than others' (p. 308). However, he minimises the significance of this: 'I was just active and on the go' and 'probably a little bit more immature' and 'I always had ants in my pants' (pp. 309–310) (see also Gray Brunton et al. 2014). These descriptions are not pathologised, but described as 'just active' or 'a little bit more' suggesting normality or only a small departure from that. Behaviours such as these can be represented as within the normal range of behaviours or they might be represented as extreme and abnormal, depending on the context of telling. As Horton-Salway (2012: 6) puts it, 'the social identity and the behaviours that define it are co-produced in the description'. Alan resists being understood as a 'bad' boy and his 'busyness' is not pathologised in his description. 'Just an active boy' is positioned against its imagined alternative, hyperactivity. Alan's account of his son's ADHD and his own similar behaviours corresponds with Singh's findings (2003) that fathers' might pathologise and normalise their own childhoods in their accounts, thereby identifying with and distancing from the ADHD label. In claiming partial identification with his son's ADHD, Alan can claim with authority that he not only understands his son's ADHD but that his son's behaviours go beyond 'normal' boyhood behaviours.

Fathers' talk of ADHD is complex, variable and designed to manage contradictory dilemmas. On the one hand, fathers portray their sons' behaviours as problematic and abnormal, while also resisting impairment discourse by normalising ADHD-like behaviours. They do this through working up their appreciation of their son's dispositional characteristics: 'but he's but he's a er a very excitable very enthusiastic boy and you know that's great about him' (Mick, cited in Davies 2014: 295). As with fathers of children with autism, Mick provides a positive evaluation of his son's characteristics (see Potter 2016b). In valuing the behaviours that might be defined as symptomatic of ADHD, fathers also demonstrate ambivalence to medication that is not so apparent in the talk of mothers. Mick, for example, explains that his son's behaviour is not so problematic (for him, at least) as to warrant medication (see also Singh 2003) and he expresses concern that his son's personality might be changed through medication: 'I don't want to see his personality change too much' (Mick, cited in Davies 2014: 295). This ambivalence is a stance identified in several studies (Hansen and Hansen 2006; Bussing and Gary 2001). Mick's hesitancy over medication demonstrates a responsibility and level of care for his son as well as a resistance to pathologised narratives of impairment.

Fathers do appear to be far more sceptical of medicalised solutions to ADHD than mothers (see also Potter 2016b; Hansen and Hansen 2006; Singh 2003). Similarly, Potter (2016b) found that fathers of children with a disability were resistant to professional interpretations and impairment discourse. According to Singh (2003), fathers of children with ADHD can be identified as either 'reluctant believers' or 'tolerant non-believers' (Singh 2003). In Chapter 4, we saw suggestions of this in mothers' (partial) non-compliance with medical prescription, for example in giving medication breaks to their children. Fathers also take up non-compliant positions in relation to dominant medicalised discourses of ADHD. For example, Mick describes how he read information:

> just to understand different psychologies…that it isn't just a hocus pocus bullshit science. (Mick, cited in Davies 2014: 291)

His willingness to be sceptical about circulating information indicates that he is not a passive consumer of professional knowledge, but an interested, and well informed father who is discriminating. His preparedness to assume a non-compliant stance makes any subsequent acceptance of medical solutions even more robust and based on reasoned choice. However, this can be a possible source of tension between parents.

Talking About Medication

A father who tests his son's medication on himself is likely to be criticised as irresponsible. However, this might also be seen as an act of rebellion and the action of a concerned father: Testing the medication not only demonstrates Alan's role as protector but it also gives him an entitlement to make evaluations about it based on first-hand experience:

> I took J's medication and… I just… I'm giving this to my son what am I giving him? So I took it…So I took it and I could actually feel my brain slow down […] it was interesting to feel my brain slow. (Alan: cited in Davies 2014: 293)

His anecdote tells us that he does not automatically accept medical authority and might be resistant to it. This kind of account works to resist one of the dominant representations of parents that appear in media reports, that of irresponsible, unscrupulous parents who want to use medication as a quick fix to control their children (see Goldberg 2011; Horton-Salway 2011). While Alan described the experience as 'interesting', he was not sure of the value of medication. When asked if the experience was positive, he indicated that this required further thought, 'uhm' before repeating the question, 'was it positive? Uhm'. Jane, his wife, supplied an answer to this, 'well I think it helped you rationalise it' (Jane, cited in Davies 2014: 293). This, Alan seemed to agree to, describing how the medication helped him prioritise tasks. However, Alan's display of scepticism and protection towards his child indicates what Singh (2003) calls a potential tension between a father's authority and medical authority. The act of taking medication can be interpreted as a way of Alan gaining some agency (for himself and for his son) within a process that renders the child and the family as 'acted upon rather than acting' (Renshaw et al. 2014). Certainly, a medical model of ADHD impacts on interventions with children and their families, 'through narratives of concern, care and specialised treatment' (Renshaw et al. 2014). As a response to the twin concerns of care and surveillance, Alan's non-compliance might be seen as an act of defiance to these disciplinary mechanisms that require parents to raise children with ADHD through a prescribed professional lens. Alan's non-compliance is only partial and based on his own experimentation with the medication. It is Jane (the child's mother) who supplies a positive evaluation of the effect that medication had on her husband, 'it helped you rationalise'.

ADHD medication seems to be a contentious topic for some mothers and fathers (Singh 2003). For example, Gill and Mick are the parents of a boy recently diagnosed with ADHD who, on account of his young age, is yet to be prescribed medication. Gill is an advocate for medication and she provided a very straightforward account of its merits:

> the medication is to get the best out of him in terms of his learning ability [...] it actually makes his br...you know ... think...focus he'll be focused he'll be able to retain information [...] it means 100% it will impact on his ability to learn. (Gill, cited in Davies 2014: 295)

Her partner, Mick, was more ambivalent. Like Alan, Mick identifies himself as having some of the traits of ADHD, entitling him to speak from experience and raise doubts about the use of medication. Gill's defence of medication is emphatic and certain, and her language is not tentative, 'it means 100% it will impact on his ability to learn'. The absence of modality, or tentative language (Woolgar 1988) represents the effects of medication as predictable, routine and, crucially, unproblematic. As with Singh's et al. (2012) concept of the 'performance niche', in which academic performance is the main preoccupation, Gill focuses on how medication can improve this. Mick's concerns are about the effect of medication on his son's 'natural' personality, character, and conduct. In this way, they correspond more to Singh's et al. (2012) 'conduct niche', which emphasises children's social behaviour. It may be that due to the association of ADHD with 'bad' boys and extreme stereotypes of masculine identities, fathers are more alert to issues of social conduct and social control.

Medication Versus Self-discipline

As with the fathers (of autistic children) in Potter's study (2016b), Mick indicates that his own characteristics might be constructed as pathological within the impairment model of ADHD. However, he resists this by focusing on how this has enabled him rather than constrained him. For example, Mick presents his 'hyperactive' behaviours as productive and valuable assets within the workplace:

> 'when I'm working there can be a million and one things well not a million but you know lots and lots of things going on in my mind' and 'I sometimes work on four computers at once [...] I always do that [...] I sometimes I shoot on a chair on wheels whizz across the room to have a look.' (Mick, cited in Davies 2014: 296)

Hyperactivity, by this account, is an asset within the workplace aligned with speed, multitasking and productivity. Redefining hyperactivity as an asset rather than impairment problematises the issue of medication. Mick, for example, claims he has managed to control potentially unhelpful behaviours through self-discipline, rather than through medication. As he says:

> I had to train myself to concentrate on 'do this' or 'do that' I have to [...] you know back to the main task and is it it's it's a what-do-you-call it? a discipline you know and I've had to learn it. (Mick: cited in Davies 2014: 296)

Mick's self regulation fits very well with neoliberal notions of responsibilisation and the 'good citizen'. The ability to self regulate or self motivate are also qualities associated with the culturally valued ideal of the entrepreneur, which have been found to correspond with Bem's (1981) inventory of culturally expected masculine characteristics (Ahl 2006). In this account, Mick produces a non-pathological version of his own behaviours, identifying them with his son's diagnosis (see also Singh 2003) but not explicitly claiming the ADHD label for himself. He suggests instead that without self discipline he would be a bit of a 'scatterbrain' (p. 296), minimising the significance of this trait. In taking this line, Mick is risking a confrontation with Gill, who has been advocating clear support for medication, but he steers a course between two statements weighing the possible benefits of medication against (self) discipline as a practical alternative:

> if I took, if I had that medication, I would be able to concentrate I would probably benefit from it because I'd be able to concentrate on one thing at once but as it is I have to discipline myself to concentrate' and 'but that's just something to learn you see not, not, you know, not drug induced. (Mick: cited in Davies 2014: 297)

In this account, however, Mick concedes that the effort to implement practices of self discipline is relentless, 'it almost takes over my life in a way'. For Mick, this has been a successful strategy and is also a way of life for him. This allows him to hold an ambivalent position in relation to medication, acknowledging the possible benefits as well as suggesting an alternative working practice. Fathers might acknowledge the biological heritability of their children's condition, but they also engage with this by promoting ideas of 'self-formation and self-improvement' (Frigerio et al. 2013: 593). Mick's proactive methods of working upon self discipline might be interpreted as a 'reflexive project of the self' (Giddens 1991). According to Giddens, there is a cultural imperative for us to assume responsibility for 'producing' our identities by working on and disciplining ourselves in order to conform to socially desired norms. The notion of self-improvement in ADHD might in some ways be at odds with the celebration of atypicality that has gained increasing momentum in disability discourse, an issue we return to in Chapter 7.

The Good Parenting Team

Expressing disagreement, or alternative views about ADHD, can be problematic for parents within the context of an interview. Argument and disagreement can threaten our public image, or 'face' as Goffman termed it. Maintaining 'face' is a condition of social interaction, and a necessary aspect of managing a plausible and consistent identity (Goffman 1955, 1959). Maintaining the 'face' of others in the interaction is equally important. As Goffman argues, a person has 'a defensive orientation towards saving his (sic) own face and a protective orientation towards saving the other's face' (Goffman 2006: 302), people 'generally cooperate with one another to maintain face' (p. 311). This mutual vulnerability means that individuals are attuned to two perspectives at the same time, their own, and the other. A fine balancing act is required to present alternative viewpoints, yet maintain the integrity of everyone involved. As we have argued throughout this volume, the integrity of parents of children with ADHD is consistently up for scrutiny, so it is especially important that parents manage to maintain 'face' when they are expressing disagreement or being critical of one another. One way they do this is by working up the integrity and skill of the parenting team, which overrides individual weakness or deficit. We saw earlier how accounts of authoritarian fathering were used in relation to accounts of more lenient mothering. In a similar way, negotiating different levels of understanding about parenting can be a relational exercise. To save 'face', parents compensate for one another's deficiencies when talking about their children. Some of these areas of deficiency and superiority resonate with the discourses pertaining to traditional fathering (and mothering), but they are also linked with newer imperatives of professionalised parenting.

Negotiating Gendered Understanding: The Parenting Team

One consequence of the cultural focus on mothers as the parent responsible for childcare and family health matters is that they are more likely to be afforded superior knowledge of these topics, despite also being represented as the blameworthy parent. Fathers are depicted as having less understanding of children and how best to manage them. One mother draws on this stereotype in order to represent her husband's more enlightened position,

> he's always accepted that there are difficulties my husband we haven't had the problem that I know a lot of families have […] dad's not involved [..] and he's just saying 'oh boys will be boys. (Caroline, cited in Davies 2014: 283)

Here Caroline resists a common stereotype of masculinity that other fathers might use to normalise their son's behaviours and dismiss concerns about ADHD. She describes her husband's more supportive approach, despite this being different from her own.

> he's been very much on board from the beginning I think we worked very well uhm because what we… he supported me and I supported the children … it had to work that way and we just held on as best we could through the worst storms […] and we did it together but the genuine real understanding was me I was the one but then that's often the case […] he didn't really get it he's never really got it [….] I mean he still doesn't […] I kind of make the rules in a way 'right ok this is what we're going to do' […] 'and these are the new rules and this is how the boundaries are going to work. (Caroline, cited in Davies 2014: 283–284)

The sailing metaphor makes a division between those who are on board and those who are not and the stormy sea that they have to weather can threaten the stability of the ship. Caroline says that her husband is 'on board' so this indicates his support, but he is positioned outside of the mother–child relationship: he 'supported me and I supported the children'. This orients to traditional notions of fathering and mothering; that a stable and reliable paternal presence assists and enables the maternal caregiving role (see Bowlby 2005; Winnicott 1984). Caroline's 'genuine real understanding' qualifies her as the parent who steers the ship and her gendered position as main caregiver and caretaker of children's health is reproduced (see also Petrassi 2012; Seymour-Smith and Wetherell 2006; O'Brien 2005 for similar discussions). Authors have claimed that it is common for mothers to position themselves (or be positioned) as the 'high-status' partner in relation to children's needs (Doucet 2006; Lupton and Barclay 1997; Petrassi 2012). The fathers in the study by Davies (2014) were rarely critical of this or the way mothers manage children; indeed, they were keen to praise them. Mothers, on the other hand, were often (indulgently or ironically) critical of their partners' (or ex- partners') management of their children, positioning them as the secondary parent.

The theme of fathers as a source of stability and support is a recurrent one in the literature on fatherhood (for example, Summers, et al. 2006) but this might also be represented as a secondary role in relation to children. Fathers' involvement and interaction with children is typically regulated and defined by their partners. As Alan remarked to his wife: 'but then you're helping me learn the right language 'cos sometimes I use the wrong language'. This supports other studies that suggest fathers rely on mothers to define their fathering (Doucet 2006) while mothers assume a maternal gatekeeping role and interpret their children's behaviour for their partners (Featherstone 2009). They also pass on their superior knowledge and expertise to their partners, whether they describe this as instinctive or learned. One mother describes how she has read up about ADHD and then passes on the relevant information to her partner: 'I've been through lots of information and then I just filtered what was interesting or relevant or different strategies for Mick (laughs)'. She provides the reason, 'cos I knew he wasn't going to read all these books' (Gill: cited in Davies 2014: 287). In Gill's account, Mick's expertise is contingent on what she passes on to him but her laughter signals that this might be seen as problematic but she is making light of it and does not mean to criticise him (see Edwards 2005). We understood from the gently ironical tone of her remarks that this is a common practice that she considers normative between parents.

In the example above, we are left to imagine why Mick has not read as much as Gill, but she is not implying that he is not a good father. The secondary role of fathers described in such examples is often justified because of the demands of their working lives and their partners' greater involvement with the children: 'you have more of the load than I do 'cos I work ....' (Alan: cited in Davies 2014: 279). The identity of out at work father is made relevant here and provides an explanation for the unequal division of child care and for why he is not so skilled at managing his child: 'I use uhm language that doesn't... probably inflames but [...] I'm at work all the time or most of the time' (Alan: 279). Alan's account of himself as a father, who might inflame the situation at home, suggests that he is not as accomplished as his partner in dealing with their son. This is partly because he spends so much time at work and has less practice, but it is a risky position in light of moral panics about absentee fathers. However, fathers are able to counter this by referring to their identity as working but involved and supportive fathers. Fathers take up of a secondary position in the home is relational to traditional forms of maternal caregiving and calls them into being, reflecting 'heavily gendered cultural discourses that are available in society' (Petrassi 2012: 525) where, for traditional forms of parenting, mothers can be understood to perform their 'socially correct' role, and with which fathers collude. Collectively, these roles establish the credentials of a family as 'hard-working' and not 'troubled' (see Runswick-Cole et al. 2016) and thus, carries moral authority, a quality that parents of children with an ADHD diagnosis are particularly invested in displaying. One mother proudly recalls the comments of a health visitor:

> 'oh you're so lucky that both ...you know that Alan is like really supportive and you're both' ...and the lady said 'I really don't need to see either of you on your own' [...] both of us sharing the load'. (Jane: cited in Davies 2014: 279)

The effectiveness of this parenting team is warranted by the story of the health visitor who makes her decision not to extend the professional monitoring of the family on this basis. It is interesting that the health visitor is quoted as saying Jane is 'lucky' that Alan is involved. This might be a reference to the cultural ideal of the two parent family, or it could be a reference to the traditional stereotype that fathers were not normatively expected to have much involvement in the domestic sphere. Either way, early years interventions, work as a disciplinary mechanism, promoting and endorsing the culturally normative ideals of good parenting. In Jane's account of the health visitor, the professional gaze was relaxed because there was evidence of a successful parenting team.

The Professionalisation of Fathers' Knowledge

Although the fathers in Davies' study seemed willing to take up the subject position of secondary parent at home, they were also keen to assert their knowledge and expertise about ADHD and their children elsewhere, for example, to inform teachers at school. For example:

> *Alan*: 'I took in books that we'd obviously bought and say 'do you want to read them? That might help you'. (cited in Davies 2014: 288)
>
> *Michael*: 'I provided some textbooks I mean it's not to say that the school would have no knowledge but I just thought whatever knowledge they had it would be useful to provide some textbooks to help them so these were books about teaching so they were more for people in the classroom.' (cited in Davies 2014: 288)

These two fathers described how they informed themselves about ADHD and passed their knowledge to education professionals. The transfer of knowledge from one site (the family) to another (the school) is a pattern that has also been identified in other research studies (Gwernan-Jones et al. 2015). These two examples of fathers supplying information about ADHD to their son's teachers concur with the observation that many teachers are called to account by parents for having 'obsolete' knowledge (Frigerio et al. 2013). Despite taking up a secondary position in relation to mothers' knowledge in the home, fathers assert equivalent parental authority in a public facing mode by passing on knowledge to the school. Fathers, like mothers, assume the status of expert on ADHD when dealing with teachers and in some cases this can take the form of a struggle between them (Bailey 2014). The acquisition of knowledge about ADHD affords fathers a level of power and resistance to the interventions of professionals. However, paradoxically, acquiring this knowledge can shape the way that their children can be known (Rose 1999).

While contemporary ideology prescribes a more active role for fathers in family life (Robb 2004) and affords them a more nurturing role (Lupton and Barclay 1997), they must still account for themselves as involved and supportive without threatening the position of the 'good mother'. They do this for the sake of the 'good parenting team' and in the examples analysed above, fathers (and mothers) do this by distinguishing the nature of fathers' caring from that of mothering, as supportive and secondary, while retaining some investment when necessary in traditionally valued masculinity (see also Doucet 2006).

Concluding Comments

In this chapter, we have seen how the fathers who participated in Alison Davies' research (2014) talked about their experiences of parenting a son with ADHD. We found that fathers drew on dilemmatic discourses of fathering that arise from traditional and contemporary ideas about new forms of fathering. Traditional fathering discourses were used to resist psychosocial explanations of ADHD that imply a lack of authority and discipline in the home and they are also used to compensate for accounts of maternal leniency. These accounts were tempered by drawing on more contemporary discourses of fathers as the secondary but supportive parent, positioning the mother as the more knowledgeable parent about their child and ADHD.

The gendering of ADHD, along with stereotypes of absent fathers and genetic inheritability explanations, appear to make the fathers of boys with ADHD, more accountable. Discourses of masculinity, (the politics of) impairment and medication converge around the category of ADHD and we found that fathers engaged with these discourses in complex and variable ways. Similar to the mothers interviewed by Davies (2014), fathers engage partially with the biomedical model of ADHD but this is troubled and they also show resistance to impairment narratives, either by emphasising the opportunities that symptoms such as hyperactivity can provide or by presenting symptoms of ADHD as characteristics of normal boyhood. Their own investment in cultural stereotypes of masculinity, either as the superhero whose ADHD traits are an asset, or the 'boisterous boy' in their own childhood, leads fathers to normalise ADHD and resist medical solutions, at least in the context of these accounts.

Fathers invoke a range of evidence to construct the authority of their claims in relation to ADHD (Frigerio and Montali 2016). They draw on both experiential and expert knowledge to display their involvement and concern for their children and both forms of warrant are used to challenge professional authority and interventions. On the one hand, the take-up of expert knowledge affords fathers some empowerment in relation to their children. However, on the other hand, fathers'

Chapters four and five have dealt with mothers and fathers separately, reflecting the different ways in which they are positioned within contemporary parenting discourses and discourses of ADHD, and the different ways in which they engage with these discourses. However, the discourses of mothers and fathers are relational and they intersect with the wider discourses of parenting. There are points of overlap.

- Both mothers and fathers draw on the biological repertoire to explain their child's ADHD.
- However, they both (in different ways) demonstrate a complex and sometimes contradictory engagement with the biological model of ADHD.
- Mothers and fathers are both subject to the discourse of deficit parenting identities, albeit in different ways. They resist this by emphasising the contribution that each parent makes to a strong parenting team. This has implications for the way that single parents are positioned by the discourse of ADHD.
- Parents resist expert and professional authority by drawing on their own parental experience and knowledge to claim a superior understanding of their children. This is often aligned with gendered discourses of good parenting.
- Parents respond to the cultural requirement to become professional parents. They develop specialised knowledge of ADHD and are proactive on behalf of their children both inside the home and also in medical, welfare and education contexts.
- While the take up of specialised knowledge around ADHD can be seen as a form of resistance to professional authority, it can also be seen as a form of compliance with forms of self-governance and the regulation of family life.

Fig. 5.2 Overlapping themes in Chapters 4 and 5

engagement with specialist knowledge relating to ADHD come to shape fathers' experiences of parenting a child with ADHD and place new responsibilities upon them (Fig. 5.2).

The association of ADHD with particular forms of masculinity and social conduct is a defining feature of the discourse of ADHD and this raises a question with regard to girls and women with ADHD. In Davies' (2014) study, no parents of girls came forward, despite several mothers from that study identifying as having ADHD themselves (see Chapter 6 and Davies and Horton-Salway 2016). We are aware that there has been an historic propensity to study problematic male populations and this, coupled with the focus on social conduct issues, can reinforce the stereotype of ADHD as a problem of boys (Horton-Salway 2012; Ohan and Visser 2009). Certainly, boys are foregrounded in the literature relating to ADHD (Bailey 2009) and some have argued that girls have been rendered invisible within the discourses of ADHD. In Chapter 6 these issues are taken up in a discussion of how gendering has impacted upon adult diagnosis and experience. We also consider the personal experience of ADHD from the viewpoint of children, adolescents and adults and take a retrospective approach to the lives of women with ADHD.

References

Ahl, H. (2006). Why research on women entrepreneurs needs new directions. *Entrepreneurship Theory and Practice, 30*(5), 595–621.

Allen, K., & Taylor, Y. (2012). Placing parenting, locating unrest: Failed femininities, troubled mothers and riotous subjects. *Studies in the Maternal, 4*(2), 1–25. https://doi.org/10.16995/sim.39.

Bailey, S. (2009). *Producing ADHD: An ethnographic study of behavioural discourses of early childhood* (Ph.D. thesis, University of Nottingham).

Bailey, S. (2014). *Exploring ADHD: An Ethnography of Disorder in Early Childhood.* Abingdon: Routledge.

Barnes, C., & Power, M. J. (2012). Internalising discourses of parental blame: Voices from the field. *Studies in the Maternal, 4*(2), 1–21. https://doi.org/10.16995/sim.36.

Bem, S. (1981). *Bem Sex-Role Inventory*. Palo Alto, CA: Mind Garden.

Bennett, J. (2007). (Dis)ordering motherhood: Mothering a child with attention deficit hyperactivity disorder. *Body Society, 13*(4), 97–110.

Berman, R. C., & Wilson, L. (2009). Pathologising or validating: Intake workers' discursive constructions of mothers. *Qualitative Health Research, 19*(4), 444–453.

Billig, M., Condor, S., Edwards, D., Gane, M., Middleton, D., & Radley, A. (1988). *Ideological Dilemmas: A Social Psychology of Everyday Thinking*. London: Sage.

Boström, P. K., & Broberg, M. (2014). Openness and avoidance—A longitudinal study of fathers of children with intellectual disability. *Journal of Intellectual Disability Research, 58*(9), 810–821.

Bowlby, J. (2005). *A Secure Base*. London: Routledge Books.

Bull, C., & Whelan, T. (2006). Parental schemata in the management of children with ADHD. *Qualitative Health Research, 16*(5), 664–676.

Bussing, R., & Gary, F. A. (2001). Practice guidelines and parental ADHD treatment evaluations: Friends or foes? *Harvard Review of Psychiatry, 9*(5), 233.

Carpenter, B., & Towers, C. (2008). Recognising fathers: The needs of fathers of children with disabilities. *Fathers and Disability, 23*(3), 118–125.

Davies, A. (2014). *It's a problem with the brain: A discursive analysis of parents' constructions of ADHD* (Unpublished Ph.D. thesis). The Open University, Milton Keynes.

Davies, A., & Horton-Salway, M. (2016). The construction of adult ADHD: Anna's story. In M. O'Reilly & J. N. Lester (Eds.), *The Palgrave Handbook of Adult Mental Health* (pp. 117–133). Basingstoke, UK: Palgrave Macmillan.

De Benedictis, S. (2012). 'Feral' parents: Austerity parenting under neoliberalism. *Studies in the Maternal, 4*(2), 1–21. https://doi.org/10.16995/sim.40.

Dixon, J., & Wetherell, M. (2004). On discourse and dirty nappies: Gender, the division of household labour and the social psychology of distributive justice. *Theory and Psychology, 14*(2), 167–189.

Doucet, A. (2006). *Do Men Mother?* London: University of Toronto Press.

Edley, N., & Wetherell, M. (1999). Imagined futures: Young men's talk about fatherhood and domestic life. *British Journal of Social Psychology, 38*, 181–194.

Edwards, D. (1994). Script formulations: An analysis of event descriptions in conversation. *Journal of Language and Social Psychology, 13*(3), 211–247.

Edwards, D. (1997). *Discourse and Cognition*. London: Sage.

Edwards, D. (2005). Moaning, whinging and laughing: The subjective side of complaints. *Discourse Studies, 7*(1), 5–29.
Featherstone, B. (2009). *Contemporary Fathering: Theory, Policy and Practice.* Bristol: Policy Press.
Foucault, M. (1980). *History of Sexuality, Vol. 1: An Introduction* (R. Hurley, Trans.). New York: Vintage.
Frigerio, A., & Montali, L. (2016). An ethnographic-discursive approach to parental self-help groups: The case of ADHD. *Qualitative Health Research, 26*(7), 935–950.
Frigerio, A., Montali, L., & Fine, M. (2013). Attention deficit/hyperactivity disorder blame game: A study on the positioning of professionals, teachers and parents. *Health, 17*(6), 584–604.
Gerdes, A. C., Hoza, B., & Pelham, W. E. (2003). Attention-deficit/hyperactivity disordered boys' relationships with their mothers and fathers: Child, mother, and father perceptions. *Developmental Psychopathology, 15*(2), 363–382.
Ghosh, M., Fisher, C., Preen, D. B., D'Arcy, J., & Holma, C. (2016). "It has to be fixed": A qualitative inquiry into perceived ADHD behaviour among affected individuals and parents in Western Australia. *BMC Health Services Research, 16,* 141.
Giddens, A. (1991). *Modernity and Self-identity*. Cambridge: Polity.
Gillies, V. (2005). Meeting parents' needs? Discourses of 'support' and 'inclusion' in family policy. *Critical Social Policy, 25*(1), 70–90.
Goffman, E. (1955). On face work. *Psychiatry, 18,* 213–231.
Goffman, E. (1959). *The Presentation of Self in Everyday Life*. Harmondsworth: Penguin.
Goffman, E. (2006). On face-work: An analysis of ritual elements in social interaction. In A. Jaworski & N. Coupland (Eds.), *The Discourse Reader* (pp. 299–310). Abingdon, Oxon: Routledge.
Goldberg, A. (2011). Unscrupulous parents seek ADHD diagnosis for benefits. *BBC News*, 6th February. Available at http://www.bbc.co.uk/news/health (Accessed 3 September 2017).
Gray, C. A. (2008). *Lay and professional constructions of childhood ADHD (attention deficit hyperactivity disorder): A discourse analysis* (Ph.D. thesis, Queen Margaret University).
Gray Brunton, C., McVittie, C., Ellison, M., & Willock, J. (2014). Negotiating parental accountability in the face of uncertainty for attention-deficit hyperactivity disorder. *Qualitative Health Research, 24*(2), 242–253.

Gwernan-Jones, R., Moore, D. A., Garside, R., Richardson, M., Thompson-Coon, J., Rogers, M., et al. (2015). ADHD, parent perspectives and parent–teacher relationships: Grounds for conflict. *British Journal of Special Education, 42*(3), 279–300.

Hansen, D. L., & Hansen, E. H. (2006). Caught in a balancing act: Parents' dilemmas regarding their ADHD child's treatment with stimulant medication. *Qualitative Health Research, 16*(9), 1267–1285.

Harden, J. (2005). Parenting a young person with mental health problems: Temporal disruption and reconstruction. *Sociology of Health & Illness, 27*(3), 351–371.

Hjorne, E. (2005). Negotiating the 'problem-child' in school: Child identity, parenting and institutional agendas. *Qualitative Social Work, 4*(4), 489–507.

Horton-Salway, M. (2011). Repertoires of ADHD in UK newspaper media. *Health (London), 15*(5), 533–549.

Horton-Salway, M. (2012). Gendering attention deficit hyperactivity disorder: A discursive analysis of UK newspaper stories. *Journal of Health Psychology, 18*(8), 1085–1099. Published online before print 1 October 2012. https://doi.org/10.1177/1359105312456326.

Karakaş, S., Bakar, E., Dinçer, E., Ülsever, H., Ceylan, A., & Taner, Y. (2015). Relationship between diagnosis of ADHD in offspring and current and retrospective self-reports of parental ADHD. *Journal of Child and Family Studies, 24*(12), 3595–3609.

Keown, L. (2011). Fathering and mothering of preschool boys with hyperactivity. *International Journal of Behavioral Development, 35*(2), 161–168.

Keown, L. (2012). Predictors of boys' ADHD symptoms from early to middle childhood: The role of father–child and mother–child interactions. *Journal of Abnormal Child Psychology, 40*, 569–581.

Litt, J. (2004). Women's carework in low-income households: The special case of children with attention deficit hyperactivity disorder. *Gender and Society, 18*(5), 625–644.

Lupton, D., & Barclay, L. (1997). *Constructing Fatherhood: Discourses and Experiences*. London: Sage.

O'Brien, M. (2005). *Shared caring: Bringing fathers in the frame* (EOC Working Paper Series No. 18). Manchester: Equal Opportunities Commission.

O'Dell, L., Stenner, P., Horton-Salway, M., & Davies, A. (2016). *Narratives of ADHD: A qualitative study of women's narrative accounts of living with ADHD*. Unpublished research report submitted to the British Academy.

Ohan, J. L., & Visser, T. A. W. (2009). Why is there a gender gap in children presenting for attention deficit hyperactivity disorder services? *Journal of Clinical Child and Adolescent Psychology, 38*(5), 650–660.

O'Reilly, M. (2008). 'I didn't violent punch him': Parental accounts of punishing children with mental health problems. *Journal of Family Therapy, 30*(3), 272–295.

Panter-Brick, C., Burgess, A., Eggerman, M., McAllister, F., Pruett, K., & Leckman, J. F. (2014). Practitioner Review: Engaging fathers—Recommendations for a game change in parenting interventions based on a systematic review of the global evidence. *Journal of Child Psychology and Psychiatry, 55,* 1187–1212.

Pedersen, D. E. (2012). The good mother, the good father, and the good parent: Gendered definitions of parenting. *Journal of Feminist Family Therapy, 24*(3), 230–246.

Petrassi, D. (2012). 'For me, the children come first': A discursive psychological analysis of how mothers construct fathers' roles in childrearing and childcare. *Feminism and Psychology, 22*(4), 518–527.

Pleck, J. H. (1987). The theory of male sex-role identity: Its rise and fall, 1936 to the present. In H. Brod (Ed.), *The Making of Masculinities: The New Men's Studies*. Boston: Allen and Unwin.

Pomerantz, A. (1986). Extreme case formulations: A way of legitimising claims. *Human Studies, 9,* 219–229.

Potter, C. (2016a). 'It's the most important thing—I mean, the schooling': Father involvement in the education of children with autism. *European Journal of Special Needs Education, 31*(4), 489–505. https://doi.org/10.1080/08856257.2016.1194573.

Potter, C. (2016b). 'I accept my son for who he is—He has incredible character and personality': Fathers' positive experiences of parenting children with autism. *Disability and Society, 31*(7), 948–965. https://doi.org/10.1080/09687599.2016.1216393.

Potter, J. (1996). *Representing Reality: Discourse, Rhetoric and Social Construction*. London: Sage.

Rafalovich, A. (2015). ADHD: Three competing discourses. In M. O'Reilly & N. Lester (Eds.), *The Palgrave Handbook of Child Mental Health* (pp. 79–99). Basingstoke: Palgrave Macmillan.

Ranson, G. (2001). Men at work: Change or no change? In the era of the 'new father'. *Men and Masculinities, 4*(3), 2–26.

Renshaw, P., Choo, J., & Emerald, E. (2014). Diverse disability identities: The accomplishment of 'child with a disability' in everyday interaction between parents and teachers. *International Journal of Educational Research, 63*, 47–58.

Riley, S. C. E. (2003). The management of the traditional male role: A discourse analysis of the constructions and functions of provision. *Journal of Gender Studies, 12*(2), 99–113.

Robb, M. (2004). Men talking about fatherhood: Discourse and identities. In M. Robb, S. Barrett, C. Komaromy, & A. Rogers (Eds.), *Communication, Relationships and Care: A Reader*. London: Routledge.

Rogers, M. A., Wiener, J., Martin, I., & Tannock, R. (2009). Parental involvement in children's learning: Comparing parents of children with and without attention-deficit and hyperactivity disorder (ADHD). *Journal of School Psychology, 47*(3), 167–185.

Rose, N. (1999). *Governing the Soul: The Shaping of the Private Self*. London: Free Association Books.

Runswick-Cole, K., Lawthom, R., & Goodley, D. (2016). The trouble with 'hard working families'. *Community, Work and Family, 19*(2), 257–260. https://doi.org/10.1080/13668803.2016.1134153.

Schmitz, M. F., Filippone, P., & Edelman, E. M. (2003). Social representations of attention deficit/hyperactivity disorder, 1988–1997. *Culture & Psychology, 9*(4), 383–406.

Seale, C. (2003). Health and media: An overview. *Sociology of Health & Illness, 25*(6), 513–531.

Seymour-Smith, S., & Wetherell, M. (2006). 'What he hasn't told you...': Investigating the micro-politics of gendered support in heterosexual couples' co-constructed accounts of illness. *Feminism and Psychology, 16*(1), 105–127.

Singh, I. (2003). Boys will be boys: fathers' perspectives on ADHD symptoms, diagnosis and drug treatment. *Harvard Review of Psychiatry, 11*(6), 308–316.

Singh, I. et al. (2012). VOICES Study: Final Report. London, UK.

Summers, J. A., Boller, K., Schiffman, R. F., & Raikes, H. H. (2006). The meaning of "good fatherhood:" Low-income fathers' social constructions of their roles. *Parenting: Science and Practice,* 6(2–3), 145–165.

Thapar, A., & Cooper, C. (2016). Attention deficit hyperactivity disorder. *The Lancet, 387*(10024), 1240–1250.

Wetherell, M. (2012). *Affect and Emotion: A New Social Science Understanding*. London: Sage.

Winnicott, D. W. (1984). Primary maternal preoccupation. In *Through Paediatrics to Psycho-Analysis* (Collected Papers). London: Karnac Books.

Winter, H., Moncrieff, J., & Speed, E. (2015). "Because you're worth it": A discourse analysis of the gendered rhetoric of the ADHD woman. *Qualitative Research in Psychology, 12*(4), 415–434.

Wooffitt, R. (1992). *Telling Tales of the Unexpected: The Organisation of Factual Discourse*. Hemel Hempstead: Harvester Wheatsheaf.

Woolgar, S. (1988). *Science: The Very Idea*. Chichester: Ellis Horwood/London: Tavistock.

Yarwood, G. A. (2011). The pick and mix of fathering identities. *Fathering, 9*(2), 150–168.

6

Voices of Experience: Narrative Lives and Selves

Mary Horton-Salway

The category of ADHD was for a long time regarded exclusively as a disorder of childhood until it was defined as a diagnosable mental health category that persists into adult life, affecting girls and women as well as men and boys. We have seen examples, in Chapters 4 and 5, where mothers and fathers have themselves identified with this diagnosis. In this chapter, our journey through the discourse of ADHD continues with a discussion of some of the issues and debates that have arisen from the emergence of adult ADHD, the consequences of gendering, and the importance of personal experience narratives.

The Emergence of ADHD as a Life-Long Condition

The persistence of ADHD into adulthood has been documented by a number of researchers since the 1980s (Dunne and Moore 2011; Henry and Jones 2011; Nussbaum 2012; Quinn 2005; Rafalovich 2001a; Sim et al. 2004; Singh 2002a; Waite 2010; Wender 1987, 1995, 1998, 2000). Wender (1998) claimed that 30–50% of children with ADHD

M. Horton-Salway and A. Davies, *The Discourse of ADHD*,
The Language of Mental Health, https://doi.org/10.1007/978-3-319-76026-1_6

in the US had symptoms that persisted into adulthood while in the UK Borrill (2000) identified only 30–40% of children with ADHD having good outcomes as adults. The prevalence of adults with ADHD in the UK population is around 4–5% according to Davidson (2008), who also suggested that adults are more often diagnosed with inattentive-type than hyperactive-type ADHD. The expansion of ADD and ADHD into adulthood came about incrementally by a series of changes in definitions and wordings of diagnostic criteria beginning with DSM-111R (American Psychiatric Association 1987). As discussed in Chapter 2, the expansion of medical categories in this way is sometimes referred to as 'bracket-creep' (Kirschner 2013). However, the criteria of DSM-111 were designed for the diagnosis of childhood ADHD (American Psychiatric Association 1980) and this had previously not allowed for adult diagnoses (see National Institute of Clinical Excellence 2009). To be inclusive, the diagnostic criteria needed to include the social context of employment (among others) rather than school (Conrad and Potter 2000). In the next version, DSM-IV (American Psychiatric Association 1994) confirmed ADHD as an adult diagnosis and it was recommended that this should be based on the 'Conners ADHD adult diagnostic interview for DSM-1V' (American Psychiatric Association 1994). In 2009 the *National Institute of Clinical Excellence* in the UK produced a report on ADHD referring to both children and adults and there were criteria for diagnosing adult ADHD in the next version, DSM-1V-TR, the latest version of ICD-10, and in the most recent version, DSM 5 (APA 2013).

The validity of adult ADHD as a diagnosis has, however, been far from uncontroversial (see Asherton et al. 2010 or Conrad and Potter 2000). Conrad and Potter (2000) outlined the social processes by which ADHD has been constructed over time as a medical category. Their concern was that the label, ADHD, medicalised the deviant behaviour of boys and this diagnosis became increasingly inclusive until it was later expanded to include adults. Adult ADHD, however, was regarded as a socially constructed 'product of collective action' between professional, lay and interest groups rather than an example of 'medical imperialism' (2000: 560). In relation to the discourse of science, Bruno Latour (1987, 1989, 1993) has described the social processes by which forms of truth and knowledge are confirmed and spread through networks of diverse actors who develop them into various 'translations' of a phenomenon. Thus, social construction arises from complexity, debate and dynamic social processes. These critical sociological observations of how knowledge and truth are established, contested and circulate pose a challenge to essentialist versions of reality.

Researchers and theorists who do not take a social constructionist view of science, medicine and mental health are nevertheless equally concerned with how people are affected by the diagnosis or the lack of it. Despite the emerging recognition of adult ADHD, there have been difficulties in obtaining a diagnosis that some argue results in barriers to care (Wiita and Parish 2008; Davidson 2008). Davidson (2008) argued, for example, that adults symptoms were more likely to be treated as indicators of several other psychiatric conditions such as anti-social behaviour disorder, borderline personality disorder, bipolar disorder, obsessional compulsive disorder and psychotic disorder (National Institute of Clinical Excellence 2009: 37). Symptoms of ADHD can also be mistaken for anxiety and undiagnosed ADHD can lead to substance misuse according to Young et al. (2003). The problems associated with a delayed diagnosis, Young et al. (2008) have argued, can result in repeated experiences of failure during childhood.

Another layer of complexity in the discourse of adult ADHD is gender bias towards boys in recognition and diagnosis. This deserves attention because of the gendered stereotypes that support definitions of ADHD and the different consequences this has for girls, women, boys and men. We continue here with a brief account of how different perspectives have viewed the gendering of ADHD and how this has merged with the discourse surrounding adult ADHD.

The Consequences of Gendering

As both Wiita and Parish (2008) and Davidson (2008) have observed, it is by no means easy for an adult to obtain a diagnosis of ADHD despite the existence of a medical label. Any undiagnosed adult would have to demonstrate the criteria for adult ADHD and obtain a referral. This is to some extent dependent on a credible account of childhood ADHD. It is less likely that women's past educational and medical histories and their health or social problems would be associated with ADHD or interpreted that way. Nadeau and Quinn (2002), for example, have argued that women who match the criteria for a diagnosis of ADHD might already have been diagnosed with other mental health conditions, such as dysthymia or bipolar disorder, so this would also influence how their 'symptoms' are interpreted.

An historical tendency to focus on the conduct of boys combined with the lack of focus on girls' conduct or instances of underachievement is worth elaborating here because it has important implications for the diagnosis of ADD or ADHD. Gender bias has arisen historically in educational settings through culturally gendered norms of femininity and masculinity that have informed academic expectations for performance and behaviours between the genders. In a medical context, there has also been a historic bias towards interpreting the problems of girls and women as a range of mental disorders (Ussher 1991). The constructive processes of gender bias are also encapsulated in the ADHD diagnosis itself as a history of 'boy-descriptive' criteria (Quinn 2005). Typically, this is a focus on the 'problematic' conduct of boys in school environments. Girls who have attentional problems but are able to 'get by' academically are likely to 'pass for normal' and be overlooked (Goffman 1963). Because their behaviours are not interpreted as socially problematic, they are less likely to be referred, diagnosed and treated (Solden 1995). Magnusson and Maracek (2012: 140) contend that gendered differences in manifesting symptoms of ADHD/ADD, for example 'internalizing' behaviours of girls, are overlooked compared with the 'externalizing' behaviours more typically displayed by boys. Although, Singh et al. (2012) have pointed out that being overlooked can be an issue for children of both genders who try to hide their 'performance' problems in order to avoid stigma and bullying from peers. Girls are still more likely to be overlooked because of lower educational expectations compared with boys and because, Solden argues (1995: 46), the symptoms of 'non-hyperactive ADD' are more 'subtle, quiet and invisible'. Is it possible, then, that more undiagnosed cases of ADHD or ADD have persisted into adulthood for women than for men who were more likely to be given a childhood diagnosis? Some suggest that it is, for example Simon et al. (2009) whose meta-analysis showed 'women comprising over 80% of adults with the diagnosis in some countries' (cited in Winter et al. 2015: 415–416). This bias also fits with Davidson's observation that adults are more often diagnosed with inattentive-type than hyperactive-type ADHD and these figures could be interpreted as evidence that a gender bias in childhood ADHD diagnosis has resulted in girls' attentional problems remaining undiagnosed until they are adults (Connolly 2010).

On the other hand as Ussher (2010) argues, 'adult ADHD is one of a number of labels ascribed to situations in which women fail to attain to normative societal explanations of how they should behave and perform' (cited in Winter et al. 2015: 416). Both lines of argument derive from the authors' concerns about gender inequality and the ways that girls and boys or men and women are positioned relative to one another. From a constructionist viewpoint, Ussher argues that 'women's misery' has, historically, been medicalised as mental illness and that ADHD is yet another example of this. She locates this bias within patriarchal cultures and the relationship of discourse, social practices and knowledge in the form of gendered 'truths' that have translated into psychiatric categories.

For Conrad and Potter (2000) and other social constructionist critics such as Timimi (2005), the labelling of boys with conduct disorders has become a cause for medical intervention in much the same way that Ussher argues that women's 'misery' has historically been labelled as mental illness in forms such as neurosis and hysteria. Ussher was commenting on the ways that patriarchal discourses and social practices have underpinned psychiatry (1991, 2010) however Conrad and Potter were also highlighting the ways that gender bias in psychiatric discourse has positioned boys and men. Clearly girls and women are positioned by mental health labels in different ways than boys and men. These categories are imbued with the social values of time and place and according to social constructionist authors they can be used as a form of 'medicalisation' of social life that functions as social control for both genders (see Chapter 2). While this social process focuses on conduct and the 'dangerous' nature of boys and men (see also Chapter 3), the socially derived distress of girls and women has been defined as so called feminine weakness. Both examples are definitions of gendering that perpetuate historicised gender stereotypes and in different ways maintain the social order.

Beyond the sociological critique of mental health categories as a gendered form of social control, others have been concerned to acknowledge the life struggles of undiagnosed adults of both genders, as they cope with being parents, in their relationships and with the workplace and at home (Johnston et al. 2012). Fedele et al. (2012), for example, identified higher impairment in women with ADHD in the contexts of family, social life, education, handling finances, and coping with daily life. Such problems arise, some argue, because gendered cultural imperatives have historically translated into women's multiple role responsibility for home, work and childcare (Solden 1995). The relative invisibility of girls and women who have symptoms of ADHD together with the gendered and stereotypical ways of defining their distress might account for many such problems. We share Ussher's concern, however, that women are more likely to have their socially derived problems defined as forms of mental illness so paradoxically 'women can be considered *both* overserved and underserved by mental health delivery systems' (Ussher 1991).

Many who do not take a constructionist sociological approach to the category of ADHD, are nonetheless equally concerned about gender bias. The less 'visible' indicators of ADHD, such as attentional or cognitive problems are reported as more likely to occur in girls, but also less likely to be noticed and referred and some claim this has resulted in 'gender-related barriers to care' that are embedded in educational practices (Groenewald et al. 2009: 767). Although these different approaches to gender bias are derived from constructionist and realist perspectives on the interpretation of ADHD, they are in agreement that there are gender issues arising from differences in the interpretation of conduct, performance and distress for girls, boys, women and men. These issues can persist into adult lives whichever way you interpret them.

Despite critiques of ADHD as a 'medicalising' label, gendered psychiatric discourse and cultural stereotypes of gendered behaviours and problems, ADHD is undoubtedly an official diagnostic category for children and adults of both genders. Matters arising from gendering and the extension of ADHD into adulthood have contributed to the circulating discourse of ADHD and this has become the cultural context of personal experience that influences how individuals understand the category of ADHD, how they interpret their lives, how others see them and how they see themselves in relation to ADHD.

Personal Experience Is Important

Forms of knowledge and the 'truths' produced by science circulate through a network of social actors (Latour 1993). As discussed in Chapter 3, there has been an increase in access to science and medical knowledge through media, online communications and global social networks that now results in yet wider networks of social actors who are able to contribute to this process as the 'producers' as well as 'consumers' of information. As we discussed in Chapter 1, science knowledge is commonly perceived to be a superior form of objective truth and medical institutions have based the integrity and legitimacy of their practice on evidence-based medicine. However, this tends to place greater emphasis on positivist forms of enquiry. In recent decades, the widespread availability of multiple truths and critiques in 'knowledge-rich' societies has undermined the authority of science and medicine in the public imagination. From a Foucauldian viewpoint, Rose (1998: 55) points out that knowledge and truth is produced by contestation as well as construction so it has been the aim of this book to unpack how knowledge and 'truths' about the meaning of ADHD have been produced by science in different 'translations', and taken up or contested in public discourse. We saw (in Chapter 3) how simplified and sensationalised versions of scientific 'truths' are taken up by the media on the publication of 'breakthrough' research (Harwood et al. 2017), while the more mundane, cumulative progressions and amendments that characterise much of science activity are less likely to be reported to the public following an initial sensational headline (Gonon et al. 2011). Despite the existence of more recent subtle and nuanced descriptions of ADHD as a complex biopsychosocial phenomenon (Ponnou and Gonon 2017), news items about ADHD have often been designed to fuel polarised debates of claim and counter-claim about biological versus social causes that whip up a storm of attention and moralistic public reaction (Horton-Salway 2011, 2012).

Therefore the re-presentations of science in popular media have often been stigmatising and unhelpful about ADHD and other mental health categories and sometimes they are quite misleading about the findings of scientific endeavour (see Chapter 3). In response to this partial and misreporting of science, a research team at *The Institute of Mental Health (UK)* (www.institutemh.org.uk) in collaboration with *The University of Nottingham* and the *Nottingham National Health Trust* attempted to address concerns about stigma and public lack of understanding. They have attempted this by conveying a more direct virtual experience of ADHD to the lay public through a project called '*In My Shoes*'; a virtual experience, based on the experience of children with ADHD, aiming to lessen the effect of stereotype and stigma.

We also consider the personal experience of people with the label, ADHD, to be important and there is a growing field of research undertaken by those who apply qualitative methods in their enquiries about individuals' lives and their subjective experiences. These studies are a valuable source of experiential knowledge based on the accounts of children and adults. For example, Singh et al. (2012) were concerned with the ethics of medicating children and designed the *Voices* project to listen to the views of school children with ADHD. Being stigmatised and bullied at school was identified as a common experience for many children who demonstrated the more visible hyperactivity and social conduct problems associated with ADHD. Those with less visible academic performance difficulties were likely to avoid negative attention by hiding this from their peers. Children described medication as mainly helpful to resolve their problems arising from hyperactivity and attentional-deficit in this study, although children who took part in studies described by Kenny (2016: 46) had sometimes reported 'emotional side effects and loss of identity'. The conduct and performance aspects of ADHD were both associated with stigma in Singh et al's study and Kenny has described similar findings arising from many other research studies of children and young people that she has reviewed. Young people's views of ADHD are however described by Kenny as 'complex and contradictory' with accounts of identity conflicts and lack of personal control in the management of their treatments. Indeed, Singh et al. (2012) reported that children did not always understand why they were being treated. Kenny, described children who managed identity conflicts by 'normalising, challenging or distancing themselves from ADHD' (Kenny 2016: 121). She was concerned that 'research presents a problem saturated picture of ADHD' (2016: 35) although this might not always reflect the ways that children and adolescents choose to describe themselves in self-reports. Research reviewed by Kenny (2016: 35) indicates that children with ADHD describe themselves in more positive terms than do their parents. This, she describes as a higher than average *Positive Illusory Bias* (PIB) that can be either protective or maladaptive. If we interpret this in discursive rather than cognitivist terms we might argue that this positive way of talking is a defence against being positioned by others in discreditable ways and it is an aspect of ADHD discourse that we have observed in media stories, parents' accounts and also in the accounts of adults with ADHD, as we go on to discuss later.

We do agree with Kenny that not enough is known about how young people, who are so labelled, make sense of ADHD. Indeed, she cites article 12 of the *United Nations Convention* on the rights of the child (United Nations 1990) and the Children and Families Act (2014) supported by the *Code of Practice* (DoE 2014) that directs professionals to take more seriously the views of children and young people. The voices of children are important in understanding more about how children are positioned by ADHD, its impact, and how parents and professionals can respond more effectively to their needs. Researchers such as Orla Kenny (2016) and Ilona Singh et al. (2012) in the UK have argued that the meaning of ADHD can only be understood within its cultural and social context and they have provided some timely and relevant observations about children's experience arising from professional practice in critical psychiatry and educational psychology respectively. Kenny (2016) observes that Educational Psychologists who work closely with children and schools are well placed to contribute to this important area of research, especially the potential to promote children's marginalised voices and inform the knowledge base of teachers and multidisciplinary healthcare teams.

Our own research on ADHD has been largely undertaken in an academic context and in the areas of media representations (Chapter 3), parents' experiences (Chapters 4 and 5) and adults with ADHD. Here, in this chapter, we draw on studies of personal experience to describe how adolescents and adults construct retrospective narratives of their lives and selves. We will begin to direct our focus towards a discursive standpoint by considering what narratives of personal experience might indicate about the issues and debates arising from the wider discourse of ADHD, mental health or disability and how people engage with these concerns.

ADHD and Transitions to Adulthood

A study by Dunne and Moore (2011) described the retrospective narrative of a young man, aged nineteen years, who had transitioned through his early years at infant school, primary school and then to secondary school, work and college. Dunne and Moore summarised his story as one of unmet needs, difficulties, stigma and social isolation. Diagnosed with special needs at the age of five years, they describe how Jake was medicated for ADHD because of conduct issues. We learned that his school experiences were variable, but after his transition to secondary school he 'came out' as gay, an event he described as life changing and isolating from his peers, 'Lads wouldn't come near me. I was uncomfortable around them. They were judgemental' (ibid.: 357). As Dunne and Moore point out, despite being described by his teachers as 'gifted and talented' in music and creative writing, by age 14–16 he was drinking, smoking and self-harming and had acquired multiple labels of ADHD and Oppositional Defiant Disorder (ODD). At age 16, 'Jake' had stopped taking medication altogether and his creative talents, according to Dunne and Moore, had been 'quashed within a system that failed to respond appropriately' (ibid. 2011: 362). This story speaks of the effects of 'public stigma' in the school setting and also, relatedly, 'self-stigma', affecting Jake's self-esteem as a consequence of this (cf. Mueller et al. 2012). Mueller et al. have described these two aspects of stigma as risk factors that aggravate the symptoms of ADHD and adversely affect mental health and life satisfaction.

The transition to work can be a chaotic time because no continuous support is available for the needs of a young adult with ADHD. Dunne and Moore described Jake's story of work related difficulties, alcohol and drug abuse that led him into money problems, conflict with family and social isolation. They noted how transformations in his life had only come about through the intervention of his mother, a mental health professional. As educationalists, Dunne and Moore were concerned that 'Jake's' problems could have been avoided with more support from educational and social institutions at key transition points. 'Jake' himself had apparently talked in a positive way about his future, expressing a wish to contribute to society and the desire to manage and organise himself. However, they argued, more recognition and emphasis of 'Jake's' creative talents would have been helpful. For young people with ADHD, attempts to study at college can be met with difficulty and failure, and as Dunne and Moore point out, success for 'Jake' was only made possible within a framework of independence combined with supported living. From 'Jake's' account, Dunne and Moore identified a need for development of self-management skills and a more integrated response from social and medical institutions to meet the needs of children with ADHD at significant transition stages of school life and into the workplace.

Although Dunne and Moore did not seek to generalise from 'Jakes' story, clearly his needs had not been met by institutional networks of support during the transition to adulthood, despite a childhood ADHD diagnosis. A similar lack of support has been reported by young women, with a previous history of troubled relationships and social isolation, in their transition to college (Shattell et al. 2008). These stories have elements in common with other transitional stories of ADHD that describe the impact of ADHD on self-esteem, difficulties with friendships and relationships, problems with memory and focus, and inability to plan and organise lives (Kelley et al. 2007). On the strength of such reports Kelley et al. recommended institutional forms of support including psychosocial interventions, skills training, education and vocational support to help with planning futures. At key transitions to adulthood, they argue, this should include the provision of both interpersonal and material support, tailored to individual needs and backed up by personal counselling. Kenny (2016) has reiterated this need for personalised support suggesting that it is managed by multidisciplinary teams that are informed by the personal experience of children and adolescents themselves.

The findings of studies such as these have given individuals the opportunity to voice their personal experiences which is important because they have provided rich insights into the lives of people who have a diagnosis of ADHD. Dunne and Moore (2011: 353) have observed, that 'asking people to tell their own stories gives access to personal and idiosyncratic understanding' and it is noteworthy that other qualitative researchers have identified the issue of unmet needs at key transitions, many arguing that this has lasting consequences for young people and adults with ADHD (see also Kenny 2016). The findings and practical suggestions of such research identify areas where improvements might better enable the transitions of young people with ADHD through school and college and onwards into the workplace (Kelley et al. 2007).

Privileged Insights or Negotiated Meanings?

Many constructionist narrative researchers have taken the view that 'the social world is an interpretive one, consisting of multiple realities' and that 'Narratives of experience allow us to gain a deeper understanding of distinct contexts via local and personal experience' (Dunne and Moore 2011: 353) so this means narratives tell us as much about the circulation of meanings in discourse and how people interpret them as they do about people's lives. For example, 'Jake's' story indicates that being different is a cultural problem. 'Jake's' highly visible conduct issues and special needs combined with his 'gay' identity defined him as 'Other' in more than one sense. His story, as recounted by Dunne and Moore, draws on these issues in their interpretation of 'Jake's' problems. As we discussed in Chapters 1 and 2, knowledge and meaning are produced and defined within an 'episteme' or 'regime of truth' and it is within such broader cultural contexts of meaning that people understand their lives and learn to recognise themselves (Foucault 1970). In other words, the parameters for who or what we might be are produced by culture and in 'Jake's' case by his sexuality and his diagnosis of ADHD. There are several kinds of subject positions that could be attributed to 'Jake' from this story, some of these are pathologised, such as those inherent in accounts of an impaired victim of unmet needs, or as a bullied and damaged child, or as a troubled adolescent. On the other hand he could be described as a creative individual and talented survivor. Cultural meanings and the identities produced by them are never singular: There are different interpretations and versions of truth that circulate in discourse, some of which are more dominant and some more negative than others, and people have to navigate their way through them in their everyday social interactions. Goodley and Rapley (2001: 230) have observed, for example, that despite the existence of dominant and pathologising constructions, 'being socially constrained does not preclude being creative. Where there is power, there is also, inevitably, resistance'. Along these lines, we value the plurality of alternative meanings that arise from accounts of personal experience and how these circulate as discourse resources that enable people to actively take up or, indeed, to resist a range of different interpretations of their lives and social identities.

We continue here from the assumption that there are cultural constructions of meaning that shape how people understand or describe their experiences and the context of social interaction is a significant aspect of how this is played out in narratives. As Gergen and Ness (in O'Reilly and Lester 2016: 510) have put it, 'meaning is …a continuously emerging achievement' and one that is worked for in the micro-politics of social interaction. With this in mind, we describe our discursive approach to a narrative of personal experience in 'Anna's' story, below.

Anna's Story: A Family Narrative of ADHD

This story was told to Alison Davies in an interview with 'Anna' who described her two sons who have ADHD and ADD. This research formed part of Davies's doctoral research on parents' experiences of having a child with ADHD (see Chapters 4 and 5; Davies 2014). The examples we use here are drawn from the original data from this interview, unless otherwise referenced (see Davies and Horton-Salway 2016, for the full and definitive analysis of 'Anna's' story).

The mothers of children with ADHD sometimes identify with their children and this example was interesting because it described one mother's late adult diagnosis. We were interested in her description of her life and experience, how she had talked about her identity and also how she constructed the meaning of ADHD. Anna described her sons' diagnoses and how these events had led to her own identification with ADHD, however the narrative was also shaped around various members of her family and ancestors (see Davies and Horton-Salway; in O'Reilly and Lester 2016). Nielsen (2016: 7) has observed that 'experiences of ADHD unfold in relation to social relationships, family struggles, cultural expectations of suffering, and contemporary expectations of being human'. This was hearable in Anna's story.

Anna explained ADHD as a genetic condition that was 'in the family' (2016: 121) establishing that her sons' problems were inherited rather than social. To support this explanation she referred to similarities that the boys had with her father, but she also identified ADHD-like traits in her mother, sister and aunt. By matching her sons' behaviours and problems with those of diverse family members she constructed the recognisable patterns of inattentive, hyperactive and combined ADHD. This body of evidence was offered to support a genetic explanation. Her own identification with this diagnosis was based on matching her own characteristics to both inattentive and hyperactive traits, describing herself as 'having all this hyperactivity' but also 'worried about my attention span…could never recall things' and being either 'very quiet in class' or as having a tendency to 'interrupt' (2016: 125). Diagnostic matching to the criteria for 'combined ADHD' arose from her identification with the experiences of two sons, each of whom had a different form of diagnosis, ADD and ADHD.

Anna's story of bereavement, grief, addiction and troubled identities was tinged with an awareness of alternative psychosocial interpretations for her sons' troubles. She told of her struggle following her husband's early death, her sons' grief, school difficulties and their substance abuse. The story contained disclosures about alcoholism and other family members who she identified with ADHD symptoms and behaviours. Her interpretation of the social and educational problems that her sons had suffered, were attributed to the lack of an early diagnosis. ADHD, she argued, had contributed to a range of social, medical and personal consequences for her sons and for her own undiagnosed ADHD.

Anna's concern about being blamed for her sons' problems was hearable in the way she told her story. Troubles and pathology were contrasted with expressions of positivity and personal achievement in a competing story of normality. This was not a normalisation of the traits of ADHD such as found in media or in fathers' representations of 'boisterous boys' and 'hyperactive' masculinity (Chapters 3 and 5). This was a normalisation of Anna's own mothering and parenting skills evidenced by her references to her other 'four normal children' (2016: 121) and 'two very normal births' for the sons with ADHD (2016: 124). This functions in her story as resistance to a 'pathologised' interpretation of her family, one that might define them as dysfunctional, one that blames her for substance abuse during pregnancy, birth trauma, or bad parenting. Her story informs us that she was very well able to distinguish between what is normal and what is not and has raised several 'normal' children.

Davies and Horton-Salway (2016: 129) indicated that Anna's awareness of the potential for 'mother-blame' (see also, Singh 2004), tells us a great deal about 'the micro-politics of [women] talking about their children's health'. These gendered cultural imperatives that mothers bear greater responsibility for children's health and well-being were apparent in Chapter 4 and echo in the focus on mothers in media representations of ADHD (see Chapter 3). These cultural biases are further compounded by the subject position of lone mother and this combines with other stereotypes of parenting that are inherent in the discourse of

ADHD. Anna's concerns to construct an account of family normality make sense in the light of potential mother-blame and 'how the story might look' to others (2016: 129). This was more apparent with her disclosure about her own history of alcoholism, expressing a concern that 'some people might look at the family circumstances and think duh duh duh'. In other words, she understands that these problems could easily be attributed to family events, dysfunction and personal troubles and not ADHD at all. By comparison, we notice that there might be alternative interpretations of 'Jake's' story (in Dunne and Moore 2011) to explain his decline at secondary school. This is not to contradict the interpretations that were made by 'Jake' or the authors of the study, but rather to emphasise that there can always be alternative interpretations when talking about lives and selves. It is also normative and commonplace that people who tell their stories are likely to be aware of how things might appear differently to other people. This must be especially so when talking of controversial topics and when navigating stigmatised identities. Anna's construction of her own version of events and her resistance to threatening or discrediting alternatives demonstrates that these culturally meaningful concerns impacted upon her world of experience as she narrated it to Alison Davies.

Narrative is as much about these kinds of micro-politics of the social interaction and the construction of a personal view as it is about describing reality. 'Anna's' resistance to discreditable alternatives is an understandable response that anyone might have, especially in talking about difficult life experiences, ADHD or any other mental health category. With accounts of mental illness, health or disability categories there is so much more at stake, including stigma and unwanted definitions of abnormal selves and identities that have their origins in cultural norms, values and stereotypes. It therefore seems significant to us that Anna talked about her embarrassment regarding a late diagnosis of ADHD, commenting that she was 'ashamed to be discovered'. This tells us something about her understanding of the category, ADHD as stigmatising or how she had managed to 'pass for normal' until this diagnosis was obtained (Goffman 1963). Whatever was implied by this expression of 'shame', rather than taking her account as a reflection of an emotional state, we note that she was clearly orienting to the social aspect of being someone with a diagnosis of ADHD, particularly as an older woman. However much she was 'ashamed', she clearly interprets the label of ADHD to be a better alternative than the negative stereotype of 'a batty old woman' (2016: 126). Her use of this latter expression conveys much about the cultural conflation of older women with mental health issues. Such negative and stigmatising social stereotypes such as 'blameworthy mother' or 'batty old woman' are categories that are embedded within the gendered norms of culture and they are powerful because they circulate in discourse and construct subject positions that can be attributed to people or taken up by them (Singh 2004; Ussher 2010). For Anna these are stereotypes to be strongly resisted in telling her story.

Stigmatising stereotypes arising from ADHD are concerns that have also been reported by children, by young adults such as 'Jake' and by older women such as 'Anna' and other adults with ADHD. As we observed earlier, Ilina Singh and her colleagues at the 'Voices Project' (2012) described children's accounts of being isolated, bullied and ridiculed by their school peers because of their ADHD. This certainly chimes with 'Jake's' story (above) as he had been medicated for conduct issues and had acquired a number of potentially stigmatising labels by the time he had reached adolescence. The sense of hidden problems and potential ridicule identified by the children in Singh et al. (2012) is also hearable in Anna's story. Both attentional and conduct aspects of children's and adult's behaviours and problems are potential sources of social difficulty. The children in Singh's study reported wanting to fit in and avoid moral judgement and stigma, sentiments that were also expressed by adolescents in Honkasilta et al. (2015). It is therefore not surprising that avoiding moral condemnation should be a concern arising in Anna's story.

It is true that the narratives of adults such as Anna describe how they identified with ADHD and they provide insightful retrospection on how their problems might be defined by others, but they also demonstrate considerable resistance to alternative negative definitions of ADHD. This was the case in children's accounts of their personal experiences at school (Singh et al. 2012) and, in other studies where we have observed, this is typically indicated by using 'positive talk' (for example,

When women such as Anna speak of their past and current troubles, many construct transformational narratives and finish on an optimistic note (Davies and Horton-Salway, 2016. O'Dell, Stenner, Horton-Salway and Davies, 2016).We also noted one of the optimistic conclusions to 'Jakes' story, where 'Jake reflected upon his 'diagnosis' and identified the positive aspects of ADHD as being outgoing, humorous, stubborn and optimistic' (Dunne and Moore, 2011: 360). Representing lives and selves to others involves the 'micro-politics' of engaging in social interactions. For example, Dunne and Moore were careful to note that 'Jake' 'may well have put a 'positive spin' on a story that was otherwise too difficult to recount in its grim, harsh reality'. We would agree that the demonstration of 'optimism' or 'positive talk' in a narrative can emerge from the context of telling troubles. This is not a cynical observation but, rather, a reference to the cultural imperative of presenting oneself to others in a positive light,and in our view, the need to manage the stigmatising definitions of self that can arise from pathologising cultural discourses. We will continue below to develop these lines of thought as we examine how people construct lives and selves by narrating troubles and contrasting them with transformations.

Fig. 6.1 Troubles and transformations

Kenny 2016). Anna's story of ADHD reflects on former troubles, unmet needs and stigma and contrasts these with her abilities and positive attributes (Davies and Horton-Salway 2016). Amidst the troubles-telling, there were references to achievements in later life, such as her success as a mature student,

> 'it was quite a challenge…I can't recall facts until I go back and painfully look them all up again uhm but it was a joy for me to go back to studying …I went back to college encouraged by somebody else uhm when I was about forty eight I think'. She described her abilities and skills, 'oh my brain is just going fifty to a dozen about things and I'll have a list of things to do which is actually quite a good way to manage'; 'I'm very active I'll always be thinking of something else or three things at once' and she told of her academic excellence, for example, 'but I have achieved I got a distinction for my Masters which surprised me'. (Extract from 'Anna's' interview with Alison Davies)

'Anna's' positive comments followed a catalogue of extreme troubles and struggle so the overall shape of her narrative trajectory was, in the end, 'progressive' as she spoke of overcoming obstacles to achieve these successes (cf. Gergen and Gergen 1986). This narrative transformed Anna into a survivor and a person to be celebrated, rather than a victim or even the perpetrator of her sons' problems (Fig. 6.1).

Troubles and Transformations: The Micro-politics of Narrating Lives and Selves

Riessman (1990, 1993), Crossley (2000), and a host of other social constructionist narrative theorists are agreed that stories about self and experience are always partial and selective. Along similar lines, Dunne and Moore (2011: 353) described their own representation of 'Jake's' story as 'to some extent fictional, because although we have attempted to 'capture' his story in textual representation and in interpretation, personal stories can never be fully replicated and something changes or is always lost in the final textual telling'. We are also aware that our account of Anna's narrative (also in Davies and Horton-Salway 2016) will be a partial view and we acknowledge that any description of the past or a researcher's representation of that should be seen as selective and constructed, depending on what is described. All stories and descriptions are situated in the cultural and interactive context of telling: 'narratives [of experience] reflect the meaning which the authors at any given point in time—consciously or unconsciously—attribute to earlier events in their own lives' (Hannas 2015: 6). At any point in their lives, people will interpret their past lives and identities in terms of their current understandings and the demands of the situated context. Biographical narratives can therefore change over time and in this sense, we regard narrative understanding as ongoing, fluid and unfinished. Narrative accounts do, however, make visible the taken for granted cultural ideas that circulate in discourse, described by Gubrium and Holstein (2001: 8–9) as the 'culturally recognizable images and culturally-endorsed formats' that shape narratives. They are not 'conjured up out of thin air' but they are based on normative forms that arise from culture, in social settings, clinical institutions, online forums and research interviews.

Story Formats

We have identified some common themes in the way that adults have described lives and selves when talking about ADHD. For example, in a clinical setting, Young et al. (2008) examined the reports of adults who described their lives prior to diagnosis of ADHD describing, how they coped, the impact of diagnosis, their adjustment and the effect of medication. They identified childhood difficulties, feeling different, being relieved at diagnosis but angry and sad about wasted years. Young et al. explained this by using Murphy's six stage process of adjustment to diagnosis involving relief and optimism, denial, anger and resentment, grief, mobilization, and accommodation (Murphy 1995; in Young et al. 2008). This study identified narratives of struggle with pathways to diagnosis and eventual triumph over adversity through successful medical treatment, cognitive behavioural therapy and adjustment (Young et al. 2008: 493–503). The shape and direction of these theorised stages of adjustment conforms to the recognisable 'progressive' narrative structure, where former obstacles are overcome and people emerge as transformed (Gergen, in Wetherell et al. 2001: 254). Since the accounts in Young et al's study were from patients in a clinical setting, it is perhaps not surprising that the stories typically pivot around the success of medical interventions. As Nielsen (2016: 4) suggests 'a diagnosis offers a certain narrative, into which the individual's life-trajectory is interpreted'. Along these lines, Wynne et al. (1992) described diagnosis as a pivot that 'reifies' a condition and triggers a retrospective review, linked to a search for causes.

Gubrium and Holstein (2001: 16) have described institutional contexts such as clinical and therapeutic ones as 'going concerns', meaning that local discourse environments generate specific kinds of formats for 'successful' narratives. The success of medical interventions is one such patterned story within a clinical context. Likewise, 'progressive' narratives are a commonly recognised story structure embedded in culture. Progressive or transformative stories are not limited to health discourse, but when they do occur in the context of troubles telling, transformational talk often pivots around a significant event or intervention such as a diagnosis of ADHD, or for instance Chronic Fatigue Syndrome (Horton-Salway 1998, 2001). 'Recovery narratives' might pivot around 'rock bottom' stories like those that feature in alcohol support groups (Denzin 1987a, b) or else a turning point might be located in an institutionalised program of 'improvement' such as therapies or addiction support organisations (Gubrium and Holstein 2001).

Fleischmann and Miller (2013) described how 'progressive' narratives of ADHD in an online group pivoted around an adult diagnosis. The 'progressive' narratives shared by adults in the online groups can be seen as one example of a 'going concern' where adults share similar stories about the moment of insight and the recognition of ADHD as the cause of current and past difficulties. Stories such as this are structured around an evaluation of past events up to a turning point like the progressive or regressive 'before and after' structures that are also a feature of many illness narratives (Horton-Salway 1998, 2001). Such stories enable people to contrast previous selves with transformed selves. In some cases this is a story of 'spoiled identity' or deterioration but in Fleischmann and Miller's study, the adults in the online group had transformed their 'spoiled identities' by representing themselves as successful survivors. This allowed them to resist being defined by impairment narratives and the negative stereotypes of ADHD (cf. 'Jake's' story in Dunne and Moore 2011). Story formats such as these are the kinds of 'going concerns' that are defined by the interests of a group or institution and they are regularly rehearsed in specific contexts (Gubrium and Holstein 2001).

Acts of Resistance

Resistance, we have seen, is a significant aspect of ADHD discourse. Mishler (2005) has referred to narrative acts of resistance as does Boschner (2000: 271) who argues that forms of resistance 'counter the domination of canonical discourse', which in this case might be medicalised or impairment narratives. For example, the 'problem saturated picture of ADHD' was identified by Kenny's research in an educational setting (2016: 121). Impairment narratives are sometimes embedded in a particular institutional order and they might contribute to the body of discourse that makes up that institution, for example, psychiatry. Acts of resistance to this take the form of widely politicised movements such as those concerned to promote 'neurodiversity' and resistance to 'normalizing ideology' (Gray 2001: 1254; see also Chapter 2 of this volume). The online communities in Fleischmann and Miller's study do share accounts of troubles, but they, like 'Anna's' story (above), also share stories of survivorship, difference, uniqueness, and even celebrate giftedness, which is reminiscent of accounts that circulate in the 'neurodiversity' movement. These kinds of discourses resist pathologising and 'deficit' definitions of self that are generated in medicalised conditions such as autism and other mental health categories (O'Dell and Brownlow 2015; see also Cromby et al. 2013).

Transformational narratives typically function to construct changed or alternative identities. For example, one such representation of a 'true' self as liberated from ADHD, implies separation and distance, for example 'Until I knew about this condition, I assumed that everything was part of my personality' (Young et al. 2008: 496). This transformed version of the self was brought about after diagnosis and medical intervention. The same participant also gave an account of 'acceptance', constructing ADHD as an authentic part of the true self, 'It's all part of me and I'm quite happy the way I am.' (2008: 497). In Nielsen's research (2016: 7) separating the self from ADHD was identified as a way of distancing the self from an entity. Although variability and conflicts are apparent in accounts of self-as-separate from ADHD but also part-of-ADHD, it is important to see them as contextual. In the context of transformational narratives these two positions are described as stages of acceptance, relief and embracing a new identity that has made sense of past troubles.

Descriptions of positivity, personal coping and self-understanding are common themes in adults' accounts and are reported as ways of acting upon ADHD, rather than being the victim of impairment. Kenny (2016: 127) has argued that the creation of positive narratives is an important way of enabling young people to focus on strengths and achievements that will counter the more usual problem saturated accounts of themselves that they usually encounter. Likewise, adults with ADHD in the Netherlands (Schrevel et al. 2016: 45) wanted their strengths and creativity recognised more, to be 'accepted for who they are, including shortcomings, and appreciated for their gifts and competences'. They identified their maturity and self-knowledge as the key to control and being able to manage their interactions with the social world, as did the women who were interviewed for a UK study of women and ADHD by O'Dell et al. (2016). An 'appreciation of the strengths of having ADHD' also arose in the accounts of women who had a diagnosis over the age of sixty (Henry and Jones 2011: 246). Although women talk of their difficulties at work, in the family and with relationships they also speak of creative strategies and their ability to manage problems. Such transformations and personal coping were contrasted with accounts of prior and ongoing troubles and struggles in the narratives of women in O'Dell et al. (2016).

ADHD as a 'Transformational Resource' in the Narratives of Women

Women's narratives of ADHD are rich and layered (O'Dell et al. 2016). In this study, women gave accounts of their experiences as part of a *British Academy* funded discourse study. The following discussion is based on the final research report and draws on examples of interview data from the study.[1] There were many interesting aspects of the women's stories, but here we will focus on one aspect that is significant from a discursive perspective. We consider how ADHD was used as a 'transformational resource' that enabled women to understand and re-construct their past lives and troubled identities.

Troubles

In telling their stories of troubles women were able to re-construct more positive representations of self and resist stigmatising ones. This aspect of narrative appeared in Anna's story and we note that it occurs in other studies of personal experience that we have discussed above. The women in O'Dell et al's study were encouraged to use a biographical structure as a framework to tell their story retrospectively. Looking back to childhood and describing their progression through lives in school, college, work, family or partner relationships, the women talked of difficulties and troubles in childhood, school, college and work transitions and also in adult lives with family, work, relationships and parenting. Like 'Anna' (above and in Davies and Horton-Salway 2016) problems sometimes included substance abuse and mental health problems, for example, 'they inter-interpreted my behaviour as, um, depression, anxiety, eating disorder' (O'Dell et al. 2016: Participant 6), or 'once I started. I wasn't able to have a couple of glasses of wine to chill out. I, I just carried on going until I passed out' (2016: Participant 3). Others referred to significant struggles at school, college or work and difficulties with relationships and disorganised or chaotic home lives. Explanations of ADHD as a problem with the brain featured accounts of difference, not fitting in, isolation and feelings of abnormality, 'when you have ADHD nothing is normal' (Participant 2), 'I felt like an alien' (O'Dell et al. 2016: 5), 'I felt that I was not an adequate human being' (O'Dell et al. 2016: 5) and 'I just thought I was just a strange person with lots of weird quirks' (Participant 4).

We observed that these accounts were very similar to the issues identified in previous research on women who had an adult diagnosis of ADHD, such as Solden (1995) who identified depression, anxiety and a constant battle with chaos as common themes. Gender roles have compounded women's problems because, in addition to their difficulties with paid work, women might be expected to take on the bulk of the household organisational responsibilities and care for children (Solden 1995). These multiple demands represent a challenge to the most organised of women and those who have additional mental health needs struggle just to keep up a façade of coping and normality. As Solden points out, 'passing for normal' requires extraordinary problem solving abilities, especially for those with challenging careers (Solden 1995). But this, she contends, is achieved at great cost to their health.

Identification with ADHD

Diagnosis, self-diagnosis or realisation of ADHD was, for most women in O'Dell et al. (2016) the means of understanding and making sense of their past experiences and current lives. Their identities as the mothers of children with ADHD were quite often the means by which they identified with ADHD, as with 'Anna's' story, above, and some of the parents in Chapters 4 and 5 of this volume. Some identification was accomplished in descriptions of a specific child, 'I mean I think because I have a son that is a mini-me' and 'from a very young age I knew my son had issues' (O'Dell et al. 2016: Participant 2). This echoes 'Anna's' story (above) and comments by 'Paula' (see Chapter 4) who identified with both hyperactive and attentional ADHD and described the more hidden aspects of that as a problem:

> When I was a child I never sat still although I read a lot I would be I'd have music on or I'd be fiddling or[I'd be doing something… at school I was quite day-dreamy I always remember missing half the lessons cos I was watching what was going on out the window… I'm quite sure that there is ADHD in me and I'm quite impulsive at times… the trouble is it is hereditary and I think there are lots of people that have gone undiagnosed and you know it's harder for women I think than it is for men… I've got the TV on and I'm on the computer and I've got a book I'm doing three or four different things but they're not obvious things to anybody. (Interview with Paula, adapted from Davies 2014)

Identifying with a child who has ADHD involves making self-comparisons as with 'Anna's' story, and by tracing symptoms and traits as genetic through a line of family inheritance, 'My brother has certainly has got traits of it but not to the severity that me, my dad and my son have it' (O'Dell et al. 2016: Participant 2). This woman also portrayed her daughter as more manageable, 'her mind is up here…then I get cross 'will you concentrate?' cos she's gone off in Lalaland but I think it's definitely more manageable'. Identification with ADHD was often built on gendered representations that defined both masculine and feminine behaviours 'I was definitely more boisterous I more associate with the boys than the girls… that's who I am but I would say the ADHD manifests itself more in a boyish, boisterous I would be having physical fights with the boys…'. Another woman represented herself as being atypical and less feminine, 'I don't really feel particularly female'… 'I was always a bit of a tomboy' (Participant 4). While fathers' identification with their sons' hyperactive ADHD (in Chapter 5) had risked their own status as good fathers to show that they had superior understanding of

ADHD, they had also used a more traditional discourse of 'macho' masculinity to depict themselves as 'normal' men with high energy levels and competence in a public facing role (Davies 2014; and Chapter 5, this volume). However, women's narratives of hyperactive type ADHD, implicate them in a double jeopardy of behavioural misconduct and lack of femininity that, according to their own definitions, threaten their identities as 'good mothers'. Their awareness of this was hearable in the way they constructed their accounts to manage these risks to their identities.

Pivotal Events

The pivotal moment (or realisation) of self-recognition for many women was frequently associated with the diagnosis of a child, 'the reason I got diagnosed was…my 13 year old was diagnosed with ADHD last June' (O'Dell et al. 2016: 6). This mother had re-interpreted her past difficulties in terms of ADHD and she described how self-understanding had generated the momentum to fight as an advocate for her child. This account of her struggle for the recognition of her child's ADHD positioned him as 'a spirited child, but no-one would have it'. Her fight for recognition was described as a therapeutic process through which past injuries and negative experiences could be healed, 'I almost feel that as I work through his problems with him, and do the things that he needs, I am healing the little girl inside of me' (O'Dell et al. 2016: 6). Mothers, spoke this way of being advocates for their children with ADHD, 'I step up and speak to his teacher about it and fight his corner' (2016: 6).

We observed how women described the difficulties arising from troubled lives and their problems meeting the demands of social, educational, work and family lives. They reflected on the meaning of ADHD and how it had 'spoiled' identities and damaged self-esteem. However, we noticed that many stories were celebratory and reconstructive using the diagnosis (or realisation and self-diagnosis) of ADHD as a 'transformative resource' to reinterpret their lives and selves. Transformational accounts were sometimes represented as 'before and after' stories, telling about troubles, identifying a realisation or a pivotal moment of transformation, for example, 'getting a diagnosis and recognising it, it's kind of made me look at things differently' (Participant 4). This resonates with ME narratives that pivot around a turning point of identification and diagnosis and denote survivorship (Horton-Salway 1998, 2001). Other kinds of turning points were identified in the lives of these women, for example, 'it almost got to the point where I, I feel like I pretty much hit my rock bottom' (O'Dell et al. 2016: Participant 3). 'Rock bottom' stories describe a pivotal moment that heralds change or transformation in one's life. They are found here in the accounts of women with late diagnosis of ADHD and also in the stories shared by members of Alcoholics Anonymous where Denzin (1987a, b) has described them as a means of re-storying the self around a pivotal moment. In narratives of ADHD diagnosis, 'rock-bottom' stories are structured towards an optimistic progressive trajectory with the self being re-conceptualised as empowered after diagnosis, 'with that comes great strength at the end of the day'; and 'I am more accepting of who I am' (O'Dell et al. 2016: Participants 2 and 3).

In common with previous studies on the experience of ADHD, the women in O'Dell et al. (2016) talked also of their abilities and creativity, 'I really really love what ADHD brings for me' (Participant 3). One woman described herself as 'enthusiastic and funny, and always had good ideas'... 'I love being an adult with ADHD actually'. She went on 'once you've got the control what's left is, um, er, a very quick, creative, innovative mind that is very engaged' (Participant 6). Others also celebrated their difference, 'oh yeah, that's me that's why I did that' and that their 'brain is just wired differently' (Participant 2). Some women represented their diagnosis of ADHD as a positive asset, 'before I always used to see who I was as a flaw' but 'it also you know is something that needs to be celebrated'. It was as though the pivotal moment of recognition allowed a re-interpretation of childhood proneness to distraction that could be transformed into useful alertness that is a positive attribute for an adult; 'because of my ADHD I, I notice everything, you know... I'm really aware of my surroundings...things like that...that's really helped me in the sense of with my job, I will remember things about people and I will notice things' (O'Dell et al. 2016: Participant 3).

Like the fathers, described by Alison Davies in Chapter 5, they represented their own ADHD-like traits as positive attributes that help them to multitask.

The narratives of women in O'Dell et al. (2016) were mostly of the progressive and transformational kind, despite lengthy descriptions of extreme troubles and struggles. But in what sense might this have been a transformation?

In What Sense Are Narratives Transformative?

We do not necessarily regard transformative narratives as a reflection of a 'recuperative' process in themselves but they are a product of narrative form and convention in response to a range of negative representations that circulate about ADHD. Critical feminist researchers such as Winter et al. (2015) see the label of ADHD as a way for overburdened women to cope with the demands placed upon them to perform and excel in multiples roles. They regard women's take up of biological explanations and medical solutions as functional in this sense. Others have interpreted ADHD as a label to justify substance abuse and excuse troublesome conduct in some contexts (Schubert et al. 2009). We think Winter et al. raise important issues about the heavy burdens placed upon women because of unequal gender relations, and Schubert et al. raise equally significant concerns about the misappropriation of the label, ADHD and the misuse of amphetamine medication. However, we did not observe much focus on medicalised solutions in the narratives of most women in O'Dell et al. (2016). On the contrary, many of them had simply described their realisation of having ADHD or diagnosis as helping them to re-shape and transform their understanding of past negative personal experience and to repair damaged self-esteem. Winter et al. have pointed out that women have traditionally been 'the largest consumers of prescribed psychotropic medication' and therefore 'may be particularly inclined to adopt 'internalised' biological explanations of their situation' (2015: 416). While we share their concerns about medicalisation and also agree with Ussher (1991) that the historical bias to define women's distress as mental illness is a significant concern, we observe that this does not necessarily translate to a consistent link between women using biological explanations of ADHD and seeking medical solutions. Unlike the women described in Winter et al. (2015) many of the women in O'Dell et al. (2016) had neither sought ADHD medication to enhance their performance nor as a quick fix to ease their overburdened lives. Like the parents described in Chapters 4 and 5, they appeared generally cautious about medical solutions for themselves or their children. Some described their effective alternative strategies, 'they try to give me anything, I'm always like, no….because I'm quite good at self-management' (O'Dell et al. 2016: 5). Nonetheless, many women, like 'Jake' in Dunne and Moore's study, have described a host of unmet needs throughout childhood, school and at significant transitional points in life. Some were not confident that they would be able to access any support as mature adults even if they felt they wanted to, 'I can't go to the doctor and say, oh by the way I think I've got ADHD. Do you want to diagnose me….what could they do for me?' (O'Dell et al. 2016: 5).

Nonetheless, the women in O'Dell et al. (2016) had mostly interpreted ADHD as a biological phenomenon, and in 'Anna's' story alcohol and substance abuse was even referred to as 'self-medication' (in Davies and Horton-Salway 2016). This medicalised interpretation echoes the use of the label, ADHD that the young offenders (in Schubert et al. 2009) had used to explain amphetamine abuse. However, the women who talked of their ADHD in O'Dell et al. (2016) did not use a biological explanation of ADHD to excuse themselves for past failures or problems. They simply acknowledged a range of social issues as contributing to their difficulties and most of them only sought recognition, support and understanding for their struggle. These women were undoubtedly proud of their abilities and achievements, but they were equally concerned about undiagnosed ADHD and unmet needs, the effects of stigma, social isolation, educational and workplace failures. Some wanted to be able to use their mature self-understanding in a useful way to mentor others, 'I would love to be able to give back because, because it is, you know, something that needs to be embraced and people do need better understanding' (Participant 3). Those women who were also mothers understandably wanted less of a struggle for their children with ADHD.

The women's stories in this study were undoubtedly organised around a troubles-telling (cf. Jefferson 1988) but they were also a celebration of difference and creativity. The construction of positive selves was accomplished to counter the impact of a troubled story and therefore we are inclined to agree with Lomas (2016: 536) that there is a 'cultural expectation that one should be upbeat' that people observe when they communicate with others. People generally work hard at presenting themselves in a positive light even when they are talking about troubling and difficult aspects of life, including a range of health and disability issues such as mothers who resisted the 'tragedy' narrative (in Chapter 4), or in illness narratives of multiple sclerosis (Riessman 1990) or in cancer talk (Wilkinson and Kitzinger 2000: 797). In talking about breast cancer for example, women use positive talk as 'a socially normative moral requirement'. This is complex because women 'who report "thinking positive" also actively resist its moral prescriptions' (2000: 797). Transformational stories of lives and selves are used to resist pathological definitions of self but while resisting these identities they are also conforming to the socially normative requirements to remain optimistic or positive when describing troubles to others (see also Lomas 2016). If these accounts are taken entirely at face value, we are concerned that this can risk overlooking the import of troubles.

Concluding Comments

Cultural constructions of meaning are drawn on as discursive resources when people talk about their experiences of ADHD and we have seen how their social identities are produced within that discourse, how they take up positive subject positions and resist pathologising subject positions through constructing their lives and selves with ADHD as a 'progressive narrative'. One significant aspect of this has been the gendering of ADHD and its differential focus on boys with conduct disorders on the one hand and hidden problems of girls and women on the other hand. Before moving to the final chapter of this book, we pause here to consider how the experiences of people with ADHD have contributed to our understanding of how the meaning of ADHD is constructed

> Across the chapters of this book, we have found it illuminating to pay attention to how the meaning of ADHD and social identities have arisen in culture and local contexts and how they speak to the wider networks of knowledge circulating in science, professional and lay discourse. The discourse of ADHD and the subject positions produced therein have had a considerable influence on how people understand and describe their own personal experience and selves. Resistance to stigmatising, gendered or discrediting stereotypes of self has now become an integral part of the ADHD experience such that adults are enabled to draw on this to build more enabling accounts of lives and selves.

Fig. 6.2 Understanding lives and selves

through narratives of lives and selves. We have examined how these personal narratives are shaped by cultural ideas, against a background of debates about ADHD and stigmatising issues arising from mental health categories (Fig. 6.2).

We conclude this chapter with a summary of the practical and discursive matters we have identified from the research on the experience of adults.

1. Hidden ADHD: Both girls and boys interviewed in Singh et al. (2012) described how they tried to hide their 'performance' problems because of bullying and stigma. In 'Anna's' story, she described herself as 'passing for normal' as an undiagnosed women with ADHD, hiding her problems for fear of ridicule (see also Solden 1995). 'Paula' (in Davies 2014; and Chapter 4 of this volume) described herself as hyperactive, 'doing three or four different things but they're not obvious things to anybody'.
2. Being blamed: Mothers with ADHD, such as 'Anna', may have concerns that they will be blamed for their children's problems because of problems in pregnancy, birth trauma or parenting. These issues are also played out in media representations of ADHD (see Chapter 3) demonstrating that there is a dominant cultural imperative holding mothers accountable for their children's health and well-being.
3. Medicalisation and gender: This can be an issue for both genders because a bias in psychiatric discourse affects them differentially. Boys and men are more likely to be medicalised for conduct disorders that are defined as ADHD while girls and women have been (historically)

less likely to be diagnosed with ADHD but more likely to have their socially derived problems diagnosed as other mental health conditions. For example, 'they inter-interpreted my behaviour as, um, depression, anxiety, eating disorder' (O'Dell et al. 2016: Participant 6). Critical constructionist feminists have also interpreted the increase in diagnosis of ADHD in women as a way of medicalising 'women's misery' while other feminists regard ADHD as overlooked or misdiagnosed in girls and women and are concerned that this is a 'barrier to care'.

4. Unmet needs in ADHD: 'Jake's' story identified unmet needs that arose at transitional stages of his life, despite his early childhood diagnosis of ADHD. His problems had consequences for stigma, self-esteem and a range of practical concerns that were far reaching into adulthood. Women with an adult diagnosis of ADHD also described their lives as a series of troubles arising from unmet needs in childhood. As adults who have had to develop ways of managing, some seem unsure that anything could be done to help, 'I can't go to the doctor and say, oh by the way I think I've got ADHD. Do you want to diagnose me....what could they do for me?' (O'Dell et al. 2016: 5). Research indicated that more institutional support networks would be helpful to help children move between schools and then into work. Kenny has suggested that Educational Psychologists are well placed to empower children by research that allows them to contribute a voice to inform teachers and healthcare teams and by enabling positive narratives that emphasise their strengths and achievements. Schrevel (2015) observes that adults with ADHD tend to choose 'strength based coaching' over public mental healthcare because clients are more empowered by defining their own problems rather than problems being defined by healthcare professionals.
5. Stigma and ADHD: Children, young men and mature women have all described the stigmatising effect of ADHD. Some children in Singh et al. (2012) suffered from 'expected stigma' hiding their diagnosis from others because they thought everyone would laugh at them or 'actual stigma' because they had experienced bullying and teasing from peers. Anna's story and the women in O'Dell et al. (2016) also described the stigmatising effect of ADHD, especially in

their attempts to 'pass for normal' especially in the workplace and feeling that symptoms of ADHD had led to difficult relationships with others.

6. Troubles telling and positive talk: We found that positive talk, optimism and progressive, transformational narratives are used alongside troubles-telling in accounts of ADHD and that they work to resist the predominantly negative discourses of deficit, impairment, abnormality and pathology that are generated by troubles telling and the need to resist stigmatising stereotypes. As Gergen and Gergen (1986) observed, the use of 'progressive narratives offer the opportunity for people to see themselves and their environment as capable of improvement'. Despite the optimistic or positive accounts that people give when they describe their troubles and health problems, it is important not to assume that this necessarily a reflection of what they feel. Face value interpretations of narratives can risk overlooking the practical and personal challenges that arise from ADHD and the ideological dilemmas that arise from talking about ADHD or other mental health issues.

The phenomenon of 'positive talk' has a much wider application than ADHD, so we will revisit this issue in the final chapter where we will also consider the function of positive talk in ADHD and discourse more generally to ask whether this is a form of discursive empowerment and resistance to negative and pathological definitions or simply a cultural imperative to be 'upbeat' that can manifest as a 'tyranny of the positive' (Lomas 2016).

Note

1. We are grateful to the women who participated in the study by O'Dell et al. (2016), who talked about their experiences of ADHD. We also acknowledge the *British Academy* who funded the project and the research team (Dr. Lindsay O'Dell, Professor Paul Stenner, Dr. Mary Horton-Salway and Dr. Alison Davies). Permission was granted for examples of anonymised interview data to be used as examples in this chapter.

References

American Psychiatric Association. (1980). *Diagnostic and Statistical Manual of Mental Disorders III* (3rd ed.). Washington, DC: Author.

American Psychiatric Association. (1987). *Diagnostic and Statistical Manual of Mental Disorders III* (3rd ed., revised). Washington, DC: Author.

American Psychiatric Association. (1994). *Diagnostic and Statistical Manual of Mental Disorders* (4th ed.). Washington, DC: Author.

American Psychiatric Association. (2013). *Attention Deficit and Hyperactivity Disorder*. Available at http://www.dsm5.org/documents/adhd%20fact%20sheet.pdf (Accessed 15 May 2016).

Asherton, P., Timimi, S., & Moncrieff, J. (2010). Is ADHD a valid diagnosis in adults. *British Medical Journal, 340,* 736–737.

Borrill, J. (2000). *All About ADHD*. Mental Health Foundation. Available at http://www.mentalhealth.org.uk.

Boschner, A. (2000). Criteria against ourselves. *Qualitative Inquiry, 6*(2), 266–272.

Connolly, M. (2010). ADHD women and girls: Late diagnosis, little treatment. *ADDitude Magazine*.

Conrad, P., & Potter, D. (2000). From hyperactive children to ADHD adults: Observations on the expansion of medical categories. *Social Problems, 47*(4), 559–582.

Cromby, J., Harper, D., & Reavy, P. (2013). *Psychology, Mental Health and Distress*. Basingstoke, UK: Palgrave Macmillan.

Crossley, M. (2000). *Introducing Narrative Psychology: Self, Trauma and the Construction of Meaning*. Buckingham: Open University Press.

Davidson, M. A. (2008). Literature review: ADHD in adults: A Review of the literature. *Journal of Attention Disorders, 11*(6), 628.

Davies, A. (2014). *It's a problem with the brain: A discursive analysis of parents' constructions of ADHD* (Unpublished Ph.D. thesis). The Open University, Milton Keynes.

Davies, A., & Horton-Salway, M. (2016). The construction of adult ADHD: Anna's story. In M. O'Reilly & J. N. Lester (Eds.), *The Palgrave Handbook of Adult Mental Health* (pp. 117–133). Basingstoke, UK: Palgrave Macmillan.

Denzin, N. K. (1987a). *The Alcoholic Self*. Newbury Park, CA: Sage.

Denzin, N. K. (1987b). *The Recovering Alcoholic*. Newbury Park, CA: Sage.

Department of Education. (2014). *Special Educational Needs and Disability, Code of Practice: 0–25*. London: The Stationery Office (TSO).

Dunne, L., & Moore, A. (2011). From boy to man: A personal story of ADHD. *Emotional and Behavioural Difficulties, 16*(4), 351–364.

Fedele, D. A., Lefler, E. K., Hartung, C. M., & Canu, W. H. (2012). Sex differences in the manifestation of ADHD in emerging adults. *Journal of Attention Disorders, 16,* 109–117. https://doi.org/10.1177/1087054710374596.

Fleischmann, A., & Miller, E. C. (2013). Online narratives by adults with ADHD who were diagnosed in adulthood. *Learning Disability Quarterly, 36*(1), 47–60.

Foucault, M. (1970). *The Order of Things*. London: Tavistock.

Gergen, K. J. (2001). Self-narration in social life. In M. Wetherell, S. Taylor, & S. Yates (Eds.), *Discourse Theory and Practice* (pp. 247–260). London: Sage.

Gergen, K. J., & Gergen, M. M. (1986). Narrative form and the construction of psychological science. In T. R. Sarbin (Ed.), *Narrative Psychology* (pp. 22–44). New York: Praeger.

Gergen, K., & Ness, O. (2016). Therapeutic practice as social construction. In M. O'Reilly & J. N. Lester (Eds.), *The Palgrave Handbook of Adult Mental Health* (pp. 502–519). Basingstoke, UK: Palgrave Macmillan.

Goffman, E. (1963). *Stigma: Notes on the Management of Spoiled Identity*. Englewood Cliffs, NJ: Prentice-Hall.

Gonon, F., Bezard, E., & Boraud, T. (2011). Misrepresentation of neuroscience data might give rise misleading conclusions in the media: The case of attention deficit hyperactivity disorder. *PLoS ONE, 6*(1), e14618. https://doi.org/10.1371/journal.pone.0014618.

Goodley, D., & Rapley, M. (2001). How do you understand "learning difficulties"? Towards a social theory of impairment. *Mental Retardation, 39*(3), 229–232.

Gray, D. E. (2001). Accommodation, resistance and transcendence: Three narratives of autism. *Social Science and Medicine, 53,* 1247–1257.

Groenewald, C., Emond, A., & Sayal, K. (2009). Recognition and referral of girls with attention deficit hyperactivity disorder: Case vignette study. *Child: Care, Health and Development, 35*(6), 767–772. https://doi.org/10.1111/j.1365-2214.2009.00984.x.

Gubrium, J. F., & Holstein, J. A. (Eds.). (2001). *Introduction in Institutional Selves: Troubled Identities in a Postmodern World* (pp. 8–9). New York: Oxford University Press.

Hannas, B. M. (2015). Youths' and adults' stories related to the background for ADHD assessment. *Sage*. Published 10 April 2015. Available at http://sgo.sagepub.com/content/5/2/2158244015579725.

Harwood, V., Jones, S., Bonney, A., & McMahon, S. (2017). Heroic struggles, criminals and scientific breakthroughs: ADHD and the medicalization of child behaviour in Australian newsprint media 1999–2009. *International Journal of Qualitative Studies on Health and Well-being, 12,* 1298262. https://doi.org/10.1080/17482631.2017.1298262.

Henry, E., & Jones, S. H. (2011). Experiences of older adult women diagnosed with attention deficit hyperactivity disorder. *Journal of Women and Aging, 23*(3), 246–262.

Honkasilta, J., Vehmas, S., & Vehkakoski, T. (2015). Self-pathologizing, self-condemning, self-liberating: Youths' accounts of their ADHD-related behavior. *Social Science and Medicine, 150,* 248–255.

Horton-Salway, M. (1998). *Mind and body in the discursive construction of ME: A struggle for authorship of an illness* (Doctoral thesis, Loughborough University).

Horton-Salway, M. (2001). Narrative identities and the management of personal accountability in talk about M.E.: A discursive approach to illness narrative. *Journal of Health Psychology, 6*(2), 261–273.

Horton-Salway, M. (2011). Repertoires of ADHD in UK newspaper media. *Health (London), 15*(5), 533–549.

Horton-Salway, M. (2012). Gendering attention deficit hyperactivity disorder: A discursive analysis of UK newspaper stories. *Journal of Health Psychology, 18*(8), 1085–1099. Published online before print 1 October 2012. https://doi.org/10.1177/1359105312456326.

Jefferson, G. (1988). On the sequential organization of troubles-talk in ordinary conversation. *Social Problems, 35*(4), 418–437.

Johnston, C., Mash, E. J., Miller, N., & Ninowski, J. E. (2012). Parenting in adults with attention-deficit/hyperactivity disorder (ADHD). *Clinical Psychology Review, 32*(4), 215–228.

Kelley, S. D. M., English, W., Schwallie-Giddis, P., & Jones, L. M. (2007). Exemplary counseling strategies for developmental transitions of young women with attention deficit/hyperactivity disorder. *Journal of Counseling and Development, 85,* 173–181.

Kenny, O. (2016). *How do young people diagnosed with ADHD perceive their condition?: An interpretative phenomenological analysis* (Doctoral thesis, University of East London).

Kirschner, S. (2013). Diagnosis and its discontents: Critical perspectives on psychiatric nosology in the DSM. *Feminism and Psychology, 23*(1), 10–28.

Latour, B. (1987). *Science in Action: How to Follow Scientists and Engineers Through Society*. Milton Keynes: Open University Press.

Latour, B. (1989). Cloaking the naked truth. In H. Lawson & L. Appignanesi (Eds.), *Dismantling Truth: Reality in the Post-modern World* (pp. 101–126). London: Weidenfeld & Nicolson.

Latour, B. (1993). *We Have Never Been Modern*. Hemel Hempstead: Harvester Wheatsheaf.

Lomas, T. (2016). Positive psychology—The second wave. *The Psychologist, 29*(7), 536.

Magnusson, E., & Maracek, J. (2012). *Gender and Culture in Psychology: Theories and Practices*. New York: Cambridge University Press.

Mishler, E. G. (2005). Patient stories, narratives of resistance and the ethics of humane care: A la recherche du temps perdu. *Health: An Interdisciplinary Journal for the Social Study of Health, Illness and Medicine, 9*(4), 431–451.

Mueller, A. K., Fuermaier, A. B. M., & Tucha, L. (2012). Stigma in attention deficit hyperactivity disorder. *Attention Deficit Hyperactivity Disorder, 4*(3), 101–114. Published online 8 July 2012. https://doi.org/10.1007/s12402-012-0085-3.

Murphy, K. (1995). *Out of the Fog: Treatment Options and Coping Strategies for Adult Attention Deficit Disorder*. New York: Hyperion.

Nadeau, K. G., & Quinn, P. O. (Eds.). (2002). *Understanding Women with ADHD*. Silver Spring, MD: Advantage Books.

National Institute of Clinical Excellence. (2009). *Attention Deficit Hyperactivity Disorder: Diagnosis and Management of ADHD in Children, Young People and Adults*. London: National Institute for Health and Clinical Excellence. Available at http://www.nice.org.uk/Guidance/CG72 (Accessed 14 September 2017).

Nielsen, M. (2016). *Experiences of ADHD in adults: Morality, temporality and neurobiology*. Aalborg Universitetsforlag (Ph.d.-serien for Det Humanistiske Fakultet, Aalborg Universitet). https://doi.org/10.5278/vbn.phd.hum.00054.

Nussbaum, N. L. (2012). ADHD and female specific concerns: A review of the literature and clinical implications. *Journal of Attention Disorders, 16*(2), 87–100.

O'Dell, L., & Brownlow, C. (2015). Normative development and the autistic child. In M. O'Reilly & J. N. Lester (Eds.), *The Palgrave Handbook of Child Mental Health* (pp. 296–309). Basingstoke, UK: Palgrave Macmillan.

O'Dell, L., Stenner, P., Horton-Salway, M., & Davies, A. (2016). *Narratives of ADHD: A qualitative study of women's narrative accounts of living with ADHD*. Unpublished research report submitted to the British Academy.

O'Reilly, M., & Lester, N. (Eds.). (2016). *The Palgrave Handbook of Adult Mental Health*. Basingstoke, UK: Palgrave Macmillan.

Ponnou, S., & Gonon, F. (2017). How French media have portrayed ADHD to the lay public and to social workers. *International Journal of Qualitative Studies on Health and Well-being, 12*(Suppl. 1), 1298244. https://doi.org/10.1080/17482631.2017.1298244.

Quinn, P. O. (2005). Treating adolescent girls and women with ADHD: Gender-specific issues. *Journal of Clinical Psychology, 61*(5), 579–587.

Rafalovich, A. (2001). Disciplining domesticity: Framing the ADHD parent and child. *The Sociological Quarterly, 42*(3), 373–393.

Riessman, C. K. (1990). Strategic uses of narrative in the presentation of self and illness: A research note. *Social Science and Medicine, 30*(11), 1195–1200.

Riessman, C. K. (1993). *Narrative Analysis*. Newbury Park, CA and London: Sage.

Rose, N. (1998). *Inventing Our Selves: Psychology, Power, and Personhood.* Cambridge, UK: Cambridge University Press.

Schrevel, S. J. C. (2015). *Surrounded by controversy: Perspectives of adults with ADHD and health professionals on mental healthcare*. Doctoral thesis, Vrije Universiteit, Amsterdam.

Schrevel, S. J. C., Dedding, C., Aken, J. A., & Broerse, J. E. W. (2016). 'Do I need to become someone else?' A qualitative exploratory study into the experiences and needs of adults with ADHD. *Health Expectations, 19*(1), 39–48.

Schubert, S. J., Hansen, S., Dyer, K. R., & Rapley, M. (2009). Categories in drug dependence services 'ADHD patient' or 'illicit drug user'? Managing medico-moral membership. *Discourse Society, 20*(4), 499–516.

Shattell, M., Bartlett, R., & Rowe, T. (2008). "I have always felt different": The experience of attention-deficit/hyperactivity disorder in childhood. *Journal of Pediatric Nursing, 23*(1), 49–57.

Sim, M. G., Hulse, G., & Khong, E. (2004). When the child with ADHD grows up. *Australian Family Physician, 33,* 615–618.

Simon, V., Czobor, P., Balint, S., & Meszaros, A. (2009). Prevalence and correlates of adult attention-deficit hyperactivity disorder: Meta-analysis. *British Journal of Psychiatry, 194,* 205–211.
Singh, I. (2002). Bad boys, good mothers, and the miracle of Ritalin. *Science in Context, 15*(4), 577–603.
Singh, I. (2004). Doing their jobs: Mothering with Ritalin in a culture of mother-blame. *Social Science and Medicine, 59*(6), 1193–1205.
Singh, I. et al. (2012). VOICES Study: Final Report. London, UK.
Solden, S. (1995). *Women with Attention Deficit Disorder: Embracing Disorganization at Home and in the Workplace.* Grass Valley, CA: Underwood.
Timimi, S. (2005). *Naughty Boys: Anti-social Behaviour, ADHD and the Role of Culture.* Basingstoke: Palgrave Macmillan.
United Nations. (1990). *Convention on the Rights of the Child.* London: UNICEF UK.
Ussher, J. M. (1991). *Women's Madness: Misogyny or Mental Illness?* Hemel Hampstead: Harvester Wheatsheaf.
Ussher, J. (2010). Are we medicalizing women's misery? A critical review of women's higher rates of reported depression. *Feminism and Psychology, 20,* 9–35.
Waite, R. (2010). Women with ADHD: It is an explanation, not the excuse du jour. *Perspectives in Psychiatric Care, 46,* 182–196.
Wender, P. H. (1987). *The Hyperactive Child, Adolescent, and Adult.* New York: Oxford University Press.
Wender, P. H. (1995). *Attention-Deficit Hyperactivity Disorder in Adults.* New York: Oxford University Press.
Wender, P. H. (1998). Pharmacotherapy of attention-deficit/hyperactivity disorder in adults. *Journal of Clinical Psychiatry, 59*(7), 76–79.
Wender, P. H. (2000). *Attention Deficit Hyperactivity Disorder in Children and Adults.* New York: Oxford University Press.
Wiita, M. D., & Parish, T. G. (2008). ADHD in young adults. *Clinician Reviews, 8*(9), 30–32.
Wilkinson, S., & Kitzinger, C. (2000). Thinking differently about thinking positive: A discursive approach to cancer patients' talk. *Social Science and Medicine, 50*(6), 797–811.
Winter, H., Moncrieff, J., & Speed, E. (2015). "Because you're worth it": A discourse analysis of the gendered rhetoric of the ADHD woman. *Qualitative Research in Psychology, 12*(4), 415–434.

Wynne, L. C., Sheilds, C. G., & Sirkin, M. I. (1992). Illness, family theory, and family therapy: I. Conceptual issues. *Family Process, 31,* 3–18. https://doi.org/10.1111/j.1545-5300.1992.00003.x.

Young, S., Bramham, J., Gray, K., & Rose, E. (2008). The experience of receiving a diagnosis and treatment of ADHD in adulthood: A qualitative study of clinically referred patients using interpretative phenomenological analysis. *Journal of Attention Disorders, 11*(4), 493–503.

Young, S., Toone, B., & Tyson, C. (2003). Comorbidity and psychosocial profile of adults with attention deficit/hyperactivity disorder. *Personality and Individual Differences, 35*(4), 743–755.

7

ADHD as the Product of Discourse

Mary Horton-Salway

In this book we have been concerned with the relationship between cultural meanings and the construction of knowledge and truth through discourse processes. Controversial histories of health categories are a window on the social processes of constructing truths, rendered more apparent when different versions are debated in science and public discourse. ADHD is one such example of a mental health category that has been shaped by a long history of controversy such that its meaning has been constructed as the product of discourse. We broadly concur with the Foucauldian position taken by Nikolas Rose, that 'truth is not only the outcome of construction but also of contestation' (Rose 1998: 55). The processes of social construction and contestation have produced and translated the meaning of ADHD as an 'epiphenomenal' product in more than one sense.

Referring to the construction of expert knowledge, Rose described 'battles over truth' that constitute the factional activity of science. This is the first sense in which the meaning of ADHD is an epiphenomenon. Such truths are produced and circulated in knowledge networks in the form of different 'translations' (Latour 1987). In Chapter 2 we described how different theories of ADHD, biological, psychological

M. Horton-Salway and A. Davies, *The Discourse of ADHD*,
The Language of Mental Health, https://doi.org/10.1007/978-3-319-76026-1_7

and social have produced a range of alternative interpretations for children's behaviours and problems. Historically, these explanations were applied individually and in various combinations in healthcare practice through the frameworks of the biomedical model and the biopsychosocial model. More contemporary theorisations of ADHD combined bio-psycho-social explanations to conceptualise complex causal relationships, a model that is used to inform clinical guidelines on ADHD and other mental health and medical conditions by the UK National Institute of Clinical Excellence (2009, 2016). This approach is now common to other parts of Europe, the USA and across many parts of the globe. By this rationale, ADHD, is seen as arising from the complex interrelation of biological, psychological and social variables and this is the second and more currently 'official' sense in which ADHD can be seen as epiphenomenal.

Within the rationale of this complex model, all kinds of health care in both general and mental health contexts should be based on a multi-perspective approach. However, the history and application of the biopsychosocial model is more complicated as we discussed in Chapter 1. According to Alvarez et al. (2012: 173), the term biopsychosocial was introduced into psychiatry by Grinker in 1954. However, at that point in the history of its application it was used to 'emphasize the biologic against psychoanalytic orthodoxy' and only later did Engel apply the rationale to general medicine in the form of a systemic model. This was introduced into general medical practice in the UK by the Royal College of General Practitioners (1972). In the translation of theory into practice, many have commented that the biopsychosocial model is more of an ideal than a reality because there is little time for practitioners to apply it's rationale in all clinical situations (Herman, cited in Soltile 2005: 401). Furthermore, the links between the sub-systems of the model proposed by Engel are not explicit enough to guide clinical decision-making method in the way that health practitioners would find practical (Alvarez et al. 2012). For this reason Alvarez et al. argue that the term 'model' is misleading while others argue that, in the practice of psychiatry, biopsychosocial is more likely to translate as bio-bio-bio because the psychological and social aspects of mental health have been subordinated to the purposes of biomedicine (Read 2005;

see also Cromby et al. 2013). This has as much to do with the socio-political history of its introduction and its basis in the rationale of positivist science as anything else. Colley (2010) has also commented on the tendency for research on the psychosocial influences that contribute to ADHD to explain causality as a linear process rather than bi-directional or circular. In other words, psychological and social variables are treated as contributory factors to individual biological pathology (see also Cromby et al. 2013). ADHD interventions are therefore based on the idea that the psychosocial environment, in the form of parenting, has room for improvement and that individual behavioural and cognitive or neurophysiological pathology can be transformed with medicine and cognitive behavioural techniques. This approach relies on positivist forms of science and social science that all too often imply linear causation rather than complex dynamic processes. In medical institutions these forms of evidence have historically been prioritised over hermeneutic, meaning-derived understandings and qualitative forms of investigation that would explore personal experience to give service users more of a voice (Lester and O'Reilly 2016).

Sociologically derived theories (Conrad and Potter 2000), and those that are rather more critical of the definitions and treatment of ADHD in psychiatric contexts (Cromby et al. 2013), emphasise the socio-cultural conditions that produced mental health categories in the first place and they challenge the underpinnings of medicalised and individualised interventions. Cromby et al. (2013) are critical of the concept of abnormal psychology that underpins psychiatric categories, while sociologists such as Conrad and Potter (2000) contend that biomedicine can function as a means of social control. For example, 'the medicalisation of masculinity' in ADHD positions boys and men as a threat to the social and moral order (Conrad and Potter 2000). In a similar way, the 'medicalisation of women's misery' has generated a range of 'feminised' mental health categories that have served the purposes of patriarchy and historically defined women's social distress as forms of mental illnesses (Ussher 1991, 2010). Social constructionist explanations such as these emphasise the role of culture and power relations, emphasising how taken for granted truths circulating in discourse constitute and legitimise forms of institutional and consensual governance and forms of intervention or self-improvement projects that function to perpetuate the social and moral order.

We have broadly agreed with these ideas and have investigated how some of these processes play out as discursive phenomena across the chapters of this book. We have found ADHD to be an epiphenomenal product in the sense that it is a meaningful but fluid category arising along with the construction of science knowledge, including the methods and explanatory models that have been applied to produce such truths, as well as cultural representations and forms of discourse in institutional, professional and public domains. Forms of knowledge about ADHD and its subjects have fuelled discourse in the public domain for a century and media representations of the science that underpins these representations are often simplistic and selective. Stories and reports circulate in formats that embody moral and cultural imperatives and they function as a powerful socialising force in the public domain. As such, they are variably taken up, resisted or translated into different versions through the circulation of discourse in the public domain. Since discourse is a powerful form of social action, these processes have consequences for those who are the subjects of its discourse, including how they are treated within healthcare and education and how they are understood and positioned in wider society (Fig. 7.1).

Consumers and Producers of Health Knowledge

As we observed in Chapter 3, the media have often used simplified versions of biological or psychosocial explanations of ADHD. These resonate with the biological and psychosocial repertoires of ADHD that were identified in Chapter 2, arising from historicised discourse. They are frequently used in an oppositional and polemic way, in the form of moral panics about the conduct of children and adults with ADHD, bad parenting or the ethics of medication, versus science reports of ADHD research that explain cognitive performance and social conduct in terms of biogenetic impairment. In the UK newspaper media psychosocial repertoires have been dominant, although this might differ in

The themes that we have focused on in this book were identified in chapter one and have been traced across the chapters of this book and informed our analysis. They were the construction of ADHD, social identities, gendering in the discourse of ADHD and forms of discursive resistance.

- We have mapped out the construction of ADHD across a range of discourse contexts through biological, psychological and social science theories (in chapter 2), in media representations (in chapter 3), in the discourse of parents who have children with ADHD (in chapters 4 and 5) and in the voices of personal experience in accounts of children and adults (in chapter 6).
- We identified competing representations of ADHD that are robust and often polarised in argument. Biological and psychosocial accounts are associated with different kinds of identity constructions that function to support competing explanations of ADHD.
- Identity constructions take the form of extreme subject positions such as disruptive boys, blameworthy mothers, absent fathers, criminal deviants, victims, or celebrity and fictional heroes. These are produced and resisted as subject positions in discourse about ADHD.
- Gender stereotypes are a significant aspect of discourse about ADHD and they are common in the way that subjects are represented in all of the contexts we analysed.
- Pathologising and stigmatising definitions are also woven through the discourse of ADHD as a significant aspect of how people understand its meaning. These are often linked with gender sterotypes.
- The discourse of ADHD is dilemmatic: When people talk about ADHD they attend to multiple contradictory concerns and navigate through a range of opposing stereotypes and cultural imperatives.
- Forms of discursive resistance are a significant aspect of all of the above. The phenomenon of resistance (or 'contestation' as Rose puts it) is a mundane aspect of constructing truths but this is compounded by the existence of controversy, the decline of scientific authority and greater public access to information networks.
- Forms of resistance in ADHD resonate with the discourse of neurodiversity and the cultural politics of impairment, matters that are relevant to wider critiques of mental health categories.

Fig. 7.1 Book themes revisited

other forms of media such as television or the Internet. Researchers in other parts of the world have reported a different media bias, for example towards biological in the US (Schmitz et al. 2003) and towards psychoanalytic explanations in France (Ponnou and Gonon 2017). Ponnou and Gonon found fewer simplistic biological representations in recent years, a trend that seems likely to follow contemporary, complex theorisations of ADHD.

There is some suggestion that children have 'contradictory views on ADHD that are reflective of portrayals of ADHD in the media.' (Kenny 2016). Kenny notes a finding of Singh et al.'s *Voices* study (2012) that children in the UK and US appear to have different concerns, about their conduct or their academic performance, respectively. This suggests a difference in emphasis between these nations in cultural priorities and imperatives that influence the children's concerns. Such priorities also appear to dominate in the UK media, for example, where there is a greater focus on social conduct and conformity rather than performance (Horton-Salway 2011, 2012).

In the UK media, we found that newsworthy stories are typically based on extreme or atypical representations that were selective, sometimes openly partisan and often sensationalist. The public are not always well informed, even by science reports that are based on 'breakthrough science' as Gonon et al. (2011) have argued (Chapter 3). One reason could be that research on ADHD has sometimes reduced complex circular, biopsychosocial processes to the form of uni-directional linear causality (Colley 2010), while (Schrevel et al. 2016: 2) observed that research itself is 'polarised with respect to the facts and values underlying ADHD and its treatments'. Where there are media reports of complex research studies, these have often been reduced to misleading headlines or slogans that can imply blame rather than nuanced explanation. Colley has expressed concerns that the media's framing of ADHD as a polemic can induce both lay people and health professionals to respond to this in defensive ways. The 'blame game' is, as we have seen, thoroughly embedded in the discourse of ADHD and both lay and professional people respond to it accordingly. We have observed that parents respond to being positioned this way by resisting psychosocial explanations of blameworthiness (Chapters 4 and 5; see also Barnes and Power 2012) and some health practitioners respond by blaming public pressure for the rise in over-prescription (see Chapter 3).

It might appear something of a paradox that a reported demand for medicalised solutions in the form of prescriptions, should thrive alongside the decline in public confidence of expert knowledge and practice. A report on public trust, by the UK Medical Research Council (2016) identified a significant decline in public trust of health professionals, scientists in universities, pharmaceutical companies, industry and also medical charities between the years 2009–2015. Public confidence is surely undermined by media framing of controversy since hardly a week goes by without headline stories of some form of health related scare, scandal or contrary advice that undermines the legitimacy of earlier health policy and practice. Changes, contradictions and competition between researchers are an integral part of the legitimate progress of science and medicine but the public have become so much more aware of the processes of claim, counter-claim and controversy that conflicting headlines about health research leads people to perceive it as unreliable (Caulfield et al. 2014). The UK Medical Research Council (2016) has recently expressed a concern about how the media have contributed to public scepticism about science and health research.

The decline of public confidence in forms of expertise and authority also arises from greater public access to a plurality of information sources on the internet whether or not they are reliable (Felt 2015) and, as Kata (2010) observes, this increases the possibility of unreliable and damaging misinformation. There is, however, also widening access to health user groups, social movements, and public access to the same forms of research that inform professional education and training (Barnes 1999: 5). This combines, in neo-liberal societies with the idea of citizens as 'consumers' and a growing sense of entitlement to choice in the form of person-centred care (Epstein 2000). In the UK, for example, Marian Barnes (1999) identified the consumerist ideology of successive governments as the driver for 'empowering' individuals as consumers of healthcare. This, combined with the pressures placed on parents as a result of educational exclusion of unruly children (Davies

2014), and 'anti-stigma' campaigns promoting brain explanations (Cromby et al. 2013) could explain why demands for prescriptions have risen in the UK. However, it is far from clear that the parents of children with ADHD are comfortable with this solution as we will discuss later (see also Davies 2014; and Chapters 4 and 5 of this volume).

For whatever reasons, the public are no longer inclined to be passive recipients of healthcare advice any more than they are the passive recipients of media representations of other forms of science, but they are an increasingly active part of how health information and forms of knowledge are discussed, defined, challenged and circulated in the public domain. The dissemination of health information in printed, digital and audio-visual forms is a burgeoning industry fuelling these processes, such that members of the public can engage with public information and health websites or independent support groups to inform themselves about health matters. Barnes (1999: 2) pointed out that community action has 'become a challenge to professional and expert authority'. The public are able to take up, question and resist different translations of knowledge and truth that, before the digital revolution, might have been represented to previous generations of the public as 'a ship in a bottle' (Collins 1985).

This is a burgeoning aspect of what Bruno Latour (1987) referred to as the networks of knowledge that actors engage with to produce different translations of truth. In post-modern 'knowledge-rich' societies the widespread circulation of discourses available online has contributed to the (often confusing) plethora of opinions and research findings that inform parents and those adults who have come to identify with an ADHD diagnosis. It is within this cultural and social context that they seek enlightenment and support. The discourse of ADHD meshes with the wider discourse of mental illness; the discourse of parenting and the cultural imperatives of neo-liberalism to inform the manner in which members of the public take up ideas about ADHD and how they use them to define their own personal experience and that of others. This was evident in the narratives we have discussed in the chapters of this book.

The Family: Forms of Institutional and 'Self-Governance'

Alison Davies described (in Chapters 2, 4 and 5) how the 'psy' disciplines have continued to set the benchmarks for normality that regulate family life and how the 'professionalisation' of child-rearing defines the knowledge and skills required for good parenting. These influences pervade family policy and institutional interventions such as 'early years' interventions and 'parenting programmes' that are designed to inform the public what it means to be a good mother or father, what is considered 'normal', and how they should manage their children (Davies 2014). We have also seen in Chapters 2 and 3 how parents and families have been positioned as problematic by the explanatory repertoires of ADHD arising from theory, institutional practice and the cultural imperatives that circulate in discourse. Kenny (2016) refers to this as a problem saturated approach to ADHD that has, historically, not taken much account of how children make sense of ADHD or how they identify with it. From our understanding of parent's accounts in Davies (2014) and in Chapters 4 and 5 of this book, this description could just as easily apply to the experience of their parents.

According to Bailey (2014: 98) parenting in general has been transformed into a 'project' that has the aim of conforming to 'medically conceived truths' and 'specialist knowledge' so it is not surprising that parents talk about their management of children with ADHD by describing their parenting as a 'project' of self-education. Taking up their own pursuit of knowledge about ADHD, through their own research and in relation to support networks, the mothers in Chapter 4 of this volume talked of developing 'expert' skills to contribute to professional partnerships with schools and medical practitioners (see also Rafalovich 2001a, 2004/2008). Parents' descriptions of 'in principle' compliance with professionals are however combined with stories of resistance and a critical stance to any professional methods that worked against their parental experience. They maintained that ordinary parenting does not work when applied to children with ADHD and prioritised parenting experience over professional advice by limiting the power and scope of parenting class and dismissing some of its methods, as one parent remarked, 'sticker charts, yeah done that, done that, done that, done that' (Davies 2014: 259). This resistance to institutionalised forms of expertise is not so much a rejection of expert knowledge, per se, but goes hand in hand with the expert or professionalised parent position, in the take up of knowledge about ADHD through online research and support networks. This focus on sharing and the expertise of experience is also observed in the discourse of mental health service users and Cromby et al. (2013) have described how a focus on personal 'distress' can challenge the kinds of treatments offered by mental health services. In online environments, Van Zoonen (2012) points out, that personal experience is afforded more value than evidence based knowledge (see also Versteeg et al. 2017). Nevertheless, the pursuit of parental expertise on ADHD involves the acquisition of science knowledge even though this might be evaluated from an experiential view. As Davies (2014) and Malacrida (2001, 2002) have both observed, mothers give accounts of themselves as skilled managers, and knowledgeable advocates for their children with ADHD. Litt (2004), Bull and Whelan (2006), and Segal (2001) similarly noted a strong emphasis on coping and learning strategies and skills.

The decline of confidence in traditional and institutional forms of expertise combined with increased public engagement with improving forms of self-help might appear paradoxical. The parents who resist the institutional interventions of professional experts often describe their take up of 'professional' forms of knowledge as empowerment but they are likely to be unaware that this could equally be regarded as a consensual form of 'self-governance' in the Foucauldian sense. The discourse of 'mental hygiene' functions as a form of governance 'educating citizens, in their professional roles and their personal lives—in the languages by which they interpret their experiences, the norms by which they should evaluate them, the techniques by which they should seek to improve them' (Rose 1998: 75–76). Even as people work to transform or liberate and empower themselves, they might be using the language of conformity to a 'regime of truth' that requires them to work upon themselves in institutionally specified ways. Against a cultural background of parental scrutiny, self-scrutiny and self-improvement technologies, parents work to manage and resist the negative and stereotypical subject positions that are generated by this discourse of ADHD. They resist the stereotypes of 'blameworthy' mother or absent, disengaged or controlling father captured by the psychosocial repertoire with all its implications of parental blame at the same time as engaging with its gendered and self-improving imperatives.

For both mothers and fathers, the 'good parent' is a, worked for but, difficult to sustain position when talking about their children with ADHD. The wider discourse of parenting positions mothers and fathers differently in relation to their children and good parenting is full of contradictions and dilemmas that are fundamentally gendered by cultural norms and imperatives (Chapters 4 and 5). The discourse of parenting a child with ADHD echoes the moral and gendered discourse that positions mothers as more accountable for childcare and health and fathers as the 'invisible' or less accountable parent in health and disability discourse. These imperatives are combined in discourse about ADHD (in the UK) with the traditional ideal of a resident father as the family authority figure because of a focus on ADHD as a 'social conduct' disorder. And yet the good father subject position is tenuous, dilemmatic and precarious and credibility depends on moving skilfully between traditional and contemporary fathering positions. Fathers' subject positions in relation to their fathering role and their relationship with the family therefore appear contradictory in many ways. Traditional strict fathering could be regarded as excessive authority and discipline on the one hand yet a less authoritative presence in a contemporary version of fatherhood could be regarded as a lack of control in relation to ADHD. Both forms of fathering have been associated with ADHD in research literature and media accounts and yet fathers manage to resolve this ideological dilemma by describing themselves as the stricter parent who is more remote from the everyday business of child care while assuming a significant role in an effective 'parenting team'. Accounts of fathers' absence is mitigated by their supportive and protective persona in relation to their families although in less traditional representations fathers assumed the subject position of 'junior parent' who relies on their partner for leadership and responsibility for childcare.

Not only does this reduce their accountability, but they are able to risk a position of relative deficiency, in relation to childcare. Nevertheless, we found that fathers only avoid being the subject of negative discourses by navigating a difficult pathway through ideological dilemmas to build their identities as good fathers. On the other hand, mothers are normatively subject to a host of negative discourses of maternal accountability for children and are caught between them (Davies 2014).

Medical Solutions

The topic of medicalisation is a significant one underpinning much of the discourse of ADHD and it is relevant to the experience of parents, children and adults with ADHD. We are aware that very little qualitative research has actually focused on children's personal viewpoints and that includes our own research. This is a significant omission, mitigated only by reference to a growing body of qualitative research studies that are beginning to inform our understanding of the child's point of view about ADHD. For example, in Chapter 6 we observed that many children who took part in Singh et al.'s (2012) '*Voices*' study, said that medication had helped them to cope but some also said they looked forward to a time when they could manage without it. On the other hand, Avisar and Lavie-Ajayi (2014) have identified reports of emotional side effects and loss of identity and Kenny (2016: 2) has found that 'young people perceive that they play a passive role in the management of their treatment'. One of the young participants in her study put it this way, 'You have to take the tablets, do what they say, go through this and that, and I don't get no input. My Mum, only my Mum my Mum my Mum gets a lot of input because that's my Mum. But I would like to have my own say' (Kenny 2016: 86).

Our own research on ADHD has allowed a glimpse of the child's experience through the accounts of parents who identified with ADHD (in Chapters 4 and 5) and by discussing the retrospective narratives of adolescents, college students, and women (in Chapter 6). We found that many of the women in a study by O'Dell et al. (2016b) had first identified with ADHD through the diagnosis of their own child, so the issue of medication, arose not so much to solve their own problems but more as an issue of how to do the best for their own children. Many were concerned with the lack of support and understanding they had experienced as children prior to developing their own coping strategies in adult life. They saw coping as an issue of maturity and looked back on their childhood self with compassion and some regret, having felt excluded and disempowered.

We also saw in Chapter 4 how mothers used the biological repertoire and the language of science to describe their child's diagnosis of ADHD, and while this positioned their child as impaired, it also allowed them to resist psychosocial explanations associated with the 'normal but naughty' stereotype and the 'blame game'. They were concerned with their identities as good mothers who are well-informed about ADHD and described their considered decisions about their children's educational and medical needs. However far they took up medical explanations to account for their children, both mothers and fathers described their reluctance to medicate, challenging professional opinion when they considered this necessary, and positioning themselves as the real experts on their children who do not automatically follow medical direction but weigh up the evidence. Versteeg et al.'s (2017) have observed, about online health forums, that people position themselves as rational and responsible citizens who are making their own choices about healthcare and they hold themselves and each other to account to provide evidence or credentials for those choices. This referred to adults, but we are sure that children and adolescents also engage with online discourse about ADHD and medication, especially those websites that have been set up to support them. Whether this has any effect on their inclusion in decisions about treatment or their sense of empowerment is another matter. Cohen and Morley (2009: 155) have observed that 'children's interests may be subsumed to those of parents, teachers and society as a whole in the course of diagnosis, treatment and labelling…' (p. 155) and they argue that the child 'internalizes the discourse and may, in fact, become an endorser of this view' (p. 165).

For adults with ADHD, medication is also one of the controversial topics frequently discussed in online health forums (Versteeg et al. 2017). This study indicated that people were not so much rejecting science and medical knowledge, as showing themselves to be making informed decisions between options. In neo-liberal societies, there is a 'moral imperative to be informed' (Hobson-West 2007: 212) and 'citizen choice is part of the discourse of healthcare in the UK under the auspices of 'professional partnerships'. So taking personal responsibility for healthcare involves deliberating about health advice and evidence in both formal institutional settings where citizens are included in policy and practice discussions, but also informally with other members of the public, as happens online and in support groups. For people who are affected by controversial health matters, it is not so much rejecting science as a question of 'which evidence' can be seen as trustworthy (Edwards and Howlett 2013: 40). For example, science knowledge about ADHD medication might be open to criticism because of the perceived interests of the funding pharmaceutical industries. However, parents who endorse or take up this option for their children justify their decisions using the evidence of their own experience, 'I did not need a scientific study to know that this worked for my child' (Versteeg et al. 2017: 7). An appeal to the evidence of outcomes operates much like the 'truth will out' arguments that scientists use to resolve the issues arising from conflicting science claims (Gilbert and Mulkay 1984) or the arguments that parents, in Chapters 4 and 5, use to resolve dilemmas arising from their complicity with medicalised solutions (see also Davies 2014). This interpretation of deliberative process, the dilemmas of treatment, and a focus on outcomes and the best interests of the child is a very different interpretation of parental experience than has been implied by the media stereotype of parents who use medication as a quick fix or 'chemical cosh'.

It was fathers (as discussed in Chapter 5) who expressed most concern about the use of medication as a 'chemical cosh' and this was closely bound up with their understanding of ADHD and masculine identities. They strongly identified themselves with the traits of hyperactive ADHD by defining it as a normal masculine characteristic of boisterous boys. This position resonates with media stories of the normal 'boisterous' boy with all of its connotations of ineffective parenting. However, fathers' accounts of medical solutions were rather troubled and concerned with how the effects of medication might 'dumb down' their sons' natural 'masculine' personality traits. Although they may have complied with medical solutions, they effectively distanced themselves from the rationale of medication in accounts of reluctance and normalisation. The parents of children with ADHD were all keenly aware of the moral condemnation associated with using ADHD medication, such that the decision to medicate or not was described as carefully considered, based on experience, initiated by a medical practitioner or explained as a consequence of exclusion from school. As we have seen, these decisions are not always completely 'owned' by parents, and as Kenny (2016) has since pointed out, they are certainly not 'owned' by children. Parents make it clear that, in the eyes of society, they are 'damned if they do and damned if they don't' (see also Taylor et al. 2006: 120) and the same idiom probably applies to health professionals.

Stigma and Resistance

We have learned more about how people respond to the stigmatising stereotypes and subject positions that arise from the discourse of ADHD across the contexts described in this book.

Symbolic interactionist theorists such as Mead (1934) and labelling theorists such as Becker (1963) theorised this as a process of being socially devalued that leads to self-devaluation because we learn to view ourselves from the perspective of the 'Other'. This explains how external social processes are internalised. Thoits described how, 'an undesirable category or label applied by others to the self becomes an undesirable social identity' (Thoits 2011: 7). Goffman (1963/1990) also described this process as self-devaluation and the outcome of a 'spoiled identity'. This was later referred to as 'self-stigmatisation' or 'internalised stigma' (Corrigan and Watson 2002; Corrigan and Calabrese 2005).

However stigma is theorised, stereotypes are also socially derived and we have seen (in Chapter 3) how they are produced in media discourse. Theoretical explanations that inform the media, such as theories of child development that rely on the discourse of normality versus abnormality, also rely on cultural values of difference but they draw on psychometric and other measures to define difference as abnormality (O'Dell and

Brownlow 2015). Cromby et al. (2013) distinguish between medical definitions of abnormality, statistical measures and social measures that appeal to social order and moral imperative. These different forms have become institutionalised and are taken for granted definitions that relate to cultural stigmatisation of ADHD and other forms of mental health conditions.

Mueller et al. (2012) has differentiated three forms of stigma; public stigma, self-stigma and courtesy stigma. Public stigma, they say, occurs at a societal level, where a discrediting stereotype is associated with a social category, such as media representations of 'boisterous' boys, difference defined as impairment, dysfunctional families, blameworthy mothers and absent fathers (Chapter 3). These stereotypes appeal to standards of normality and morality and they fuel the public imagination, through the everyday discourse of ADHD. They are produced and re-produced in all kinds of texts and social contexts and interactions as we have seen across the chapters of this book.

In this book, we are treating stigma and 'spoiled identity' as a discursive product rather than a socio-cognitive process. Even though people might not themselves always take up such identities in discourse, they still have to manage the way stigmatising discourse and 'spoiled identities' are applied to them. In relation to mental health categories, Thoits (2011: 6) described resistance to stigma as 'opposition to the imposition of mental illness stereotypes by others' and she categorised some forms of resistance as 'challenging' ('fighting back') and others as 'deflecting' ('guarding the fort') (2011: 11). Goffman's (1963) observations about 'passing for normal' and 'withdrawal from social interactions' are also relevant to this process. In a school context, for example, the children with ADHD who took part in Illina Singh et al.'s *Voices* research (2012; see also Chapter 6, this book) indicated their awareness of the stigma associated with their ADHD by describing how they had hidden their special needs and academic performance problems from their peers. In doing this they also take up the position of a victim of peer bullying. In Chapter 6, women with ADHD described 'passing for normal' when they were children and some have referred to themselves as outsiders who had become socially isolated as a result (O'Dell et al. 2016b). Thoits (2011: 12) might interpret this as 'withdrawal from social interactions' in order to avoid being devalued by others, although we note that the women often spoke of being excluded or marginalised by others rather than avoiding others themselves. They did not usually blame other people for this, but explained it as an understandable consequence of their chaotic lives and their personal impact on those around them in social and work situations. In these accounts they describe taking personal responsibility for their own actions, but in order to do this they are recognising themselves as the subjects of 'self-stigmatising' discourse and blame. In other parts of their interviews we saw them work hard to produce more positive accounts of their personal coping, strategies and transformations, describing skilled, positive and creative selves who overcame difficulties and battled on. Such accounts functioned in their narratives to resist being defined by 'spoiled identities' arising from their experiences and accounts of ADHD (O'Dell et al. 2016b).

'Fighting back' and 'guarding the fort' were also identified by Thoits (2011) as two alternative forms of resistance that are used to protect the self from stigma. These can be theorised as socio cognitive processes of identity formation and stigmatisation, but we have explained fighting and defensive talk alternatively as forms of discursive resistance that are common in social interactions. Mothers, for example, might describe being affected by stigma as a result of their children's behaviour and the negative stereotypes about bad parents and 'mother-blame'. They describe themselves as the front line victims of intimidation from other parents at the school gates because of their children with ADHD. We noted how mothers take up this victim position in their accounts of troubled interactions with other parents, but they do so while resisting the subject position of 'mother-blame' through their valourised accounts of family life and parenting. Such accounts 'guard the fort' against discrediting identities but they also dismiss the views of other parents as lacking understanding. More 'challenging' forms of resistance are described in accounts of campaigning advocates who have to fight back on behalf of their children. Educating others is a form of 'fighting back' to the stigma of mental illness (Thoits 2011), in much the same way that 'fighting talk', according to Ribbens-MacCarthy et al. (2000), is a way for the mothers of disabled children to establish a positive moral identity and avoid the stigmatising effect of mother-blame discourse. Paradoxically, when mothers take up valourised accounts they are resisting the accountability of 'mother-blame' but they implicate themselves in a further gendered cultural imperative of responsibility that 'holds mothers responsible for families and future citizens, maintaining this "natural" care at the center of normative femininity' (Blum 2007). Mothers are captured by this cultural imperative for maternal accountability that arises as something of a defining theme when they talk about their children with ADHD. In the chapters of this book, we have identified a range of such gendered dilemmas and cultural imperatives along with the resistance strategies that parents of both genders and people with ADHD might use to protect themselves against the stigmatising stereotypes that arise in the discourse of ADHD.

What Does Resistance Discourse Really Tell Us?

If we were to take resistance stories entirely at face value, we might risk overlooking important issues.

1. The social, cultural and interactional context of describing troubles and difficulties is highly relevant to the interpretation of meaning. Wilkinson and Kitzinger (2000: 797), in their analysis of coping talk, noted that one function of positive talk is to close down troubles-telling in compliance with a 'socially normative requirement' to be positive. They also identified expressions of 'fighting spirit' along with 'gaining a sense of mastery' and 'transformational' or 'silver lining' outlooks as idioms that have a dual function to 'round off and close down "troubles-telling" while making it possible for troubles telling to take place' (p. 805). Since positivity is a cultural imperative, speakers might also use positive talk to pre-empt an exhortation from their interlocutor to 'have a positive attitude' (p. 807).
2. Additionally, there is a specific cultural imperative not to express ambivalence towards ones' own child, especially for mothers. Davies (2014) observed that parents began interviews by describing difficulties and trauma but frequently ended by describing positive

experiences, thereby 'rescuing' their own identities as good parents who have an engaging child who they like, and a positive family life that they enjoy, for example, 'I actually find him quite funny, a little comedian and he's really quirky and he's full of beans and he's wild… I quite enjoy it he's very spirited he's good fun' (Davies 2014: 267).

3. Positive and enabling narratives might be celebrated as a form of resistance to the implications of stigmatising impairment discourse, but there is also a danger that a face value interpretation of these stories could risk acknowledgement of people's needs. Referring to people on the autistic spectrum, Jarratt (2014: 749) has cautioned 'just because people want their strengths acknowledged does not mean they don't want help and support'. We make these observations not to detract in any way from the importance of promoting enabling or 'ability focused narratives'. These are important therapeutic and socio-political tools that are highly valued by members of the neurodiversity movement who want to resist being defined by impairment discourse (see O'Dell et al. 2016a). Indeed, a concern to advance this cause and promote enabling narratives is one of the stated aims of the critical disability movement along with a concern about unequal power relations and the need to develop non-reductive and inclusive methods of enquiry that give people with disabilities a voice (O'Dell et al. 2016a). We concur with these sentiments with the caveat that positive talk and ability focused narratives should be treated as discursive forms of resistance that have a situated meaning and whose function might be dilemmatic as well as empowering.
4. Transformative narratives are as much a product of the micropolitics of social interaction as a description of lives or mental states. We have observed that when talking about their troubles, parents and adults with ADHD make efforts to counter the implications of troubles-telling through valourised or normalised accounts. The wider discursive context for this is a cultural 'tyranny of the positive' that demands an optimistic outlook (Lomas 2016). Being positive has become a socially and morally desirable response (Wilkinson and Kitzinger 2000) and being positive is valued in a therapeutic and clinical environment, but it also has the potential to function in discourse as a form of 'moral oppression' (De Raeve 1997). Despite the

vast literature that describes the health benefits of positivity, the discourse of positivity might not tell us as much about mental states as some assume (Wilkinson and Kitzinger 2000).

Pathology and Normalisation: The Cultural Politics of Impairment

Describing troubles was a significant aspect of ADHD discourse across all of the contexts we examined and with the caveats above in mind we ought not to ignore it. Like Wilkinson and Kitzinger (2000) we have however observed that when people describe their troubles, they also resist being 'captured' as the subjects of such discourses. This tells us quite a lot about the status of distress within our culture (see also Cromby et al. 2013). Within a culture of positivity, troubles-telling can be problematic. One way people accomplish this is to re-establish normality alongside the constructions of abnormality or pathology that tend to arise in the process of telling troubled accounts of ADHD. As we have observed, representations of the 'impaired' child that are embedded in parents' accounts of troubles are typically linked to biological interpretations and their efforts to represent themselves as 'good parents'. However, parents also demonstrate an awareness of the stigmatising stereotypes generated by this impairment discourse and they work hard to resist this as the defining representation of their child. Fathers appeared rather more resistant to the idea of impairment and medicalised interventions than were mothers, although, as we discussed above, this might be an expression of mothers' frontline position in childcare and fathers' identification with ADHD as a stereotypical form of traditional 'boisterous' masculinity. However, parents all typically work to manage dilemmas arising from the discourse of ADHD that pivot around issues of impairment and blame. They represent their child and family variably through talk of troubles along with stories that describe normality and their family life as business-as-usual. Troubles-telling involves definitions of impairment, pathology and difficult family lives and school experience, while normalising accounts resist the 'spoiled identities' that might be implied by this. Normalising accounts can, however, risk acknowledgement of needs.

Parents have also described their children in accounts of exceptional creativity and special abilities and we noted that this form of representation also appears in adults' accounts of their own ADHD. Talking about difference, creativity and special skills affords a significant form of parental resistance to impairment discourse. Parents express appreciation of traits in their child that they might elsewhere, in the context of troubles-telling, identify as problematic. Fathers who identified with their sons' hyperactive ADHD traits, for example, defined these as problematic behaviours in children that could be harnessed to improve their performance in adult life. However, such celebrations of difference and skill were frequently constructed alongside accounts of how improvements might be made. Similar paradoxes arose in the self-management narratives of adults who described their lives as a trajectory of troubles and transformations in Chapter 6. These kinds of account conform to a culturally recognisable 'progressive' narrative shape (Gergen and Gergen 1986) and they comply with an imperative for improvement or coping that can be generated as much by a response to the culture of positivity as they are a form of resistance to the discourse of impairment and pathology. The talk of difference and creativity that we observed in parents' narratives and the accounts of creativity and multitasking spoken of by adults with ADHD can work to re-define the meaning of ADHD as an asset rather than impairment, but still one that must be worked upon.

O'Reilly and Lester (2015: 258) have pointed out that the, 'biomedical categories in psychiatry have provided the foundation for defining pathological behaviour' and they have also 'provided the boundaries for normality and abnormality' (see also Cromby et al. 2013). What counts as normal, and what is regarded as 'ability', arise from the norms of culture and they are underpinned by taken for granted ideas about what it means to be human (O'Dell et al. 2016a: 174). As O'Dell et al. argue 'culturally specific ideas are translated into developmental science' producing atypicality as disability. Thus, the social construction of 'normality' is only achieved by Othering 'difference' (O'Dell and

Brownlow 2015: 296). This has resulted in a social world organised to accommodate typicality and encourage conformity and it is the reason why the term 'neurologically typical' has been preferred by people on the autistic spectrum because they prefer to acknowledge and celebrate their 'difference' as atypicality rather than be defined as abnormal (O'Dell and Brownlow 2015: 299–306). Nonetheless, the discourse of normality as defined by psychometrics has historically carried with it all the power of a taken for granted truth and informs practice. Such definitions circulate in mental health and disability discourse and we have seen how people take up ideas about both normality and difference in their accounts of ADHD. Paradoxically, the concepts of normality and difference are both used as a form of resistance to stigmatising stereotypes of abnormality and impairment in the discourse of ADHD.

The neurodiversity movement is a growing sociopolitical service user movement that resists the pathologising effects of disability discourse (Goodley and Roets 2008) and it challenges the 'Othering' power of mental health categories such as autism and ADHD (O'Dell and Brownlow 2015). O'Dell and Brownlow have suggested that it would be helpful if more attention was given by professionals to the abilities and strengths of neurodiversity that provide possibilities for crafting 'positive identities' (2015: 307). We concur with these ideas with two caveats: First, that a focus on strengths and a 'positive identity' does not risk acknowledging troubles and needs (Jarratt 2014), and second that positive identities do not turn out to be those defined by the discourse of cultural and institutional imperative imposed by the 'psy' disciplines, individualistic ideology and neoliberal regimes of truth. These contexts make up the wider discursive framework for understanding how people talk about ADHD and other forms of mental illness and health categories.

Relevance for Practice

We can certainly endorse the idea of encouraging more 'enabling' narratives and of forms of professional practice that are built on effective forms of collaboration between professionals and service users. This has the potential to promote marginalised voices and inform practice, with the proviso that service users are listened to and allowed to define their own identities and needs and inform their own solutions (see O'Dell and Brownlow 2015; Todd 2006). Kenny (2016: 25) suggests that Educational Psychologists are well placed to facilitate this process for children with ADHD. Such ideals comply with recommendations of the *Nuffield Trust* enquiry, as outlined, for example, in a paper by Barnes (1999) identifying a lack of co-ordination and fit with the needs identified by citizens and users, and a need to take less powerful users more seriously. This involves inclusive methods of practice informed by qualitative forms of social science and the perspectives of service users rather than imposing expert forms of knowledge as a superior form (see also Schrevel et al. 2016: 33).

Education is an important aspect of putting theory into practice. Kenny (2016) has, for example, reviewed studies of general practitioners' and teachers' knowledge and understandings of ADHD across the globe and found that 50% said that they did not know as much as they would like. Moldavsky and Sayal (2013) also found misconceptions, amongst children, adolescents, parents, healthcare professionals and the general public that were likely to reinforce stigma. In any society where people feel the need to hide their problems because of negative and stigmatising labels, clearly something needs to change (Singh et al. 2012; Davies and Horton-Salway 2016). Thus, educating children, adolescents and the general public about the stigmatising effects of mental health labels and how these socially define children and families is a step forward that is currently on the social and political agenda in the UK. However 'anti-stigma' campaigns have focused on biomedical and brain explanations of mental health conditions and this is not likely to promote a better public understanding and sympathy for psychosocial influences on distress (Cromby et al. 2013). The impact of negative media stereotyping is also a significant contribution to the discourse of mental health and ADHD is an example of how ideas about psychosocial influences can translate into stigmatising representations that feed moral panics. These are both areas of discourse that have room for improvement. Cromby et al. (2013) have suggested public education campaigns should focus more on distress arising from society and environment by treating the experience of distress as an understandable response to adverse life events. From this view widening public awareness and education about the harmful effects of discriminatory practices and the blame culture could help to reduce public fear and increase understanding.

Cromby et al. (2013: 11) also observe that 'people might end up receiving services, not because they themselves are distressed, but because their behaviour and experiences are distressing to those around them' (see also Cohen and Morley 2009). This certainly applies to disempowered social categories, for example, young people report that they are neither involved in making decisions about the management of their ADHD nor educated about the labels applied to them, less still consulted about the definition of their identities (Kenny 2016: 126). Cohen and Morley (2009: 165) described how 'the child is acted upon by the relatively powerful adults around them, who in effect create the discourse of problems associated with the child'. Kenny therefore recommends 'self-advocacy', informed by children's own experiences, to be promoted through schools, Educational Psychologists and members of health professions. Along similar lines, Schrevel et al. (2016: 63) has suggested forms of strength-based coaching that are preferred by adults with ADHD because these methods allow them to identify their own problems, goals and solutions. Coaching and some post-structuralist forms of narrative therapy (Gergen and Ness 2016) are not based on the superiority of expert knowledge but instead they aim to engage with clients' understandings and how they might construct the meaning of their experience in more empowering ways.

In the context of mental healthcare, the education of health professionals is an important issue for the future. Todd (2006) has described an application of post-structuralist theory and narrative practices to effect change in the way that health professionals think about the health categories they work with and the models that guide their practice. In workshops, they are challenged to consider how these categories have come to be afforded the status of truths in healthcare institutions. Todd has had some success with this and at the time of writing suggested that there was professional goodwill to engage with ideas that re-direct the focus away from individualising practices. Kenny (2016) further suggests that Educational Psychologists are well placed to liaise with health professionals to consider how systemic forms of thinking can more effectively include the experience of children as service users. The ideas of Todd and Kenny as well as others (such as Cromby et al. 2013; O'Dell and Brownlow 2015) who have critiqued mental health services, or who themselves work as health professionals in this field, have provided practical suggestions that have the potential to transform theoretical ideas into a form that can empower individual health professionals as well as their service users.

Perhaps post-structural methods of analysis might also be helpful to support health professionals, policy makers, managers and senior health educators to consider what exactly is meant by biopsychosocial complexity in the context of mental health and disability conditions? As we have indicated at the start of this chapter, a truly epiphenomenal understanding of ADHD, disability and mental health categories would include a cultural understanding of how the category definitions themselves have come to be afforded the status of truth, how these ideas have emerged historically from the constructive practices of science and culture and how they define people. This view of complexity is in addition to the more familiar understanding of how the psychosocial environs are considered to impact upon biology and inform biopsychosocial explanation and treatment. Colley (2010) has previously observed that unidirectional rather than bi-directional or circular and systemic explanations have been common in research on ADHD and that these may have contributed to polarised claim and counter-claim in biological versus psychosocial explanations of ADHD. In this way, psychosocial explanations are inclined to translate, at least in the media and public imagination, as parental blame and stereotypes of children with spoiled identities. Colley argues that it is not helpful to position parents in this way, because they are much more uniquely challenged by children with ADHD and require 'extraordinary parenting skills'. This observation is endorsed by the parents, in Chapter 4 of this volume, who have indicated that, 'normal parenting does not apply'.

We will conclude by acknowledging the people who have contributed their stories of experience for the research we have described and we thank them for helping us understand what ADHD means for them. Providing enabling forms of support throughout their difficult transitions of life requires greater public appreciation of the challenges people face and this can only happen if they are allowed to voice their experiences of distress without fear of being blamed or stigmatised. A co-ordinated multi-agency approach that is properly funded and responsive to the task of promoting enabling forms of person-centred support is a goal (Epstein 2000; Epstein et al. 2010), although we are aware that this is not always easy to implement in practice. To this end, however, we agree with Cromby et al. (2013) and O'Dell and Brownlow (2015) that the personal experience of service users should be treated as a valuable and legitimate resource of knowledge. This has the potential to inform self-advocacy, peer support and also to inform the understanding and practice of health professionals, educators and policy-makers. We suggest that personal accounts of ADHD by children, parents and adults with ADHD can tell us more about the cultural meaning of ADHD as a mental health category and the impact of this discourse upon its subjects. From our perspective, accounts of experience should be heard as culturally situated, discursive, and inherently dilemmatic, arising as they do from a culture of 'Othering', gendered discourse, stigma and blame.

References

Alvarez, A. S., Pagani, M., & Meucci, P. (2012). The clinical application of the biopsychosocial model in mental health: A research critique. *American Journal of Physical Medicine and Rehabilitation, 91*(2), 173–180.

Avisar, A., & Lavie-Ajayi, M. (2014). The burden of treatment: Listening to stories of adolescents with ADHD about stimulant medication use. *Ethical Human Psychology and Psychiatry, 16*(1), 37–50.

Bailey, S. (2014). *Exploring ADHD: An Ethnography of Disorder in Early Childhood*. Abingdon: Routledge.

Barnes, C., & Power, M. J. (2012). Internalising discourses of parental blame: Voices from the field. *Studies in the Maternal, 4*(2), 1–21. https://doi.org/10.16995/sim.36.

Barnes, M. (1999). *Public Expectations. From Paternalism to Partnership: Changing Relationships in Health and Health Services*. Paper 10 in a series edited by Charlotte Dargie (In Policy Futures for UK Health). London: The Nuffield Trust.

Becker, H. (1963). *Outsiders*. Glencoe, NY: Free Press.

Blum, L. (2007). Mother-blame in the Prozac nation: Raising kids with invisible disabilities. *Gender and Society, 21*(2), 202–226.

Bull, C., & Whelan, T. (2006). Parental schemata in the management of children with ADHD. *Qualitative Health Research, 16*(5), 664–676.

Caulfield, T. C., Clark, M. I., McCormack, J. P., Rachul, C., & Field, C. J. (2014, December). Representations of the health value of vitamin D supplementation in newspapers: Media content analysis. *BMJ Open, 4*(12), e006395.

Cohen, E. F., & Morley, C. P. (2009). Children, ADHD and citizenship. *Journal of Medicine and Philosophy, 34*, 155–180. https://doi.org/10.1093/jmp/jhp013.

Colley, B. (2010). ADHD, Science and the common man. *Emotional and Behavioural Difficulties, 15*(2), 83–94.

Collins, H. M. (1985). *Changing Order: Replication and Induction in Scientific Practice*. London: Sage.

Conrad, P., & Potter, D. (2000). From hyperactive children to ADHD adults: Observations on the expansion of medical categories. *Social Problems, 47*(4), 559–582.

Cromby, J., Harper, D., & Reavy, P. (2013). *Psychology, Mental Health and Distress*. Basingstoke: Palgrave Macmillan.

Corrigan, P. W., & Calabrese, J. P. (2005). Strategies for assessing and diminishing self-stigma. In *On the Stigma of Mental Illness: Practical Strategies for Research and Change* (pp. 239–256). Washington, DC: American Psychological Association.

Corrigan, P. W., & Watson, A. C. (2002). Stigma. The paradox of self-stigma and mental illness. *Clinical Psychology: Science and Practice, 9*, 35–53.

Davies, A. (2014). *It's a problem with the brain: A discursive analysis of parents' constructions of ADHD* (Unpublished Ph.D. thesis). The Open University, Milton Keynes.

Davies, A., & Horton-Salway, M. (2016). The construction of adult ADHD: Anna's story. In M. O'Reilly & J. N. Lester (Eds.), *The Palgrave Handbook of Adult Mental Health* (pp. 117–133). Basingstoke: Palgrave Macmillan.

De Raeve, L. (1997). Positive thinking and moral oppression in cancer care. *European Journal of Cancer Care, 6*, 249–256.

Edwards, C., & Howlett, E. (2013). Putting knowledge to trial: "ADHD parents" and the evaluation of alternative therapeutic regimes. *Social Science and Medicine, 81*, 34–41.

Epstein, R. M. (2000). The Science of patient centered care. *Journal of Family Practice, 49*(9), 805–810.

Epstein, R. M., Fiscella, K., Lesser, C. S., & Stange, K. C. (2010). Why the nation needs a policy push on patient-centered health care. *Health Affairs, 29*(8), 1489–1495.

Felt, U. (2015). Sociotechnical imaginaries of "the internet", digital health information and the making of citizen-patients. In S. Hilgartner, C. Miller, & R. Hagendijk (Eds.), *Science and Democracy: Making Knowledge and Making Power in the Biosciences and Beyond* (pp. 176–197). New York: Routledge.

Gergen, K. J., & Gergen, M. M. (1986). Narrative form and the construction of psychological science. In T. R. Sarbin (Ed.), *Narrative Psychology* (pp. 22–44). New York: Praeger.

Gergen, K., & Ness, O. (2016). Therapeutic practice as social construction. In M. O'Reilly & J. N. Lester (Eds.), *The Palgrave Handbook of Adult Mental Health* (pp. 502–519). Basingstoke, UK: Palgrave Macmillan.

Gilbert, G. N., & Mulkay, M. (1984). *Opening Pandora's Box: A Sociological Analysis of Scientists' Discourse*. Cambridge: Cambridge University Press.

Goffman, E. (1963). *Stigma: Notes on the Management of Spoiled Identity*. Englewood Cliffs, NJ: Prentice-Hall.

Goffman, E. (1990). *Stigma: Notes on the Management of Spoiled Identity*. London: Penguin Group.

Goodley, D., & Roets, G. (2008). The (be)comings and goings of developmental disabilities': The cultural politics of 'impairment'. *Discourse, 29*(2), 239–255.

Gonon, F., Bezard, E., & Boraud, T. (2011). Misrepresentation of neuroscience data might give rise to misleading conclusions in the media: The case of attention deficit hyperactivity disorder. *PLoS ONE, 6*(1), e14618. https://doi.org/10.1371/journal.pone.0014618.

Hobson-West, P. (2007). Trusting blindly can be the biggest risk of all: Organized resistance to childhood vaccination in the UK. *Sociology of Health & Illness, 29*(2), 198–215.

Horton-Salway, M. (2011). Repertoires of ADHD in UK newspaper media. *Health (London), 15*(5), 533–549.

Horton-Salway, M. (2012). Gendering attention deficit hyperactivity disorder: A discursive analysis of UK newspaper stories. *Journal of Health Psychology, 18*(8), 1085–1099. Published online before print 1 October 2012. https://doi.org/10.1177/1359105312456326.

Jarratt, C. (2014). Autism: Myth and reality. *British Psychological Society, 27*(10), 749.

Kata, A. (2010). A postmodern Pandora's box: Anti-vaccination misinformation on the internet. *Vaccine, 28,* 1709–1716.

Kenny, O. (2016). *How do young people diagnosed with ADHD perceive their condition?: An interpretative phenomenological analysis* (Doctoral thesis, University of East London).

Latour, B. (1987). *Science in action: How to follow scientists and engineers through society*. Milton Keynes: Open University Press.

Lester, J. N., & O'Reilly, M. (2016). The history and landscape of conversation and discourse analysis. In M. O'Reilly & J. N. Lester (Eds.), *The Palgrave Handbook of Adult Mental Health* (pp. 23–44). Basingstoke: Palgrave Macmillan.

Litt, J. (2004). Women's carework in low-income households: The special case of children with Attention Deficit Hyperactivity Disorder. *Gender and Society, 18*(5), 625–644.

Lomas. (2016). Positive Psychology—The second wave. *The Psychologist, 29*(7), 536.

Malacrida, C. (2001). Motherhood, resistance and attention deficit disorder: Strategies and limits. *Canadian Review of Sociology and Anthropology, 38*(2), 141–165.

Malacrida, C. (2002). Alternative therapies and attention deficit disorder: Discourses of maternal responsibility and risk. *Gender & Society, 16,* 366–385.

Mead, G. H. (1934). *Mind, Self and Society.* Chicago: University of Chicago Press.

Medical Research Council. (2016). *Public Trust in Scientific Research.* Report by MRC/BBSRC/AMS/WT. Available at www.mrc.ac.uk/documents/pdf/public-trust-in-science-2016 (Accessed 26 October 2017).

Moldavsky, M., & Sayal, K. (2013). Knowledge and attitudes about attentiondeficit/hyperactivity disorder (ADHD) and its treatment: The views of

children, adolescents, parents, teachers and healthcare professionals. *Current Psychiatry Reports, 15*(8), 337–344.
Mueller, A. K., Fuermaier, A. B. M., & Tucha, L. (2012). Stigma in attention deficit hyperactivity disorder. *Attention Deficit Hyperactivity Disorder, 4*(3), 101–114. Published online 8 July 2012. https://doi.org/10.1007/s12402-012-0085-3.
National Institute of Clinical Excellence. (2009). *Attention Deficit Hyperactivity Disorder: Diagnosis and Management of ADHD in Children, Young People and Adults*. London: National Institute for Health and Clinical Excellence. Available at http://www.nice.org.uk/Guidance/CG72 (Accessed 14 September 2017).
National Institute for Health and Care Excellence. (2016). *Attention Deficit Hyperactivity Disorder: Diagnosis and Management NICE Guideline (CG72)*. Available at https://www.nice.org.uk/guidance/cg72/ifp/chapter/Information-for-parents-of-children-with-ADHD (Accessed 14 September 2017).
O'Dell, L., & Brownlow, C. (2015). Normative development and the autistic child. In M. O'Reilly & J. N. Lester (Eds.), *The Palgrave Handbook of Child Mental Health* (pp. 296–309). Basingstoke, UK: Palgrave Macmillan.
O'Dell, L., Bertilsdotter Rosqvist, H., Ortega, F., Brownlow, C., & Orsini, M. (2016a). Critical autism studies: Exploring epistemic dialogues and intersections, challenging dominant understandings of autism. *Disability and Society, 31*(2), 166–179.
O'Dell, L., Stenner, P., Horton-Salway, M., & Davies, A. (2016b). *Narratives of ADHD: A qualitative study of women's narrative accounts of living with ADHD*. End of project report to the British Academy.
O'Reilly, M., & Lester, N. (2015). *The Palgrave Handbook of Child Mental Health* (M. O'Reilly & J. N. Lester, Eds.). Basingstoke, UK: Palgrave Macmillan.
Ponnou, S., & Gonon, F. (2017). How French media have portrayed ADHD to the lay public and to social workers. *International Journal of Qualitative Studies on Health and Well-being, 12*(Suppl. 1), 1298244. https://doi.org/10.1080/17482631.2017.1298244.
Rafalovich, A. (2001). Disciplining domesticity: Framing the ADHD parent and child. *The Sociological Quarterly, 42*(3), 373–393.
Rafalovich, A. (2004/2008). *Framing ADHD Children: A Critical Examination of the History, Discourse and Everyday Experience of Attention Deficit/Hyperactivity Disorder*. Plymouth: Lexington Books.

Read, J. (2005). The bio-bio-bio model of madness. *The Psychologist, 8*(10), 596–597.

Ribbens McCarthy, J., Edwards, R., & Gillies, V. (2000). Moral tales of the child and the adult: Narratives of contemporary family lives under changing circumstances. *Sociology, 34,* 785–803.

Rose, N. (1996/1998). *Inventing Our Selves: Psychology, Power, and Personhood.* Cambridge, UK: Cambridge University Press.

Rose, N. (1999). *Governing the Soul: The Shaping of the Private Self.* London: Free Association Books.

Royal College of General Practitioners (RCGP). (1972). *The Future General Practitioner: Learning and Teaching.* Exeter: British Medical Journal.

Schmitz, M. F., Filippone, P., & Edelman, E. M. (2003). Social representations of attention deficit/hyperactivity disorder, 1988–1997. *Culture & Psychology, 9*(4), 383–406.

Schrevel, S. J. C., Dedding, C., Aken, J. A., & Broerse, J. E. W. (2016). 'Do I need to become someone else?' A qualitative exploratory study into the experiences and needs of adults with ADHD. *Health Expectations, 19*(1), 39–48.

Segal, E. S. (2001). Learned mothering: Raising a child with ADHD. *Child and Adolescent Social Work Journal, 18*(4), 263–279.

Singh, I. et al. (2012). VOICES study: Final report. London, UK.

Soltile, W. M. (2005). Biopsychosocial care of heart patients: Are we practicing what we preach? *Families, Systems and Health, 23*(4), 400–403.

Taylor, M., O'Donoghue, T., & Houghton, S. (2006). To medicate or not to medicate? The decision making process of Western Australian parents following their child's diagnosis with an attention deficit hyperactivity disorder. *International Journal of Disability, Development and Education, 53*(1), 111–128.

Thoits, P. A. (2011). Mechanisms linking social ties and support to physical and mental health. *Journal of Health and Social Behavior, 52,* 145–161.

Todd, L. (2006). Enabling practice for professionals: The need for practical post-structuralist theory. In D. Goodley & R. Lawthom (Eds.), *Disability and Psychology: Critical Introductions and Reflections* (pp. 141–154). Basingstoke, UK: Palgrave Macmillan.

Ussher, J. M. (1991). *Women's Madness: Misogyny or Mental Illness?* Hemel Hampstead: Harvester Wheatsheaf.

Ussher, J. (2010). Are we medicalizing women's misery? A critical review of women's higher rates of reported depression. *Feminism and Psychology, 20,* 9–35.

Van Zoonen, L. (2012). I-pistemology: Changing truth claims in popular and political culture. *European Journal of Communication, 27*(3), 56–67.
Versteeg, W., te Molder, H., & Sneijder, P. (2017). "Listen to your body": Participants' alternative to science in online health discussions. *Health*, 1–17. https://doi.org/10.1177/1363459317695632.
Wilkinson, S., & Kitzinger, C. (2000). Thinking differently about thinking positive: A discursive approach to cancer patients' talk. *Social Science and Medicine, 50*(6), 797–811.

Glossary

ADHD: Attention Deficit and Hyperactivity Disorder one of several terms used to describe a collection of characteristics, behaviours and 'symptoms' displayed by individuals who are considered hyperactive and to have difficulty concentrating (see also hyperkinetic disorder).

Advocacy: Activity which supports an individual or cause by expressing views and wishes on their behalf.

Bandwagon effect: When people do specific things or express specific views because other people are doing so, or to gain an advantage.

Before-and-after stories: People give accounts of what life was like before and after and event (see also transformative/transformational stories).

Bio-bio-bio model (of mental health): A phrase used by critics to describe an approach to mental health which they claim neglects psychological and social factors and emphasises biological ones.

Biomedical model: An approach to health which focuses on biological factors, and classification and treatment.

Biopsychosocial model (of mental health): An approach that explains mental distress in terms of the interaction between a person's psychology, biology and social context.

M. Horton-Salway and A. Davies, *The Discourse of ADHD*,
The Language of Mental Health, https://doi.org/10.1007/978-3-319-76026-1

Blameworthy mother: A cultural stereotype which holds mothers primarily responsible and accountable for their children's care, health and development, including negative outcomes.

Blended approach to discourse: An approach to the study of discourse which blends micro and macro levels of analysis.

BPS (British Psychological Society): Representative professional body of psychologists and psychology in the UK.

'Bracket-creep': A term used by Kirschner (2013) to describe the way that medical categories expand. Compare with Conrad and Potter (2000) and the ideas about medicalisation of social phenomena.

Cognitivist psychology/cognitivism: Theoretical approach within psychology which seeks to explain behaviour in terms of underlying mental processes and states.

Combined ADHD: This type of ADHD combines inattentive, hyperactive and impulsive symptoms.

Conduct disorder: According to the DSM 5, a behavioural and emotional disorder identified in young people who do not conform to legal and social norms.

Conduct niche: This refers to one of the two ecological niches identified by Ilina Singh and her colleagues (2012). These were conduct and performance niches where conduct niche refers to children's social behaviour as a focus of attention and context for children's experience of education.

Contestation: The process whereby the meanings of social phenomena, identities and actions are disputed and resisted in discourse (see also resistance).

Contingent repertoire: This is a discursive strategy identified by Gilbert and Mulkay (1984) in their sociological study of scientists discourse and practice. It is a pattern of discourse and argument drawn on to explain why there can be errors or mistakes in science, drawing on the idea that beliefs, actions or claims (of only some scientists) are dependent on subjective bias or error. This repertoire was used by scientists to point out the 'contingent' nature of error and protect the idea of science is an objective empirical method providing that the scientific method is used correctly by good scientists (contrast this with 'empiricist repertoire').

Courtesy stigma: Concept used by Erving Goffman (1963) where stigma is extended to those close to the stigmatised person.

Critical discursive psychology (CDP): An approach which explores how cultural resources are drawn on in discourse and social interaction and identifies how some forms of discourse and cultural representations are more powerful than others (for example, dominant discourses or repertoires). Studies using CDP can combine micro and macro analysis of discourse.

Disciplinary gaze: Originating with Michel Foucault, a concept referring to the ubiquity of power as it is exercised through particular bodies of knowledge. Individuals come to discipline their behaviour in accordance with dominant social norms as if they were being observed (see also 'panoptican').

Disciplinary mechanism: Relating to the operation of power, techniques and institutions which come to regulate the behaviour of individuals.

Discursive psychology: A discipline that emerged as a critique of the dominant cognitivist approach to psychology (Edwards and Potter 1992). Taking a discursive approach, DP studies how psychological topics such as memories, causal attributions, accounts of self and identity and emotion states are constructed in social interactions, text and representations of reality. Discursive psychology rejects a realist approach to language and instead understands language to be constitutive in the sense that it is a form of social action.

DSM: Diagnostic and Statistical Manual of Mental Disorders used in diagnosing mental health conditions.

EBM: Evidence Based Medicine is the approach favoured within medical/ health contexts which privileges positivist, quantitative research methods to inform clinical practice and treatment.

Empiricist repertoire: As used by scientists in a study by Gilbert and Mulkay (1984), this is a discursive strategy to construct events and phenomena (in science) as empirical observations, facts and neutral accounts of method and outcomes in order to construct their science findings as empirical truths based on rigorous method. (Contrast with 'contingent repertoire'.)

Epiphenomenon: An event or process that may arise alongside another phenomenon or process. This can sometimes be in a correlational sense, or it can mean that the phenomenon occurs independently and is not related to the primary phenomenon. In this book it is used to describe various phenomena such as how ADHD is a product of biopsychosocial processes, or how it has been constructed through models of medicine, and how it has also been developed through social processes in parallel to science discourse and 'official' definitions. The term is being used here to denote a discursive phenomenon rather than a specific relationship between mind and body as with the philosophical position of 'epiphenomenalism'.

Extreme case formulation (ECF): This describes expressions and accounts using extreme terms such as 'all, every, none' which work to legitimise accounts and claims (see Pomerantz 1986).

Face: A term used by Goffman (1953) to describe how people present a positive social identity to others in social interactions.

Face-threatening: Instances of social interaction or descriptions that challenge the public image of the speaker or listener.

Fear-of-harm narratives: This refers to a form of meta-narrative or story that focuses on dangers and risks to the public.

Gendering: This refers to the power relations inherent in culturally defined meanings of male and female, or masculine and feminine which constrain how people's identities are represented and how the normative social practices of a culture operate with respect to boys and girls or men and women.

Genealogy: A term used by Foucault to describe an approach to writing history and to understanding the present by looking at the discursive traces and processes left by the past.

Governmentality/governance: A term coined by Michel Foucault to describe the way the state exercises control over its citizens through their willing participation, self-regulation and self-governance.

Historicised discourse: Referring to ideas and discourse generated in a previous period of history, yet remaining influential.

Hyperkinetic disorder: One of several terms used historically to describe a collection of characteristics, behaviours and 'symptoms' displayed by individuals who are considered hyperactive and to have difficulty concentrating (see also ADHD).

Hyperactive-impulsive ADHD: One of the main types of ADHD characterised by symptoms of hyperactivity and impulsivity.

Ideological dilemma: A key theoretical concept of critical discursive psychology referring to the contrary and competing arguments that exist within common sense and everyday knowledge.

Inattentive ADHD: one of the main types of ADHD characterised by symptoms which indicate difficulty in sustaining and focusing attention.

Interpretative repertoire: A key theoretical concept originating in the sociological study of scientists by Gilbert and Mulkay (1984) and later applied in a discourse analytic approach to social psychology and critical discursive psychology. Interpretative repertoires can be used to characterise, define and evaluate phenomena and they are used in lay discourse as well as in scientists' discourse.

ME: Myalgic Encephalomyelitis is a chronic condition with a wide-range of symptoms that has a controversial history (also referred to as CFS or Chronic Fatigue Syndrome).

Mediatisation: Process by which the media comes to control or influence how people think about the world.

Medicalisation: The interpretation of social phenomenon in medical terms.

Meta-narratives: An overarching, universal, or superordinate storyline based on cultural myths and stereotypes.

Micro-politics: The operation of power within small-scale or local social interactions, such as ordinary conversations or social interactions in institutional settings.

Mind-body dualism: Refers to the idea that the mind and body are two distinct substances, each with a different essential nature.

Minimal brain damage/dysfunction: A diagnostic label formerly used to describe a collection of symptoms that are today associated with ADHD.

Moral imperative: A socially prescribed way to act, think or behave that is embedded in the taken for granted norms of culture.

Moral panic: Referring to public anxiety or concern about an issue that is seen to threaten the moral standards of society.

Mother-blame/brain-blame binary: Relating to the transformation of blame from mother to brain in explanations of ADHD.

Mother-valour/mother-blame binary: Relating to the idea that mothers are responsible for their families' welfare and health. For example, the valourised mother is responsible for good outcomes; the blameworthy mother is held accountable for negative outcomes.

Narrative: An account of events, often of past events that has a structure, plot and trajectory, such as biographical accounts or personal experience stories. In this context, narratives are analysed to see how they draw on cultural ideas and discourse and how they are used to constitute a perspective or version of events.

Neoliberalism: A pervasive ideology referring to a set of social and economic values which emphasises free market competition over and above state intervention. It is based on a socio-economic theory incorporating individualism and emphasising the values of individual responsibility and personal control.

Networks of knowledge: An expression used by Latour (1987) to describe how knowledge circulates around networks of social actors.

Neurodiversity: Is a term used to describe diverse neurological brains and is drawn on to highlight the idea that neurological difference need not be defined in terms of deficit, impairment or pathology (see also 'politics of impairment').

Neurotechnologies: Technologies which research and aim to develop understanding of the brain.

NICE: The National Institute for Health and Care Excellence is a public body of the Department of Health in the UK which publishes guidelines relating to health and treatment.

Normalisation: Referring to social processes through which actions and ideas come to be understood as 'normal'.

Oppositional defiant disorder: A type of conduct disorder usually attributed to children and characterised by disobedience to and arguing with adults.

Othering: The process of defining individuals or groups of people as different and distinct from the self, often emphasising ways in which the different individual or group is inferior or deficient.

Panopticon: Jeremy Bentham's prison design which comprises one guard tower, which can be seen by all prisoners who do not know if they are themselves being watched. Foucault used this concept as a metaphor for the way society governs itself via individuals regulating their behaviour as if they were being observed.

Parenting-as-project: The idea that parenting and parenting identities are reflexive projects which have to be made and consciously developed according to cultural imperatives.

Pathologise: To regard or treat a phenomenon or person as socially or psychologically abnormal.

Performance niche: Expression used by Ilina Singh and her colleagues (2012) to describe one of two 'ecological niches' or contexts in which children with ADHD experience their educational environment. In a 'performance niche' it is children's academic achievement or ability that is the focus (see also 'conduct niche').

Politics of impairment: A critical approach within disability activism and disability studies that challenges and interrogates the historical, social and cultural formations of impairment (see also neurodiversity).

Positioning: A theoretical concept within critical discursive psychology referring to the way an individual can be described within interpretative repertoires and cultural discourse; also how they take up representations of themselves and others within discourse, and in doing so how they negotiate their identities in social interactions.

Positive talk: A cultural imperative to talk positively about events in order to present an upbeat and positive identity.

Positivism/positivist science: A philosophical approach to the study of society which favours scientific forms of enquiry such as experiments and statistics.

Poststructuralism: A relativist approach concerned with the plurality of constructed meanings and representations in different historical and socio/cultural contexts.

Professonalisation of parenting/professional parenting: A term used to describe how external and professional authority is increasingly privileged over parents' own informal knowledge of how to parent, resulting in parenting becoming a skill to be learned (see also parenting-as-project).

Progressive narratives: A positive account of how a situation improves over time (see Gergen and Gergen 1986).

Proximate blame: A term used to describe the blame attached to mothers of children with an ADHD diagnosis, not for causing their child's ADHD but for their subsequent management of it.

Psy-complex: See psy-disciplines.

Psy-disciplines: A term used by Nikolas Rose to refer to refer to the developing influence of knowledge that came from within the disciplines of psychology, psychiatry and psychotherapy and shaped new understandings of children and family life in the UK.

Psychodynamic/psychoanalysis: Related practices, originating in the work of Sigmund Freud, which amongst other things, emphasise the significance of early relationships on our emotional and psychological development.

Psychosocial: Relating to both psychological and social factors. Psychosocial is used in this book to describe a way of representing reality that draws on psychological or social explanations, for example, 'psychosocial repertoire'.

Public stigma: A type of stigma that occurs at a societal level, where a discrediting stereotype is associated with a social category.

Regimes of truth: Foucault regarded the historically specific social mechanisms that produce and perpetuate dominant common sense discourses and taken-for-granted knowledge within a given society as a 'regime of truth'.

Representation(s): Referring to the way language is used to assign meaning to phenomena or people/groups of people. Meaning is constructed through linguistic representation.

Resistance: See 'contestation', in this context referring to the process whereby the meanings of social phenomena, identities and actions are disputed and resisted in discourse.

Responsibilisation: A term used to refer to a cultural imperative for individuals to be responsible for themselves and their families.

Script formulation: A description of an action or event which constructs it as predictable and recurring.

Social actors: A person who performs an action (implies agency). Talk and discourse is regarded as a form of social action is discursive psychology.

Social constructionism: Referring to theories which emphasise the socially constituted nature of social life and phenomena.

Sociology of scientific knowledge (SSK): An approach which emphasises the social construction of scientific knowledge.

Spoiled identity: A term coined by Erving Goffman (1963) to refer to the process by which stigma and the reactions of others attacks or spoils 'normal' identities. For example, the stigma of mental illness arises from cultural ideas and definitions.

Stake or interest: A term used to note a personal reason for or investment in holding a particular point of view.

Stake inoculation: A linguistic device used to downplay a speaker's potential stake in holding a particular viewpoint and make the speaker appear neutral and unbiased.

Stimulant medication: Medication most often associated with the treatment of ADHD. See also Ritalin.

Subject positions: A key theoretical concept of critical discursive psychology referring to the identity slots which are constructed when people use discourse. Identities are taken up or resisted while explaining or negotiating the social world.

Technologies of self: A Foucauldian concept referring to the techniques and interventions used to manage and regulate the behaviour and thinking of populations and so render them governable, for example as described by Nikolas Rose (1999).

Transformative/transformational stories: Stories or accounts which describe how troubled and problematic pasts are overcome and resolved leading to a less problematic present or future trajectory. These accounts perform several interactive functions including distancing the self from a 'spoiled' or troubled identity (see also before-and -after stories).

Troubles-talk: Descriptions of events which are problematic in some way, and which might invite negative appraisal of the speaker.

Troubles-talk package: Referring to the way that troubles-talk is organised in interaction (Jefferson 1988). Troubles-talk is typically followed by accounts of resolution or easing of troubles and the concept is applied here to the way that narratives are organised.

Notes

Conrad, P., & Potter, D. (2000). From hyperactive children to ADHD adults: Observations on the expansion of medical categories. *Social Problems, 47*(4), 559–582.

Edwards, D. & Potter, J. (1992). *Discursive Psychology*. London: Sage.

Foucault, M. (1970). *The Order of Things*. London: Tavistock.

Gergen, K. J., & Gergen, M. M. (1986). Narrative form and the construction of psychological science. In T. R. Sarbin (Ed.), *Narrative Psychology* (pp. 22–44). New York: Praeger.

Gilbert, G. N., & Mulkay, M. (1984). *Opening Pandora's Box: A Sociological Analysis of Scientists' Discourse*. Cambridge: Cambridge University Press.

Goffman, E. (1955). On face work. *Psychiatry, 18,* 213–231.

Goffman, E. (1963). *Stigma: Notes on the Management of Spoiled Identity*. Englewood Cliffs, NJ: Prentice-Hall.

Jefferson, G. (1988). On the sequential organization of troubles-talk in ordinary conversation. *Social Problems, 35*(4), 418–437.

Kirschner, S. (2013). Diagnosis and its discontents: Critical perspectives on psychiatric nosology in the DSM. *Feminism and Psychology, 23*(1), 10–28.

Latour, B. (1987). *Science in Action: How to Follow Scientists and Engineers Through Society*. Milton Keynes: Open University Press.

Pomerantz, A. (1986). Extreme case formulations: A way of legitimising claims. *Human Studies, 9,* 219–229.

Rose, N. (1996/1998). *Inventing Our Selves: Psychology, Power, and Personhood*. Cambridge: Cambridge University Press.

Rose, N. (1999). *Governing the Soul: The Shaping of the Private Self*. London: Free Association Books.

Singh, I. et al. (2012). VOICES Study: Final Report. London, UK.

Bibliography

Adams, P. (2008). Positioning behaviour: Attention deficit/hyperactivity disorder in the post welfare educational era. *International Journal of Inclusive Education, 12*(2), 113–125.

Ahl, H. (2006). Why research on women entrepreneurs needs new directions. *Entrepreneurship Theory and Practice, 30*(5), 595–621.

Allen, K., & Taylor, Y. (2012). Placing parenting, locating unrest: Failed femininities, troubled mothers and riotous subjects. *Studies in the Maternal, 4*(2), 1–25. https://doi.org/10.16995/sim.39.

Alvarez, A. S., Pagani, M., & Meucci, P. (2012). The clinical application of the biopsychosocial model in mental health: A research critique. *American Journal of Physical Medicine and Rehabilitation, 91*(2), 173–180.

American Psychiatric Association. (1968). *Diagnostic and Statistical Manual of Mental Disorders II* (2nd ed.). Washington, DC: Author.

American Psychiatric Association. (1980). *Diagnostic and Statistical Manual of Mental Disorders III* (3rd ed.). Washington, DC: Author.

American Psychiatric Association. (1987). *Diagnostic and Statistical Manual of Mental Disorders III* (3rd ed., revised). Washington, DC: Author.

American Psychiatric Association. (1994). *Diagnostic and Statistical Manual of Mental Disorders* (4th ed.). Washington, DC: Author.

M. Horton-Salway and A. Davies, *The Discourse of ADHD*,
The Language of Mental Health, https://doi.org/10.1007/978-3-319-76026-1

American Psychiatric Association. (2000). *Diagnostic and Statistical Manual of Mental Disorders: DSM IV* (Text Revision). Washington, DC: Author.

American Psychiatric Association. (2013a). *Attention Deficit and Hyperactivity Disorder.* Available at http://www.dsm5.org/documents/adhd%20fact%20sheet.pdf (Accessed 15 May 2016).

American Psychiatric Association. (2013b). *Diagnostic and Statistical Manual of Mental Disorders* (5th ed.). Washington, DC: Author.

Antaki, C., & Widdicombe, S. (Eds.). (1998). *Identities in Talk.* London: Sage.

Armon, R. (2015). Expert positions and scientific contexts: Storying research in the news media. *Discourse and Communication, 10*(1), 3–21.

Arruda, M. A., Querido, C. N., Bigal, M. E., & Polanczyk, G. V. (2015). ADHD and mental health status in Brazilian school-age children. *Journal of Attention Disorders, 19*(1), 11–17.

Asherton, P., Timimi, S., & Moncrieff, J. (2010). Is ADHD a valid diagnosis in adults. *British Medical Journal, 340,* 736–737.

Atkinson, P. (1995). *Medical Talk and Medical Work: The Liturgy of the Clinic.* London: Sage.

Austin, H., & Carpenter, L. (2008). Troubled, troublesome, troubling mothers: The dilemma of difference in women's personal motherhood narratives. *Narrative Inquiry, 18*(2), 378–392.

Austin, J. L. (1962). *How to Do Things with Words.* Oxford: Clarendon Press.

Avisar, A., & Lavie-Ajayi, M. (2014). The burden of treatment: Listening to stories of adolescents with ADHD about stimulant medication use. *Ethical Human Psychology and Psychiatry, 16*(1), 37–50.

Babinski, D. E., Pelham, W. E., Jr., Molina, B. S. G., Waschbusch, D. A., Gnagy, E. M., Yu, J., et al. (2011). Women with childhood ADHD: Comparisons by diagnostic group and gender. *Journal of Psychopathology and Behaviour Assessment, 33,* 420–429. https://doi.org/10.1007/s10862-011-9247-4.

Bailey, S. (2009). *Producing ADHD: An ethnographic study of behavioural discourses of early childhood* (Ph.D. thesis, University of Nottingham).

Bailey, S. (2010). The DSM and the dangerous school child. *International Journal of Inclusive Education, 14*(6), 581–592.

Bailey, S. (2014). *Exploring ADHD: An Ethnography of Disorder in Early Childhood.* Abingdon: Routledge.

Barnes, C., & Power, M. J. (2012). Internalising discourses of parental blame: Voices from the field. *Studies in the Maternal, 4*(2), 1–21. https://doi.org/10.16995/sim.36.

Barthes, R. (1964). *Elements of Semiology*. New York: Hill and Wang.

Barthes, R. (1972). *Mythologies*. London: Paladin.

Baruch, G. (1981). Moral tales: Parents' stories of encounters with the health professions. *Sociology of Health and Illness, 3*(3), 275–295.

Becker, Howard S. (1963). *Outsiders: Studies in the Sociology of Deviance*. New York: Macmillan.

Bennett, J. (2007). (Dis)ordering motherhood: Mothering a child with attention deficit hyperactivity disorder. *Body Society, 13*(4), 97–110.

Benwell, B. (2012). Common-sense anti-racism in book group talk: The role of reported speech. *Discourse Society, 23*(4), 359–376.

Berger, N. P. (2015). The creative use of the ADHD diagnosis in probationers' self-narratives. *Journal of Scandinavian Studies in Criminology and Crime Prevention, 16*(1), 122–139.

Berger, P. L., & Luckmann, T. (1966). *The Social Construction of Reality*. Garden City: Doubleday.

Berger, P. L., & Luckmann, T. (1971). *The Social Construction of Reality*. Harmondsworth: Penguin.

Berman, R. C., & Wilson, L. (2009). Pathologising or validating: Intake workers' discursive constructions of mothers. *Qualitative Health Research, 19*(4), 444–453.

Berry, C. A., Shaywitz, S. E., & Shaywitz, B. A. (1985). Girls with attention deficit disorder: A silent minority? A report on behavioral and cognitive characteristics. *Pediatrics, 76*, 801–809.

Bettelheim, B. (1959). Feral children and autistic children. *American Journal of Sociology, 64*(5), 455–467.

Biderman, A., Yeheskel, A., & Herman, J. (2005). The biopsychosocial model—Have we made any progress since 1977? *Families, Systems and Health, 23*(4), 379–386.

Billig, M. (1996). *Arguing and Thinking: A Rhetorical Approach to Social Psychology*. Cambridge: Cambridge University Press.

Billig, M., Condor, S., Edwards, D., Gane, M., Middleton, D., & Radley, A. (1988). *Ideological Dilemmas: A Social Psychology of Everyday Thinking*. London: Sage.

Billington, T., & Pomerantz, M. (2004). Resisting social exclusion. In T. Billington & M. Pomerantz (Eds.), *Children at the Margins: Supporting Children, Supporting Schools* (pp. 1–14). Stoke on Trent: Trentham Books.

Bishop, F. L., & Yardley, L. (2004). Constructing agency in treatment decisions: Negotiating responsibility in cancer. *Health: An Interdisciplinary Journal for the Social Study of Health Illness and Medicine, 8*(4), 465–482.

Blum, L. (2007). Mother-blame in the Prozac nation: Raising kids with invisible disabilities. *Gender and Society, 21*(2), 202–226.

Borrill, J. (2000). *All About ADHD.* Mental Health Foundation. Available at http://www.mentalhealth.org.uk.

Boschner, A. (2000). Criteria against ourselves. *Qualitative Inquiry, 6*(2), 266–272.

Boström, P. K., & Broberg, M. (2014). Openness and avoidance—A longitudinal study of fathers of children with intellectual disability. *Journal of Intellectual Disability Research, 58*(9), 810–821.

Bourdaa, M., Konsman, J. P., Sécail, C., Venturini, T., Veyrat-Masson, I., & Gonon, F. (2015). Does television reflect the evaluation of scientific knowledge? The case of attention-deficit hyperactivity disorder coverage on French television. *Public Understanding of Science, 24*(2), 200–209.

Bourdieu, P. (1979). Symbolic power. *Critique of Anthropology, 4,* 77–85.

Bowlby, J. (2005). *A Secure Base*. London: Routledge Books.

BPS (The British Psychological Society). (2012). *Response to the American Psychiatric Association: DSM The Future of Psychiatric Diagnosis (Final Consultation).* Retrieved from http://apps.bps.org.uk/_publicationfiles/consultation-responses/DSM-5%202012%20-%20BPS%20response.pdf.

Bracken, P., & Thomas, P. (2010). From Szasz to Foucault: On the role of critical psychiatry. *Philosophy, Psychiatry, and Psychology, 17*(3), 219–228.

Bradley, C. (1937). The behaviour of children receiving benzedrine. *American Journal of Psychiatry, 941,* 577–581.

Bradley, L., & Butler, C. W. (2015). Managing and normalising emotions and behaviour: A conversation analytic study of ADHD coaching. In M. O'Reilly & J. N. Lester (Eds.), *The Palgrave Handbook of Child Mental Health* (pp. 480–499). Basingstoke, UK: Palgrave Macmillan.

British Broadcasting Corporation (BBC), *Radio 5 Live.* (2011, February 6). *ADHD Drug Cheats.*

British Broadcasting Corporation. (2011, November). *Newsbeat.*

Broberg, M. (2011). Expectations of and reactions to disability and normality experienced by parents of children with intellectual disability in Sweden. *Child: Care Health and Development, 37*(3), 410–417.

Brod, M., Schmitt, E., Goodwin, M., Hodgkins, P., & Niebler, G. (2012). ADHD burden of illness in older adults: A life course perspective. *Quality of Life Research, 21,* 795–799.

Broomhead, K. (2013). Blame, guilt and the need for "labels"; Insights from parents of children with special educational needs and educational practitioners. *British Journal of Special Education, 40,* 14–21.

Brownlow, C., & Lamont-Mills, A. (2015). The production of the 'normal child': Exploring co-constructions of parents, children, and therapists. In M. O'Reilly & J. N. Lester (Eds.), *The Palgrave Handbook of Child Mental Health* (pp. 233–251). Basingstoke: Palgrave Macmillan.

Bull, C., & Whelan, T. (2006). Parental schemata in the management of children with ADHD. *Qualitative Health Research, 16*(5), 664–676.

Burman, E. (2008). *Deconstructing Developmental Psychology* (2nd ed.). London: Routledge.

Burr, V. (2003). *Social Constructionism* (2nd ed.). Hove: Routledge.

Bussing, R., & Gary, F. A. (2001). Practice guidelines and parental ADHD treatment evaluations: Friends or foes? *Harvard Review of Psychiatry, 9*(5), 233.

Carabine, J. (2001). Unmarried motherhood 1830–1990: A genealogical analysis. In Wetherell, Taylor, & Yates (Eds.), *Discourse as Data: A Guide for Analysis* (pp. 267–310). London: Sage.

Carpenter, B., & Towers, C. (2008). Recognising fathers: The needs of fathers of children with disabilities. *Fathers and Disability, 23*(3), 118–125.

Castle, L., Aubert, R., Verbrugge, R., & Khalid, M. (2007). Trends in medication treatment for ADHD. *Journal of Attention Disorders, 10*(4), 335–342.

Caulfield, T. C., Clark, M. I., McCormack, J. P., Rachul, C., & Field, C. J. (2014, December). Representations of the health value of vitamin D supplementation in newspapers: Media content analysis. *BMJ Open, 4*(12), e006395.

Chamberlain, Z. (2010, April 25). Juggling cured our girl's temper tantrums. *The Sunday Mercury*, p. 34.

Clarke, J. N. (2011). Magazine portrayal of attention deficit/hyperactivity disorder (ADD/ADHD): A post-modern epidemic in a post-trust society. *Health, Risk and Society, 13*(7–8), 621–636.

Clout, L. (2008, September 24). Parents warned over the dangers of Ritalin. *The Express (UK)*, 1st ed., p. 30.

Cohen, E. F., & Morley, C. P. (2009). Children, ADHD and citizenship. *Journal of Medicine and Philosophy, 34,* 155–180. https://doi.org/10.1093/jmp/jhp013.

Colley, B. (2010). ADHD, science and the common man. *Emotional and Behavioural Difficulties, 15*(2), 83–94.

Collins, H. M. (1985). *Changing Order: Replication and Induction in Scientific Practice.* London: Sage.

Comstock, E. J. (2011). The end of drugging children: Toward the genealogy of the ADHD subject. *Journal of the History of the Behavioral Sciences, 47*(1), 44–69.

Connolly, M. (2010). ADHD women and girls: Late diagnosis, little treatment. *ADDitude Magazine.*

Conrad, P. (1975). The discovery of hyperkinesis: Notes on the medicalisation of deviant behaviour. *Social Problems, 23,* 12–21.

Conrad, P. (2006). From hyperactive children to ADHD adults: Observations on the expansion of medical categories. In *Identifying Hyperactive Children: The Medicalisation of Deviant Behaviour* (Expanded edition, pp. 101–126). Aldershot: Ashgate Publishing.

Conrad, P. (2007). *The Medicalisation of Society on the Transformation of Human Conditions into Treatable Disorders.* Baltimore: The Johns Hopkins University Press.

Conrad, P., & Bergey, M. R. (2014). The impending globilization of ADHD: Notes on the expansion and growth of a medicalized disorder. *Social Science and Medicine, 122,* 31–43.

Conrad, P., & Potter, D. (2000). From hyperactive children to ADHD adults: Observations on the expansion of medical categories. *Social Problems, 47*(4), 559–582.

Cooper, P. (2001). Understanding AD/HD: A brief critical review of the literature. *Children and Society, 15*(5), 387–395.

Cooper, P. (2008). Like alligators bobbing for poodles? A critical discussion of education, ADHD and the biopsychosocial perspective. *Journal of Philosophy of Education, 42*(3–4), 457–474.

Corrigan, P. W., & Calabrese, J. D. (2005). Strategies for assessing and diminishing self-stigma. In P. W. Corrigan (Ed.), *On the Stigma of Mental Illness. Practical Strategies for Research and Social Change* (pp. 239–256). Washington, DC: American Psychological Association.

Corrigan, P. W., & Watson, A. C. (2002). The paradox of self-stigma and mental illness. *Clinical Psychology: Science & Practice, 9,* 35–53.

Cromby, J., Harper, D., & Reavy, P. (2013). *Psychology, Mental Health and Distress.* Basingstoke: Palgrave Macmillan.

Crossley, M. (2000). *Introducing Narrative Psychology: Self, Trauma and the Construction of Meaning.* Buckingham: Open University Press.

Danforth, S., & Navarro, V. (2001). Hyper talk: Sampling the social construction of ADHD in everyday language. *Anthropology and Education Quarterly, 32*(2), 167–190.

Davidson, M. A. (2008). Literature review: ADHD in adults: A review of the literature. *Journal of Attention Disorders, 11*, 628.

Davies, A. (2014). *It's a problem with the brain: A discursive analysis of parents' constructions of ADHD* (Unpublished Ph.D. thesis). The Open University, Milton Keynes.

Davies, A., & Horton-Salway, M. (2016). The construction of adult ADHD: Anna's story. In M. O'Reilly & J. N. Lester (Eds.), *The Palgrave Handbook of Adult Mental Health* (pp. 117–133). Basingstoke, UK: Palgrave Macmillan.

Davies, B. (2007, November 19). The Scandal of Kiddy Coke. *The Daily Mail (London)*, p. 17.

De Benedictis, S. (2012). 'Feral' parents: Austerity parenting under neoliberalism. *Studies in the Maternal, 4*(2), 1–21. https://doi.org/10.16995/sim.40.

DeGrandpre, R. J. (2000). *Ritalin Nation*. New York: W. W. Norton.

Denzin, N. K. (1987a). *The Alcoholic Self*. Newbury Park, CA: Sage.

Denzin, N. K. (1987b). *The Recovering Alcoholic*. Newbury Park, CA: Sage.

Department of Education. (2014). *Special Educational Needs and Disability Code of Practice: 0–25*. London: The Stationery Office (TSO).

De Raeve, L. (1997). Positive thinking and moral oppression in cancer care. *European Journal of Cancer Care, 6*, 249–256.

De Sanctis, V. A., Nomura, Y., Newcorn, J. H., & Halperin, J. M. (2012). Childhood maltreatment and conduct disorder: Independent predictors of criminal outcomes in ADHD youth. *Child Abuse and Neglect, 36*(11/12), 782–789.

Dillon, A., & Craven, R. G. (2014). Examining the genetic contribution to ADHD. *Ethical Human Psychology and Psychiatry, 16*(1), 20–28. https://doi.org/10.1891/1559-4343.16.1.20.

Dixon, J., & Wetherell, M. (2004). On discourse and dirty nappies: Gender, the division of household labour and the social psychology of distributive justice. *Theory and Psychology, 14*(2), 167–189.

Donnelly, L. (2013, August 13). Students taking 'smart drugs' may be behind soaring Ritalin use. *The Telegraph*. Available at http://www.telegraph.co.uk/health/healthnews/10238660/Students-taking-smart-drugs-may-be-behind-soaring-Ritalin-use.html (Accessed 21 November 2013).

Doucet, A. (2006). *Do Men Mother?* London: University of Toronto Press Inc.

Doward, J. (2013, May 12). Psychiatrists under fire in mental health battle. *The Guardian*. Available at https://www.theguardian.com/society/2013/may/12/psychiatrists-under-fire-mental-health (Accessed 20 May 2017).

Dunne, L., & Moore, A. (2011). From boy to man: A personal story of ADHD. *Emotional and Behavioural Difficulties, 16*(4), 351–364.

Edley, N., & Wetherell, M. (1999). Imagined futures: Young men's talk about fatherhood and domestic life. *British Journal of Social Psychology, 38,* 181–194.

Edwards, C., & Howlett, E. (2013). Putting knowledge to trial: "ADHD parents" and the evaluation of alternative therapeutic regimes. *Social Science and Medicine, 81,* 34–41.

Edwards, D. (1994). Script formulations: An analysis of event descriptions in conversation. *Journal of Language and Social Psychology, 13*(3), 211–247.

Edwards, D. (1997). *Discourse and Cognition*. London: Sage.

Edwards, D. (2005). Moaning, whinging and laughing: The subjective side of complaints. *Discourse Studies, 7*(1), 5–29.

Edwards, D., & Potter, J. (1992). *Discursive Psychology*. London: Sage.

Edwards, D., & Potter, J. (1993). Language and causation: A discursive action model of description and attribution. *Psychological Review, 100*(1), 23–41.

Einarsdottir, J. (2008). Teaching children with ADHD: Icelandic early childhood teachers' perspectives. *Early Child Development and Care, 178*(4), 375–397.

Elston, M. A. (1991). The politics of professional power: Medicine in a changing health service. In J. Gabe, M. Calnan, & M. Bury (Eds.), *The Sociology of the Health Service*. London: Routledge.

Engel, G. L. (1977). The need for a new medical model: A challenge for biomedicine. *Science, 196,* 129–136.

Engel, G. L. (1980). The clinical application of the biopsychosocial model. *American Journal of Psychiatry, 137,* 535–544.

Epstein, R. M. (2000). The science of patient centered care. *Journal of Family Practice, 49*(9), 805–810.

Epstein, R. M., Fiscella, K., Lesser, C. S., & Stange, K. C. (2010). Why the nation needs a policy push on patient-centered health care. *Health Affairs, 29*(8), 1489–1495.

Featherstone, B. (2009). *Contemporary Fathering: Theory, Policy and Practice*. Bristol: Policy Press.

Fedele, D. A., Lefler, E. K., Hartung, C. M., & Canu, W. H. (2012). Sex differences in the manifestation of ADHD in emerging adults. *Journal of Attention Disorders, 16,* 109–117. https://doi.org/10.1177/1087054710374596.

Feingold, B. F. (1974). *Why Your Child Is Hyperactive*. New York: Random House.

Felt, U. (2015). Sociotechnical imaginaries of "the internet", digital health information and the making of citizen-patients. In S. Hilgartner, C. Miller, & R. Hagendijk (Eds.), *Science and Democracy: Making Knowledge and Making Power in the Biosciences and Beyond* (pp. 176–197). New York: Routledge.

Feltz, V. (2007, July 31). Scandal of using drugs to replace parenting. *The Express (UK)*, 1st ed., Leader, p. 11.

Fernando, S. (2010). *Mental Health, Race and Culture* (3rd ed.). Basingstoke: Palgrave Macmillan.

Fleischmann, A., & Miller, E. C. (2013). Online narratives by adults with ADHD who were diagnosed in adulthood. *Learning Disability Quarterly, 36*(1), 47–60.

Foley, P. (2011). A viral infection of the mind? The curious case of encephalitis lethargica. *The Conversation*. Available at http://theconversation.com/a-viral-infection-of-the-mind-the-curious-case-of-encephalitis-lethargica-660 (Accessed 21 May 2017).

Foroushani, P. S. (2008). The internet: A place for different voices in health and medicine? A case study of attention deficit hyperactivity disorder. *Mental Health Review Journal, 13*(1), 33–40.

Foucault, M. (1970). *The Order of Things*. London: Tavistock.

Foucault, M. (1973). *The Birth of the Clinic*. London: Tavistock.

Foucault, M. (1980). *History of Sexuality, Vol. 1: An Introduction* (R. Hurley, Trans.). New York: Vintage.

Foucault, M. (1988). *"Technologies of the Self" in Technologies of the Self: A Seminar with Michel Foucault* (L. H. Martin, H. Gutman, & P. Hutton, Eds., pp. 16–49). Amherst: University of Massachusetts Press.

Foucault, M. (1991). *Discipline and Punish: The Birth of the Prison*. London: Penguin Books.

Foucault, M. (2003). *The Birth of the Clinic*. Abingdon: Routledge Classics.

Foucault, M. (2006). *The History of Madness*. Abingdon: Routledge.

Francis, A. (2012). Stigma in an era of medicalisation and anxious parenting: How proximity and culpability shape middle-class parents' experiences of disgrace. *Sociology of Health and Illness, 34*(6), 927–942.

Frankel, H. (2010, May 7). Doctors, leave them kids alone. *TES Magazine*. Available at http://www.tes.co.uk/article.aspx?storycode=6043074 (Accessed 20 June 2010).

Frigerio, A., & Montali, L. (2016). An ethnographic-discursive approach to parental self-help groups: The case of ADHD. *Qualitative Health Research, 26*(7), 935–950.

Frigerio, A., Montali, L., & Fine, M. (2013). Attention deficit/hyperactivity disorder blame bame: A study on the positioning of professionals, teachers and parents. *Health, 17*(6), 584–604.

Furnham, A., & Sarwar, T. (2011). Beliefs about attention-deficit hyperactivity disorder. *Counselling Psychology Quarterly, 24*(4), 301–311.

Garfinkel, H. (1967). *Studies in Ethnomethodology*. Englewood Cliffs, NJ: Prentice-Hall.

Geertz, C. (1973). *The Interpretation of Cultures*. New York: Basic Books.

Gelo, O. C. G., Vilei, A., Maddux, J. E., & Gennaro, A. (2015). Psychopathology as social construction: The case of anorexia nervosa. *Journal of Constructivsist Psychology, 28*(2), 105–125.

Gerdes, A. C., Hoza, B., & Pelham, W. E. (2003). Attention-deficit/hyperactivity disordered boys' relationships with their mothers and fathers: Child, mother, and father perceptions. *Developmental Psychopathology, 15*(2), 363–382.

Gergen, K. J., & Gergen, M. M. (1986). Narrative form and the construction of psychological science. In T. R. Sarbin (Ed.), *Narrative Psychology* (pp. 22–44). New York: Praeger.

Gergen, K., & Ness, O. (2016). Therapeutic practice as social construction. In M. O'Reilly & J. N. Lester (Eds.), *The Palgrave Handbook of Adult Mental Health* (pp. 502–519). Basingstoke, UK: Palgrave Macmillan.

Ghosh, M., Fisher, C., Preen, D. B., & Holman, C. A. J. (2016). "It has to be fixed": A qualitative inquiry into perceived ADHD behaviour among affected individuals and parents in Western Australia. *BMC Health Services Research, 16,* 141.

Giddens, A. (1991). *Modernity and Self-identity*. Cambridge: Polity.

Gilbert, G. N., & Mulkay, M. (1984). *Opening Pandora's Box: A Sociological Analysis of Scientists' Discourse*. Cambridge: Cambridge University Press.

Gillies, V. (2005). Meeting parents' needs? Discourses of 'support' and 'inclusion' in family policy. *Critical Social Policy, 25*(1), 70–90.

Gillies, V., Edwards, R., & Horsley, N. (2016). Brave new brains: Sociology, family and the politics of knowledge. *The Sociological Review, 64,* 219–237.

Goffman, E. (1955). On face work. *Psychiatry, 18,* 213–231.

Goffman, E. (1959). *The Presentation of Self in Everyday Life*. Harmondsworth: Penguin.

Goffman, E. (1961). *Asylums*. Harmondsworth: Penguin.

Goffman, E. (1963). *Stigma: Notes on the Management of Spoiled Identity*. Englewood Cliffs, NJ: Prentice-Hall.

Goffman, E. (1990). *Stigma: Notes on the Management of Spoiled Identity*. London: Penguin Group.

Goffman, E. (2006). On face-work: An analysis of ritual elements in social interaction. In A. Jaworski & N. Coupland (Eds.), *The Discourse Reader* (pp. 299–310). Abingdon, Oxon: Routledge.

Goldberg, A. (2011, February 6). Unscrupulous parents seek ADHD diagnosis for benefits. *BBC News*. Available at http://www.bbc.co.uk/news/health (Accessed 3 September 2017).

Gonon, F., Bezard, E., & Boraud, T. (2011). Misrepresentation of neuroscience data might give rise to misleading conclusions in the media: The case of attention deficit hyperactivity disorder. *PLoS ONE, 6*(1), e14618. https://doi.org/10.1371/journal.pone.0014618.

Goodley, D., & Rapley, M. (2001). How do you understand 'learning difficulties'? Towards a social theory of impairment. *Mental Retardation, 39*(3), 229–232.

Goodley, D., & Roets, G. (2008). The (be)comings and goings of 'developmental disabilities': The cultural politics of 'impairment'. *Discourse, 29*(2), 239–255.

Goodley, D., & Tregaskis, C. (2006). Storying disability and impairment: Retrospective accounts of disabled family life. *Qualitative Health Research, 16*(5), 630–646.

Graham, L. J. (2006). Caught in the net: A foucaultian interrogation of the incidental effects of limited notions of 'inclusion'. *International Journal of Inclusive Education, 10*(1), 3–24.

Graham, L. J. (2007). *Schooling attention deficit hyperactivity disorders: Educational systems of formation and the 'behaviourally disordered' school child* (Doctoral thesis, Queensland University of Technology).

Graham, L. J. (2008). Drugs, labels and (p)ill-fitting boxes: ADHD and children who are hard to teach. *Discourse: Studies in the Cultural Politics of Education, 29*(1), 85–106.

Gray, C. A. (2008). *Lay and professional constructions of childhood ADHD (Attention Deficit Hyperactivity Disorder): A discourse analysis* (Ph.D. thesis, Queen Margaret University).

Gray, D. E. (2001). Accommodation, resistance and transcendence: Three narratives of autism. *Social Science and Medicine, 53,* 1247–1257.

Gray, D. E. (2002a). Ten years on: A longitudinal study of families of children with autism. *Journal of Intellectual and Developmental Disability, 27*(3), 215–222.

Gray, D. E. (2002b). 'Everybody just freezes. Everybody is just embarrassed': Felt and enacted stigma among parents of children with high functioning autism. *Sociology of Health and Illness, 24*(6), 734–749.

Gray Brunton, C., McVittie, C., Ellison, M., & Willock, J. (2014). Negotiating parental accountability in the face of uncertainty for attention-deficit hyperactivity disorder. *Qualitative Health Research, 24*(2), 242–253.

Groenewald, C., Emond, A., & Sayal, K. (2009). Recognition and referral of girls with attention deficit hyperactivity disorder: Case vignette study. *Child: Care, Health and Development, 35*(6), 767–772. https://doi.org/10.1111/j.1365-2214.2009.00984.x.

Gubrium, J. F., & Holstein, J. A. (2001). *Introduction in Institutional Selves: Troubled Identities in a Postmodern World* (J. F Gubrium & J. A Holstein, Eds., pp. 8–9). New York: Oxford University Press.

Gwernan-Jones, R., Moore, D. A., Garside, R., Richardson, M., Thompson-Coon, J., Rogers, M., et al. (2015). ADHD, parent perspectives and parent–teacher relationships: Grounds for conflict. *British Journal of Special Education, 42*(3), 279–300.

Halasz, G., Anaf, G., Ellingson, P., Manne, A., & Thomson Salo, F. (2002). *Cries Unheard: A New Look at Attention Deficit Hyperactivity Disorder*. Altona: Common Ground.

Hall, J. (2008). Mental deficiency changing the outlook. *The Psychologist, 21*(11), 1006–1007.

Hall, S. (2001). Foucault: Power knowledge and discourse. In M. Wetherell, S. Taylor, & S. J. Yates (Eds.), *Discourse Theory and Practice: A Reader* (pp. 72–81). London: Sage.

Hannas, B. M. (2015, April 10). Youths' and adults' stories related to the background for ADHD assessment. *Sage*. Available at http://sgo.sagepub.com/content/5/2/2158244015579725.

Hansen, D. L., & Hansen, E. H. (2006). Caught in a balancing act: Parents' dilemmas regarding their ADHD child's treatment with stimulant medication. *Qualitative Health Research, 16*(9), 1267–1285.

Harborne, A., Wolpert, M., & Clare, L. (2004). Making sense of ADHD: A battle for understanding? Parents' views of their children being diagnosed with ADHD. *Clinical Child Psychology and Psychiatry, 9*(3), 327–339.

Harden, J. (2005). Parenting a young person with mental health problems: Temporal disruption and reconstruction. *Sociology of Health and Illness, 27*(3), 351–371.

Harper, D. J. (1995). Discourse analysis and 'mental health'. *Journal of Mental Health, 4*(4), 347–358.

Harper, D. J. (2013). On the persistence of psychiatric diagnosis: Moving beyond a zombie classification system. *Feminism and Psychology, 23*(1), 78–85.

Hartman, D., & Zimberoff, D. (2009). The hero's journey of self-transformation: Models of higher development from mythology. *Journal of Heart Centered Therapies, 12*(2), p. 3(91).

Hartman, K. L. (2008). *The rhetorical myth of the athlete as a moral hero: The implications of steroids in sport and the threatened myth* (Ph.D. thesis, Louisiana State University and Agricultural and Mechanical College).

Hartmann, T. (1994). *Attention Deficit Disorder: A Different Perception.* New York: Underwood Books.

Harwood, V., Jones, S., Bonney, A., & McMahon, S. (2017). Heroic struggles, criminals and scientific breakthroughs: ADHD and the medicalization of child behaviour in Australian newsprint media 1999–2009. *International Journal of Qualitative Studies on Health and Well-being, 12,* 1298262. https://doi.org/10.1080/17482631.2017.1298262.

Hawthorne, S. (2010). Embedding values: How science and society jointly valence a concept—The case of ADHD. *Studies in History and Philosophy of Biological and Biomedical Sciences, 41*(1), 21–31.

Hawthorne, S. (2014). *Accidental Intolerance: How We Stigmatize ADHD and How We Can Stop.* Print publication date: 2013 Print ISBN-13: 9780199977383. Published to Oxford Scholarship Online January 2014. https://doi.org/10.1093/acprof:oso/9780199977383.001.0001.

Henry, E., & Jones, S. H. (2011). Experiences of older adult women diagnosed with attention deficit hyperactivity disorder. *Journal of Women and Aging, 23*(3), 246–262.

Hepburn, A., & Wiggins, S. (Eds.). (2007). *Discursive Research in Practice: New Approaches to Psychology and Interaction.* Cambridge, UK: Cambridge University Press.

Heritage, J. C. (1984). *Garfinkel and Ethnomethodology.* Cambridge: Polity.

Hjorne, E. (2005). Negotiating the 'problem-child' in school: Child identity, parenting and institutional agendas. *Qualitative Social Work, 4*(4), 489–507.

Hobson-West, P. (2007). Trusting blindly can be the biggest risk of all: Organized resistance to childhood vaccination in the UK. *Sociology of Health and Illness, 29*(2), 198–215.

Hodge, N., & Runswick-Cole, K. (2008). Problematising parent-professional partnerships in education. *Disability and Society, 23*(6), 637–647.

Holst, J. (2008). Danish teachers' conception of challenging behaviour and DAMP/ADHD. *Early Child Development and Care, 178*(4), 363–374.

Holt, A. (2010). Managing 'spoiled identities': Parents' experiences of compulsory parenting support programmes. *Children and Society, 24*(5), 413–423.

Hong, Y. (2008). Teachers' perceptions of young children with ADHD in Korea. *Early Child Development and Care, 178*(4), 399–414.

Honkasilta, J., Vehmas, S., & Vehkakoski, T. (2015). Self-pathologizing, self-condemning, self-liberating: Youths' accounts of their ADHD-related behavior. *Social Science and Medicine, 150,* 248–255.

Hopton, J. (2006). The future of critical psychiatry. *Critical Social Policy, 26*(1), 57–73.

Horton-Salway, M. (1998). *Mind and body in the discursive construction of ME: A struggle for authorship of an illness* (Doctoral thesis, Loughborough University).

Horton-Salway, M. (2001a). Narrative identities and the management of personal accountability in talk about M.E.: A discursive approach to illness narrative. *Journal of Health Psychology, 6*(2), 261–273.

Horton-Salway, M. (2001b, March). The Construction of ME: The discursive action model. In M. Wetherell, S. Taylor, & S. J. Yates (Eds.), *Discourse as Data: A Guide to Analysis.* London: Sage and The Open University.

Horton-Salway, M. (2002). Bio-psycho-social reasoning in GPs' case narratives: The discursive construction of M.E. patients' identities. *Health. An Interdisciplinary Journal for the study of Health, Illness and Medicine, 6*(4), 401–421.

Horton-Salway, M. (2004). Expertise and experience: The local production of knowledge and identities in ME support group talk. *Health. An Interdisciplinary Journal for the Study of Health, Illness and Medicine, 8*(3), 351–371.

Horton-Salway, M. (2007). The ME bandwagon and other labels: Constructing the authentic case in talk about a controversial illness. *British Journal of Social Psychology., 46*(4), 895–914.

Horton-Salway, M. (2011). Repertoires of ADHD in UK newspaper media. *Health (London), 15*(5), 533–549.

Horton-Salway, M. (2012). Gendering attention deficit hyperactivity disorder: A discursive analysis of UK newspaper stories. *Journal of Health Psychology, 18*(8), 1085–1099. Published online before print 1 October 2012. https://doi.org/10.1177/1359105312456326.

Horton-Salway, M., & Davies, A. (2015). Moral evaluations in repertoires of ADHD. In M. O'Reilly & J. N. Lester (Eds.), *The Palgrave Handbook of Child Mental Health* (pp. 158–174). Basingstoke, UK: Palgrave Macmillan.

Hoyle, A. (2005, November 30). Tantrums…or do they need treatment? *The Mirror*, pp. 28–29.

Jarratt, C. (2014). Autism: Myth and reality. *British Psychological Society, 27*(10), 749.

Jaworski, A., & Coupland, N. (2006). Editors' introduction to Part Four. In A. Jaworski & N. Coupland (Eds.), *The Discourse Reader* (pp. 289–298). Abingdon, Oxon: Routledge.

Jefferson, G. (1984). On the organisation of laughter in talk about troubles. In J. M. Atkinson & J. Heritage (Eds.), *Structures of Social Action: Studies in Conversation Analysis* (pp. 346–369). Cambridge: Cambridge University Press.

Jefferson, G. (1988). On the sequential organization of troubles-talk in ordinary conversation. *Social Problems, 35*(4), 418–437.

Johnston, C., Mash, E. J., Miller, N., & Ninowski, J. E. (2012). Parenting in adults with attention-deficit/hyperactivity disorder (ADHD). *Clinical Psychology Review., 32*(4), 215–228.

Jones, S. C., & Harwood, V. (2009). Representations of autism in Australian print media. *Disability & Society, 24*(1), 5–18. https://doi.org/10.1080/09687590802535345.

Justman, S. (2015). Attention deficit/hyperactivity disorder: Diagnosis and stereotypy. *Ethical Human Psychology and Psychiatry, 17*(2), 135–144.

Karakaş, S., Bakar, E., Dinçer, E., Ülsever, H., Ceylan, A., & Taner, Y. (2015). Relationship between diagnosis of ADHD in offspring and current and retrospective self-reports of parental ADHD. *Journal of Child and Family Studies, 24*(12), 3595–3609.

Karim, K. (2015). The value of conversation analysis: A child psychiatrist's perspective. In M. O'Reilly & J. N. Lester (Eds.), *The Palgrave Handbook of Child Mental Health* (pp. 25–41). Basingstoke, UK: Palgrave Macmillan.

Kata, A. (2010). A postmodern Pandora's box: Anti-vaccination misinformation on the internet. *Vaccine, 28,* 1709–1716.

Kean, B. (2005). The risk society and attention deficit hyperactivity disorder (ADHD): A critical social research analysis concerning the development and social impact of the ADHD diagnosis. *Ethical Human Psychology and Psychiatry, 7*(2), 131–142.

Kelley, S. D. M., English, W., Schwallie-Giddis, P., & Jones, L. M. (2007). Exemplary counseling strategies for developmental transitions of young women with attention deficit/hyperactivity disorder. *Journal of Counseling and Development, 85,* 173–181.

Kenny, O. (2016). *How do young people diagnosed with ADHD perceive their condition?: An interpretative phenomenological analysis* (Doctoral thesis, University of East London).

Keown, L. (2011). Fathering and mothering of preschool boys with hyperactivity. *International Journal of Behavioral Development, 35*(2), 161–168.

Keown, L. (2012). Predictors of boys' ADHD symptoms from early to middle childhood: The role of father-child and mother-child interactions. *Journal of Abnormal Child Psychology, 40,* 569–581.

Kirschner, S. (2013). Diagnosis and its discontents: Critical perspectives on psychiatric nosology in the DSM. *Feminism and Psychology, 23*(1), 10–28.

Kiyimba, N. (2015). The value of discourse analysis: A clinical psychologist's view. In M. O'Reilly & J. N. Lester (Eds.), *The Palgrave Handbook of Child Mental Health* (pp. 42–58). Basingstoke: Palgrave Macmillan.

Klapp, O. E. (1962). *Heroes, Villains, and Fools.* Englewood Cliffs, NJ: Prentice-Hall.

Klapp, O. E. (1964). *Symbolic Leaders: Public Dramas and Public Men.* Chicago: Aldine.

Klasen, H., & Goodman, R. (2000). Parents and GPs at cross-purposes over hyperactivity: A qualitative study of possible barriers to treatment. *British Journal of General Practice, 50*(452), 199–202.

Kuhn, T. S. (1962/1970). *The Structure of Scientific Revolutions* (2nd ed.). Chicago: University of Chicago Press.

Laing, R. D. (1960). *The Divided Self.* London: Tavistock Publications.

Lange, K. W., Reichl, S., Lange, K. M., Tucha, L., & Tucha, O. (2010). The history of attention deficit hyperactivity disorder. *Attention Deficit and Hyperactivity Disorders, 2*(4), 241–255.

Lareau, A. (2003). *Unequal Childhoods.* Berkeley: University of California Press.

Latour, B. (1987). *Science in Action: How to Follow Scientists and Engineers Through Society.* Milton Keynes: Open University Press.

Latour, B. (1989). Cloaking the naked truth. In H. Lawson & L. Appignanesi (Eds.), *Dismantling Truth: Reality in the Post-modern World* (pp. 101–126). London: Weidenfeld and Nicolson.

Latour, B. (1993). *We Have Never Been Modern*. Hemel Hempstead: Harvester Wheatsheaf.

Lemma, A. (1996). *Introduction to Psychopathology*. London: Sage.

Leo, J., & Lacasse, J. R. (2015). *The New York Times* and the ADHD Epidemic. *Society, 52*, 3–8. Springer Science: Business Media New York.

Lester, J. N., & O'Reilly, M. (2016). The history and landscape of conversation and discourse analysis. In O'Reilly & Lester (Eds.), *The Palgrave Handbook of Adult Mental Health* (pp. 23–44). Basingstoke, UK: Palgrave Macmillan.

Levant, R. F. (2011, November). Research in the psychology of men and masculinity using the gender role strain paradigm as a framework. *American Psychologist, 66*, 765–776.

Lichtenstein, P., Halldner, L., & Zetterqvist, J. (2013). Criminality reduced when ADHD patients are on medication. *Psychopharmacology Update, 24*(3), 1–3.

Litt, J. (2004). Women's carework in low-income households: The special case of children with attention deficit hyperactivity disorder. *Gender and Society, 18*(5), 625–644.

Lloyd, G., & Norris, C. (1999). Including ADHD? *Disability and Society, 14*(4), 505–517.

Locke, A., & Edwards, D. (2003). Bill and Monica: Memory, emotion and normativity in Clinton's Grand Jury testimony. *British Journal of Social Psychology, 42*(2), 239–256.

Locke, A., & Horton-Salway, M. (2010). 'Golden age' versus 'bad old days': A discursive examination of advice giving in antenatal classes. *Journal of Health Psychology, 15*(8), 1214–1224.

Lomas, T. (2016). Positive psychology—The second wave. *The Psychologist, 29*(7), 536.

Lupton, D., & Barclay, L. (1997). *Constructing Fatherhood: Discourses and Experiences*. London: Sage.

MacMillan, K., & Edwards, D. (1998). 'Designer families': A discourse study of fact and accountability. *Journal of Sociolinguistics, 2*(3), 323–345.

MacRae, F. (2008, April 29). Fathers can't find time for family life. *The Daily Mail (London)*, p. 31.

Magnusson, E., & Maracek, J. (2012). *Gender and Culture in Psychology: Theories and Practices*. New York: Cambridge University Press.

Mailonline. (2014, November). *The rise in ADHD cases due to marketing not medicine* by Madlen Davies for Mailonline. 19 November 2014 at 16.02 hours (updated at 18.00 hours).

Malacrida, C. (2001). Motherhood, resistance and attention deficit disorder: Strategies and limits. *Canadian Review of Sociology and Anthropology, 38*(2), 141–165.

Malacrida, C. (2002). Alternative therapies and attention deficit disorder: Discourses of maternal responsibility and risk. *Gender & Society, 16*, 366–385.

Malacrida, C. (2004). Medicalisation, ambivalence and social control: Mothers' descriptions of educators and ADD/ADHD. *Health: An Interdisciplinary Journal for the Social Study of Health Illness and Medicine, 8*(61), 61–79.

Marcer, H., Finlay, F., & Baverstock, A. (2008). ADHD and transition to adult services—The experience of community paediatricians. *Child: Care, Health and Development, 34*, 564–566.

Mayes, R., & Rafalovich, A. (2007). Suffer the restless children: The evolution of ADHD and paediatric stimulant use, 1900–80. *History of Psychiatry, 18*(4), 435–457.

McCarthy, S., Asherson, P., Coghill, D., Hollis, C., Murray, M., Potts, L., et al. (2009). Attention-deficit hyperactivity disorder: Treatment discontinuation in adolescents and young adults. *The British Journal of Psychiatry, 194*(3), 273–277.

Mchoul, A., & Rapley, M. (2005). A case of attention-deficit hyperactivity disorder diagnosis: Sir Karl and Francis B. Slug it out on the consulting room floor. *Discourse and Society, 16*(3), 419–449.

McKeever, P., & Miller, K. (2004). Mothering children who have disabilities: A Bourdieusian interpretation of maternal practices. *Social Science and Medicine, 59*(6), 1177–1191.

McKinstry, L. (2005a). Not ill—Just naughty: Leo McKinstry on the scandal of attention deficit hyperactivity disorder, whereby parents are paid to bring up their children badly. *Spectator, 297*, 18–24.

McKinstry, L. (2005b, March 2). Why have we created a medical condition to excuse our spoilt brats? *The Express (UK)*, 1st ed., p. 12.

McLeod, J. D., Fettes, D. L., Jensen, P. S., Pescosolido, B. A., & Martin, J. K. (2007, May). Public knowledge, beliefs and treatment preferences concerning attention deficit hyperactivity disorder. *Psychiatric Services, Psychiatryonline.org, 58*(5), 626–631.

McVittie, C., Goodall, K. E., & McKinlay, A. (2008). Resisting having learning disabilities by managing relative abilities. *British Journal of Learning Disabilities, 36*(4), 256–262.

Mead, G. H. (1934). *Mind, Self and Society.* Chicago: University of Chicago Press.

Medical Research Council. (2016). *Public Trust in Scientific Research.* Report by MRC/BBSRC/AMS/WT. Available at www.mrc.ac.uk/documents/pdf/public-trust-in-science-2016 (Accessed 26 October 2017).

Meredith, C. (2013, August 13). Ritalin use more than doubles in six years sparking 'smart drug' fears. *The Huffington Post UK.* Available at http://www.huffingtonpost.co.uk/2013/08/13/adhd-ritalin-smart-drugs_n_3747748.html (Accessed 20 November 2013).

Merleau-Ponty, M. (1945/1962). *The Phenomenology of Perception* (C. Smith, Trans.). New York: Humanities Press.

Metzl, J., & Angel, J. (2004). Assessing the impact of SSRI antidepressants on popular notions of women's depressive illness. *Social Science and Medicine, 58,* 577–584.

Miller, G., & Silverman, D. (1995). Troubles talk and counselling discourse: A comparative study. *Sociological Quarterly, 36*(4), 725–747.

Mishler, E. G. (2005). Patient stories, narratives of resistance and the ethics of humane care: a la recherche du temps perdu. *Health: An Interdisciplinary Journal for the Social Study of Health Illness and Medicine, 9*(4), 431–451.

Moghaddam, M. F., Assareh, M., Heidaripoor, A., Rad, R. E., & Pishjoo, M. (2013). The study comparing parenting styles of children with ADHD and normal children. *Archives of Psychiatry and Psychotherapy, 4,* 45–49.

Moldavsky, M., & Sayal, K. (2013). Knowledge and attitudes about attention deficit/hyperactivity disorder (ADHD) and its treatment: The views of children, adolescents, parents, teachers and healthcare professionals. *Current Psychiatry Reports, 15*(8), 337–344.

Moncrieff, J., & Timimi, S. (2013). The social and cultural construction of psychiatric knowledge: An analysis of NICE guidelines on depression and ADHD. *Anthropology and Medicine, 20*(1), 59–71.

Mordre, M., Groholt, B., Kjelsberg, E., Standstad, B., & Myhre, A. M. (2011). The impact of ADHD and conduct disorder in childhood on adult delinquency rates: A 30 years follow-up study using official crime records. *BMC Psychiatry, 11*(1), 57–66.

Morrow, R. L., Garland, E. J., Wright, J. M., Maclure, M., Taylor, S., & Dormuth, C. R. (2012). Influence of relative age on diagnosis and treatment of attention-deficit/hyperactivity disorder in children. *CMAJ: Canadian Medical Association Journal, 184*(7), 755–762.

Morton, E. (2010, Thursday, February 4). Genuises boosted by ADHD says Prof. *The Sun (England)*, p. 22.

Mueller, A. K., Fuermaier, A. B. M., & Tucha, L. (2012). Stigma in attention deficit hyperactivity disorder. *Attention Deficit Hyperactivity Disorder, 4*(3), 101–114. Published online 8 July 2012. https://doi.org/10.1007/s12402-012-0085-3.

Murphy, K. (1995). *Out of the Fog: Treatment Options and Coping Strategies for Adult Attention Deficit Disorder*. New York: Hyperion.

Nadeau, K. G., & Quinn, P. O. (Eds.). (2002). *Understanding Women with ADHD*. Silver Spring, MD: Advantage Books.

Nadeau, K., & Quinn, P. (2005). Women and ADHD. Retrieved from National resource center of AD/HD: A program of CHADD (www.chadd.org). http://209.126.179.230/documents/WWK19.pdf.

National Health Service. (2012). *Attention Deficit and Hyperactivity Disorder (ADHD)*. Available at www.nhs.uk/Conditions/Attention-deficit-hyperactivity-disorder/Pages/Introduction.aspx (Accessed 14 September 2017).

National Health Service. (2014). *Attention Deficit and Hyperactivity Disorder (ADHD)—Treatment*. Available at http://www.nhs.uk/conditions/attention-deficit-hyperactivity-disorder/Pages/Treatment.aspx (Accessed 14 September 2017).

National Institute for Health and Care Excellence. (2016). *Attention Deficit Hyperactivity Disorder: Diagnosis and Management NICE Guideline (CG72)*. Available at https://www.nice.org.uk/guidance/cg72/ifp/chapter/Information-for-parents-of-children-with-ADHD (Accessed 14 September 2017).

National Institute of Clinical Excellence. (2009). *Attention Deficit Hyperactivity Disorder: Diagnosis and Management of ADHD in Children, Young People and Adults*. London: National Institute for Health and Clinical Excellence. Available at http://www.nice.org.uk/Guidance/CG72 (Accessed 14 September 2017).

Neophytou, K., & Webber, R. (2005). Attention deficit and hyperactivity disorder: The family and social context. *Australian Social Work, 58*(3), 313–325.

Nielsen, M. (2016). *Experiences of ADHD in Adults: Morality, Temporality and Neurobiology*. Aalborg Universitetsforlag (Ph.d.-serien for Det Humanistiske Fakultet, Aalborg Universitet). https://doi.org/10.5278/vbn.phd.hum.00054.

Norris, C., & Lloyd, G. (2000). Parents, professionals and ADHD: what the papers say. *European Journal of Special Needs Education, 15*(2), 123–137.

Nussbaum, N. L. (2012). ADHD and female specific concerns: A review of the literature and clinical implications. *Journal of Attention Disorders, 16*(2), 87–100.

O'Brien, M. (2005). *Shared caring: Bringing fathers in the frame* (EOC Working Paper Series No. 18). Manchester: Equal Opportunities Commission.

O'Dell, L., & Brownlow, C. (2005). Media reports of links between MMR and autism: A discourse analysis. *British Journal of Learning Disabilities, 33*(4), 194–199.

O'Dell, L., & Brownlow, C. (2015). Normative development and the autistic child. In M. O'Reilly & J. N. Lester (Eds.), *The Palgrave Handbook of Child Mental Health* (pp. 296–309). Basingstoke, UK: Palgrave Macmillan.

O'Dell, L., Bertilsdotter Rosqvist, H., Ortega, F., Brownlow, C., & Orsini, M. (2016). Critical autism studies: Exploring epistemic dialogues and intersections, challenging dominant understandings of autism. *Disability and Society, 31*(2), 166–179.

O'Dell, L., Stenner, P., Horton-Salway, M., & Davies, A. (2016). *Narratives of ADHD: A qualitative study of women's narrative accounts of living with ADHD*. End of project report to the British Academy.

O'Reilly, M. (2008). 'I didn't violent punch him': Parental accounts of punishing children with mental health problems. *Journal of Family Therapy, 30*(3), 272–295.

O'Reilly, M., & Lester, N. (2015). *The Palgrave Handbook of Child Mental Health* (M. O'Reilly & J. N. Lester, Eds.). Basingstoke, UK: Palgrave Macmillan.

O'Reilly, M., & Lester, N. (2016). *The Palgrave Handbook of Adult Mental Health* (M. O'Reilly & J. N. Lester, Eds.). Basingstoke, UK: Palgrave Macmillan.

O'Reilly, M., Lester, J. N., Muskett, T., & Karim, K. (2017). How parents build a case for autism spectrum disorder during initial assessments: 'We're fighting a losing battle'. *Discourse Studies, 19*(1), 69–83.

Ogden, J. (2000). *Health Psychology: A Textbook*. Buckingham: Open University Press.

Ohan, J. L., & Johnston, C. (2007). What is the social impact of ADHD in girls? A multi-method assessment. *Journal of Abnormal Child Psychology, 35*, 239–250.

Ohan, J. L., & Visser, T. A. W. (2009). Why is there a gender gap in children presenting for attention deficit hyperactivity disorder services? *Journal of Clinical Child and Adolescent Psychology, 38*(5), 650–660.

Olstead, R. (2002). Contesting the text: Canadian media depictions of the conflation of mental illness and criminality. *Sociology of Health and Illness, 4*(5), 621–643.

Palmer, S. (2006, May 4). The Toxic Generation. *Daily Mail*, London, 1st ed., p. 58.

Panter-Brick, C., Burgess, A., Eggerman, M., McAllister, F., Pruett, K., & Leckman, J. F. (2014). Practitioner review: Engaging fathers—Recommendations for a game change in parenting interventions based on a systematic review of the global evidence. *Journal of Child Psychology and Psychiatry, 55,* 1187–1212.

Parker, N., & O'Reilly, M. (2012). 'Gossiping' as a social action in family therapy: The pseudo-absence and pseudo-presence of children. *Discourse Studies, 14*(4), 457–475.

Partridge B. J., Bell S. K., Lucke J. C., Yeates S., & Hall W. D. (2011). Smart drugs 'as common as coffee': Media hype about neuroenhancement. *PLoS ONE, 6*(11), e28416. https://doi.org/10.1371/journal.pone.0028416. https://www.ncbi.nlm.nih.gov/pubmed/22140584.

Petrassi, D. (2012). 'For me, the children come first': A discursive psychological analysis of how mothers construct fathers' roles in childrearing and childcare. *Feminism and Psychology, 22*(4), 518–527.

Phillips, D. P., Kanter, E. J., & Bednarczyk, B. (1991). Importance of the lay press in the transmission of medical knowledge to the scientific community. *The New England Journal of Medicine, 325,* 1180–1183.

Pleck, J. H. (1987). The theory of male sex-role identity: Its rise and fall, 1936 to the present. In H. Brod (Ed.), *The Making of Masculinities. The New Men's Studies*. Boston: Allen and Unwin.

Polanczyk, G., Silva de Lima, M., Lessa Horta, B., Biederman, J., & Augusto Rohde, L. (2007). The worldwide prevalence of ADHD: A systematic review and metaregression analysis. *American Journal of Psychiatry, 164*(6), 942–948.

Pomerantz, A. (1986). Extreme case formulations: A way of legitimising claims. *Human Studies, 9,* 219–229.

Ponnou, S., & Gonon, F. (2017). How French media have portrayed ADHD to the lay public and to social workers. *International Journal of Qualitative Studies on Health and Well-being, 12*(Suppl. 1), 1298244. https://doi.org/10.1080/17482631.2017.1298244.

Potter, C. (2016). 'It's the most important thing—I mean, the schooling': Father involvement in the education of children with autism. *European*

Journal of Special Needs Education, 31(4), 489–505. https://doi.org/10.1080/08856257.2016.1194573.

Potter, C. A. (2016). 'I accept my son for who he is—He has incredible character and personality': Fathers' positive experiences of parenting children with autism. *Disability and Society, 31*(7), 948–965. https://doi.org/10.1080/09687599.2016.1216393.

Potter, J. (1996). *Representing Reality: Discourse, Rhetoric and Social Construction*. London: Sage.

Potter, J., & Wetherell, M. (1987). *Discourse and Social Psychology: Beyond Attitudes and Behaviour*. London: Sage.

Poulin, C. (2007). From attention-deficit/hyperactivity disorder to medical stimulant use to the diversion of prescribed stimulants to non-medical stimulant use: Connecting the dots. *Addiction, 102*(5), 740–751.

Prosser, B. (2015). Attention deficit hyperactivity disorder in Australia: Perspectives from the sociology of deviance. *Journal of Sociology, 51*(3), 596–612.

Quinn, P. O. (2005). Treating adolescent girls and women with ADHD: Gender-specific issues. *Journal of Clinical Psychology, 61*(5), 579–587.

Radley, A. (1994). *Making Sense of Illness: The Social Psychology of Health and Disease*. London: Sage.

Radley, A., & Billig, M. (1996). Accounts of health and illness: Dilemmas and representations. *Sociology of Health and Illness, 18*(2), 220–240.

Rafalovich, A. (2001a). Disciplining domesticity: Framing the ADHD parent and child. *The Sociological Quarterly, 42*(3), 373–393.

Rafalovich, A. (2001b). The conceptual history of attention deficit hyperactivity disorder: Idiocy, imbecility, encephalitis and the child deviant, 1877–1929. *Deviant Behaviour an Interdisciplinary Journal, 22*(2), 93–115.

Rafalovich, A. (2004/2008). *Framing ADHD Children: A Critical Examination of the History, Discourse and Everyday Experience of Attention Deficit/Hyperactivity Disorder.* Plymouth: Lexington Books.

Rafalovich, A. (2005). Exploring clinician uncertainty in the diagnosis and treatment of attention deficit hyperactivity disorder. *Sociology of Health Illness, 27*(3), 305–323.

Rafalovich, A. (2015). ADHD: Three competing discourses. In M. O'Reilly & N. Lester (Eds.), *The Palgrave Handbook of Child Mental Health* (pp. 79–99). Basingstoke: Palgrave Macmillan.

Ragg, R. (2006, September 23). How we'd handle William now. *Daily Telegraph News*, p. 4.

Ramundo, P., & Helly, K. (1995/1996). *You Mean I'm Not Lazy, Stupid or Crazy: A Self-help Book for Adults with Attention Deficit Disorder*. Hardback: Scriber, ISBN 0-68488 116-7. Paperback: Fireside, ISBN 0-68481-531-1.

Ranson, G. (2001). Men at work: Change or no change? In the era of the 'new father'. *Men and Masculinities, 4*(3), 2–26.

Ray, L., & Hinnant, A. (2009). Media representation of mental disorders: A study of ADD and ADHD coverage in magazines from 1985 to 2008. *Journal of Magazine & New Media Research, 11*(1), 1–21.

Read, J. (2005). The bio-bio-bio model of madness. *The Psychologist, 8*(10), 596–597.

Remschmidt, H. (2005). Global consensus on ADHD/HKD. *European Child and Adolescent Psychiatry, 14*(3), 127–137.

Renshaw, P., Choo, J., & Emerald, E. (2014). Diverse disability identities: The accomplishment of 'child with a disability' in everyday interaction between parents and teachers. *International Journal of Educational Research, 63,* 47–58.

Resnick, R. J. (1993). 'Fidgety Phil' to DSM-IV: 135 years of hyperactivity. *The School Psychologist, 2*(4), 3–9.

Ribbens McCarthy, J., Edwards, R., & Gillies, V. (2000). Moral tales of the child and the adult: Narratives of contemporary family lives under changing circumstances. *Sociology, 34,* 785–803.

Ricoeur, P. (1967). *The Symbolism of Evil.* New York: Harper and Row.

Riessman, C. K. (1990). Strategic uses of narrative in the presentation of self and illness: A research note. *Social Science and Medicine, 30*(11), 1195–1200.

Riessman, C. K. (1993). Narrative analysis. Newbury Park, CA and London: Sage.

Riley, S. C. E. (2003). The management of the traditional male role: A discourse analysis of the constructions and functions of provision. *Journal of Gender Studies, 12*(2), 99–113.

Robb, M. (2004). Men talking about fatherhood: Discourse and identities. In M. Robb, S. Barrett, C. Komaromy, & A. Rogers (Eds.), *Communication, Relationships and Care: A Reader*. London: Routledge.

Robertson, J., Walkham, E. J., Bevan, M. D., & Newby, D. A. (2013). Medicines and the media: News reports of medicines recommended for government reimbursement in Australia. *BMC Public Health, 13,* 489.

Rodriguez, T. L. (2010, January 1). Resisting negative images and stereotypes: One latina prospective teacher's story. *Brock Education: A Journal of Educational Research and Practice, 19*(2), 1183–1189.

Rogers, M. A., Wiener, J., Martin, I., & Tannock, R. (2009). Parental involvement in children's learning: Comparing parents of children with and without attention-deficit and hyperactivity disorder (ADHD). *Journal of School Psychology, 47*(3), 167–185.

Rose, D. (2010, January 7). Calm voices that turn unruly children into model pupils: Counsellors bring reason to troubled young lives. *The Times*, 1st ed., p. 17.

Rose, N. (1996/1998). *Inventing Our Selves: Psychology, Power, and Personhood.* Cambridge, UK: Cambridge University Press.

Rose, N. (1999). *Governing the Soul: The Shaping of the Private Self.* London: Free Association Books.

Rose, N. (2007). *The Politics of Life Itself: Biomedicine, Power and Subjectivity in the Twenty First Century.* Princeton, NJ: Princeton University Press.

Rose, N. (2013). The human sciences in a biological age. *Theory, Culture and Society, 30*(1), 3–34.

Rose, N., & Abi-Rached, J. M. (2013). *Neuro: The New Brain Sciences and the Management of the Mind.* Princeton, NJ: Princeton University Press.

Rose, S. (2012). Commentary on Singh: Not robots: Childrens' perspective on authenticity, moral agency and stimulant drug treatments. *Journal of Medical Ethics.* Published online 9 November 2012. https://doi.org/10.1136/medethics-2012-100961. http://jme.bmj.com/content/39/6/371.

Royal College of General Practitioners (RCGP). (1972). *The Future General Practitioner: Learning and Teaching.* Exeter: British Medical Journal.

Rucklidge, J. J., & Kaplan, B. J. (1997). Psychological functioning in women identified in adulthood with attention-deficit/hyperactivity disorder. *Journal of Attention Disorders, 2,* 167–176.

Runswick-Cole, K., Lawthom, R., & Goodley, D. (2016). The trouble with 'hard working families'. *Community, Work and Family, 19*(2), 257–260. https://doi.org/10.1080/13668803.2016.1134153.

Ryan, S. (2006). People don't do odd, do they? Mothers making sense of the reactions of others towards their learning disabled children in public places. *Children's Geographies, 3*(3), 291–305.

Ryan, S., & Runswick-Cole, K. (2008). Repositioning mothers: Mothers, disabled children and disability studies. *Disability and Society, 23*(3), 199–210.

Sacks, H. (1995). *Lectures on Conversation.* Oxford: Blackwell.

Saul, H. (2013, August 13). Use of ADHD drugs soars by more than 50% in six years. *The Independent.* Available at http://www.independent.co.uk/news/uk/home-news/use-of-adhd-drugs-soars-by-more-than-50-in-six-years-8758768.html (Accessed 21 November 2013 and 14 September 2017).

Schlachter, S. (2008). Diagnosis, treatment and educational implications for students with attention-deficit/hyperactivity disorder in the USA, Australia and the UK. *Peabody Journal of Education, 83*(1), 154–169.

Schmitz, M. F., Filippone, P., & Edelman, E. M. (2003). Social representations of attention deficit/hyperactivity disorder, 1988–1997. *Culture & Psychology, 9*(4), 383–406.

Schrevel, S. J. C., Dedding, C., Aken, J. A., & Broerse, J. E. W. (2016). 'Do I need to become someone else?' A qualitative exploratory study into the experiences and needs of adults with ADHD. *Health Expectations, 19*(1), 39–48.

Schubert, S. J., Hansen, S., Dyer, K. R., & Rapley, M. (2009). Categories in drug dependence services 'ADHD patient' or 'illicit drug user'? Managing medico-moral membership. *Discourse Society, 20*(4), 499–516.

Seale, C. (2003). Health and media: An overview. *Sociology of Health and Illness, 25*(6), 513–531.

Segal, E. S. (2001). Learned mothering: Raising a child with ADHD child and adolescent. *Social Work Journal, 18*(4), 263–279.

Seymour-Smith, S., & Wetherell, M. (2006). 'What he hasn't told you…': Investigating the micro-politics of gendered support in heterosexual couples' co-constructed accounts of illness. *Feminism and Psychology, 16*(1), 105–127.

Shattell, M., Bartlett, R., & Rowe, T. (2008). "I have always felt different": The experience of attention-deficit/hyperactivity disorder in childhood. *Journal of Pediatric Nursing, 23*(1), 49–57.

Sheriff, M., & Weatherall, A. (2009). A feminist discourse analysis of popular-press accounts of postmodernity. *Feminism & Psychology, 19,* 89–108.

Shotter, J. (1997). The social construction of our inner selves. *Journal of Constructivist Psychology, 10*(1), 7–24.

Sim, M. G., Hulse, G., & Khong, E. (2004). When the child with ADHD grows up. *Australian Family Physician, 33,* 615–618.

Simon, V., Czobor, P., Balint, S., & Meszaros, A. (2009). Prevalence and correlates of adult attention-deficit hyperactivity disorder: Meta-analysis. *British Journal of Psychiatry, 194,* 205–211.

Singh, I. (2002). Bad boys, good mothers, and the miracle of Ritalin. *Science in Context, 15*(4), 577–603.

Singh, I. (2002). Biology in context: Social and cultural perspectives on ADHD. *Children and Society, 16*(5), 360–367.

Singh, I. (2003). Boys will be boys: Fathers' perspectives on ADHD symptoms, diagnosis and drug treatment. *Harvard Review of Psychiatry, 11*(6), 308–316.

Singh, I. (2004). Doing their jobs: Mothering with Ritalin in a culture of mother-blame. *Social Science and Medicine, 59*(6), 1193–1205.

Singh, I. (2005). Will the 'real boy' please behave: Dosing dilemmas for parents of boys with ADHD. *The American Journal of Bioethics, 5*(3), 34–47.

Singh, I. (2008a). Beyond polemics: Science and ethics of ADHD. *Nature Reviews Neuroscience, 9,* 957–964.

Singh, I. (2008b). ADHD culture and education. *Early Child Development and Care, 178*(4), 339–346.

Singh, I. et al. (2012). VOICES Study: Final Report. London, UK.

Slaby, J. (2010). Steps towards a critical neuroscience. *Phenomenology and the Cognitive Sciences, 9,* 397–416.

Smith, D. E. (1978). 'K is mentally ill': The anatomy of a factual account. *Sociology, 12*(1), 23–53.

Smith, E., Koerting, J., Latter, S., Knowles, M. M., McCann, D. C., Thompson, M., & Sonuga-Barke, E. J. (2014). Overcoming barriers to effective early parenting interventions for attention-deficit hyperactivity disorder (ADHD): Parent and practitioner views. *Child: Care, Health and Development, 41*(1), 93–102.

Solden, S. (1995). *Women with Attention Deficit Disorder: Embracing Disorganization at Home and in the Workplace.* Grass Valley, CA: Underwood.

Soltile, W. M. (2005). Biopsychosocial care of heart patients: Are we practicing what we preach? *Families, Systems and Health, 23*(4), 400–403.

Sonuga-Barke, E. J. S. (2005). Causal models of attention-deficit/hyperactivity disorder: From common simple deficits to multiple developmental pathways. *Biological Psychiatry, 57*(11), 1231–1238.

Sternadori, M. (2014). The witch and the warrior. *Feminist Media Studies, 14*(2), 301–317.

Still, G. F. (1902). Some abnormal psychiatric conditions in children. *Lancet, 1,* 1008–1012, 1077–1082, 1163–1168.

Stokoe, E., & Edwards, D. (2007). Black this, black that: Racial insults and reported speech in neighbour complaints and police interrogations. *Discourse Society, 18*(3), 337–372.

Storey, J. (1993). *An Introductory Guide to Cultural Theory and Popular Culture* (pp. 73–74). Athens: University of Georgia Press.

Strate, L. (1994). Heroes: A communication perspective. In S. J. Drucker & R. S. Cathcart (Eds.), *American Heroes in a Mediated Age* (pp. 15–23). Cresol, NJ: Hampton Press.

Strong, T., & Sesma-Vazquez, M. (2015). Discourses in children's mental health: A critical review. In M. O'Reilly & N. Lester (Eds.), *The Palgrave Handbook of Child Mental Health* (pp. 99–117). Basingstoke: Palgrave Macmillan.

Summers, J. A, Boller, K., Schiffman, R. F., & Raikes, H. H. (2006). The meaning of "good fatherhood:" Low-income fathers' social constructions of their roles parenting. *Science and Practice, 6*(2 and 3), 145–165.

Sunderland, J. (2006). 'Parenting' or 'mothering'? The case of modern childcare magazines. *Discourse & Society, 17*(4), 503–527.

Swain, J., & French, S. (2000). Towards an affirmation model of disability. *Disability and Society, 15*(4), 569–582.

Szasz, T. S. (1974). *The Myth of Mental Illness: Foundations of a Theory of Personal Conduct*. New York: Harper and Row.

Tait, G. (2001). Pathologising difference, governing personality. *Asia-Pacific Journal of Teacher Education, 29*(1), 93–101.

Tancred, E.-M., & Greeff, A. P. (2015). Mothers' parenting styles and the association with family coping strategies and family adaptation in families of children with ADHD. *Clinical Social Work Journal, 43,* 442–451.

Tarver, J., Daley, D., & Sayal, K. (2014). Beyond symptom control for attention-deficit hyperactivity disorder (ADHD): What can parents do to improve outcomes? *Child: Care, Health and Development, 41*(1), 1–14.

Taylor, E. W., & Keltner, N. L. (2002). Messy purse girls: Adult females and ADHD. *Perspectives in Psychiatric Care, 38*(2), 69–71.

Taylor, M., O'Donoghue, T., & Houghton, S. (2006). To medicate or not to medicate? The decision making process of Western Australian parents following their child's diagnosis with an attention deficit hyperactivity disorder. *International Journal of Disability, Development and Education, 53*(1), 111–128.

Thapar, A., & Cooper, C. (2016). Attention deficit hyperactivity disorder. *The Lancet, 387*(10024), 1240–1250.

Thoits, P. A. (2011). Mechanisms linking social ties and support to physical and mental health. *Journal of Health and Social Behavior, 52,* 145–161.

Thomas, P., Bracken, P., & Timimi, S. (2012). The limits of evidence-based medicine in psychiatry. *Philosophy, Psychiatry and Psychology, 19*(4), 295–308.

Thompson, L., & McCabe, R. (2016). 'Good' communication in schizophrenia: A conversation analytic definition. In M. O'Reilly & J. N. Lester (Eds.), *The Palgrave Handbook of Adult Mental Health* (pp. 394–418). Basingstoke: Palgrave Macmillan.

Timimi, S. (2005). *Naughty Boys: Anti-social Behaviour, ADHD and the Role of Culture*. Basingstoke: Palgrave Macmillan.

Timimi, S. (2007). The medicalization of childhood. *Healthcare, Counselling and Psychotherapy Journal, 7*(1), 7–9.

Timimi, S., & Taylor, E. (2004). ADHD is best understood as a cultural construct. *The British Journal of Psychiatry, 184,* 8–9.

Timimi, S., & Timimi, S. (2015). The social construction of attention deficit hyperactivity disorder. In M. O'Reilly & N. Lester (Eds.), *The Palgrave Handbook of Child Mental Health* (pp. 139–158). Basingstoke: Palgrave Macmillan.

Todd, L. (2006). Enabling practice for professionals: The need for practical post-structuralist theory. In D. Goodley & R. Lawthom (Eds.), *Disability and Psychology: Critical Introductions and Reflections* (pp. 141–154). Basingstoke, UK: Palgrave Macmillan.

Todd, S., & Jones, S. (2003). Mum's the word!: Maternal accounts of dealings with the professional world. *Journal of Applied Research in Intellectual Disabilities, 16,* 229–244.

Travell, C., & Visser, J. (2006). 'ADHD does bad stuff to you': Young people's and parents' experiences and perceptions of attention deficit hyperactivity disorder (ADHD). *Emotional and Behavioural Difficulties, 11*(3), 205–216.

United Nations. (1990). *Convention on the Rights of the Child.* London: UNICEF UK.

Ussher, J. M. (1991). *Women's Madness: Misogyny or Mental Illness?* Hemel Hampstead: Harvester Wheatsheaf.

Ussher, J. (2010). Are we medicalizing women's misery? A critical review of women's higher rates of reported depression. *Feminism and Psychology, 20,* 9–35.

Valentine, J. (2001). Disabled discourse: Hearing accounts of deafness constructed through Japanese television and film. *Disability and Society, 16*(5), 707–727.

Vander Ploeg Booth, K., Chronis-Tuscano, A., & Stein, M. A. (2010). ADHD and mood symptoms in mothers of children with ADHD. *CML—Psychiatry, 21*(1), 1–13.

Van Zoonen, L. (2012). I-pistemology: Changing truth claims in popular and political culture. *European Journal of Communication, 27*(3), 56–67.

Venter, C. (2007, October 16). What my genes tell me about my destiny. *The Daily Telegraph (London),* p. 31.

Versteeg, W., te Molder, H., & Sneijder, P. (2017). "Listen to your body": Participants' alternative to science in online health discussions. *Health,* 1–17. https://doi.org/10.1177/1363459317695632.

Vickery, A. (1993). Golden age to separate spheres? A review of the categories and chronology of English women's history. *Historical Journal, 36,* 383–414.

Vingilis, E., Erickson, P. G., Toplak, M., Kolla, N. J., Mann, R. E., Seeley, J., et al. (2015). ADHD symptoms, comorbidities, substance use and social outcomes among men and women in a Canadian sample. *BioMed Research International, 2015,* Article ID 982072, 8 pages. http://dx.doi.org/10.1155/2015/982072.

Visser, J., & Jehan, Z. (2009). ADHD: A scientific fact or a factual opinion? *A Critique of the Veracity of Attention Deficit Hyperactivity Disorder Emotional and Behavioural Difficulties, 14*(2), 127–140.

Voysey, M. (1972). Impression management by parents with disabled children. *Journal of Health and Social Behaviour, 13*(1), 80–89.

Waite, R. (2010). Women with ADHD: It is an explanation, not the excuse du jour. *Perspectives in Psychiatric Care, 46,* 182–196.

Waite, R., & Ivey, N. (2009). Unveiling the mystery about adult ADHD: One woman's journey. *Issues in Mental Health Nursing, 30,* 547–553.

Waite, R., & Tran, M. (2010). ADHD among a cohort of ethnic minority women. *Women and Health, 50*(1), 71–87.

Wang, L. J., Lee, S. Y., Yuan, S. S., Yang, C. J., Yang, K. C., Lee, T. L., & Shyu, Y. C. (2016). Impact of negative media publicity on attention-deficit/hyperactivity disorder medication in Taiwan. *Pharmacoepidemiology and Drug Safety, 25,* 45–53.

Watermeyer, B. (2009). Claiming loss in disability. *Disability and Society, 24*(1), 91–102.

Watson, C. (2011). Home–school partnership and the construction of deviance: Being and becoming the Goldfish family. *Journal of Research in Special Educational Needs, 11*(1), 20–29.

Weaver, D. (2007). Thoughts on agenda setting, framing, and priming. *Journal of Communication, 57,* 142–147.

Weiss, M. D. et al. (2009). The soft underbelly of research in the psychosocial treatment of ADHD. *Journal of Attention Disorders, 12*(5), 391–393.

Wender, P. H. (1987). *The Hyperactive Child, Adolescent, and Adult*. New York: Oxford University Press.

Wender, P. H. (1995). *Attention-Deficit Hyperactivity Disorder in Adults*. New York: Oxford University Press.

Wender, P. H. (1998). Pharmacotherapy of attention-deficit/hyperactivity disorder in adults. *Journal of Clinical Psychiatry, 59*(7), 76–79.

Wender, P. H. (2000). *Attention Deficit Hyperactivity Disorder in Children and Adults*. New York: Oxford University Press.

Wetherell, M. (1998). Positioning and interpretative repertoires: Conversation analysis and post-structuralism in dialogue. *Discourse and Society, 9*(3), 387–412.

Wetherell, M. (2007). A step too far: Discursive psychology, linguistic ethnography and questions of identity. *Journal of Sociolinguistics, 11*(5), 661–681.

Wetherell, M. (2012). *Affect and Emotion: A New Social Science Understanding*. London: Sage.

Wetherell, M., & Potter, E. (1992). *Mapping the Language of Racism*. Chichester: Columbia University Press.

Wetherell, M., Taylor, S., & Yates, S. (2001). *Discourse Theory and Practice*. London: Sage.

Weusten, J. (2011). Narrative constructions of motherhood and autism. Reading embodied language beyond binary oppositions. *Journal of Literary Cultural Disability Studies, 5*(1), 53–70.

Weyandt, L., Swentosky, A., & Gudmundsdottir, B. G. (2013). Neuroimaging and ADHD: fMRI, PET, DTI Findings, and Methodological Limitations. *Developmental Neuropsychology, 38*(4), 211–225. https://doi.org/10.1080/87565641.2013.783833.

Wheeler, L. (2010). Critique of the article by Visser and Jehan (2009): 'ADHD: A scientific fact or a factual opinion? A critique of the veracity of attention deficit hyperactivity disorder'. *Emotional and Behaviour Difficulties, 15*(3), 257–267.

White, W. (2014). Myths of masculinity and superheroes. In D. Whitt & J. Perlich (Eds.), *Myth and the Modern World: Essays on the Intersection with Ideology and Culture*. Jefferson, NC: McFarland.

Whitely, M. (2015). Attention deficit hyperactive disorder diagnosis continues to fail the reliability and validity tests. *Australian and New Zealand Journal of Psychiatry, 49*(6), 497–498.

Whitt, D., & Perlich, J. (Eds.). (2014). *Myth and the Modern World: Essays on the Intersection with Ideology and Culture*. Jefferson, NC: McFarland.

Widdicombe, S., & Wooffitt, R. (1995). *The Language of Youth Subcultures: Social Identity in Action*. London: Harvester Wheatsheaf.

Wigginton, B., & Lafrance, N. (2016). How do women manage the spoiled identity of a 'pregnant smoker'? An analysis of discursive silencing in women's accounts. *Feminism and Psychology, 26*(1), 30–51.

Wiita, M. D., & Parish, T. G. (2008). ADHD in young adults. *Clinician Reviews, 8*(9), 30–32.

Wilkinson, S., & Kitzinger, C. (2000). Thinking differently about thinking positive: A discursive approach to cancer patients' talk. *Social Science and Medicine, 50*(6), 797–811.

Williams, S. J., Seale, C., Boden, S., Lowe, P., & Steinberg, D. L. (2008). Waking up to sleepiness: Modafinil, the media and the pharmaceuticalisation of everyday/night life. *Sociology of Health & Illness, 30*(6), 839–855. ISSN 0141–9889.

Williamson, D., & Johnston, C. (2015). Gender differences in adults with attention-deficit/hyperactivity disorder: A narrative review. *Clinical Psychology Review, 40*, 15–27.

Willig, C. (2013). *Introducing Qualitative Research in Psychology* (3rd ed.). Maidenhead: Open University Press/McGraw-Hill Education.

Winnicott, D. W. (1984). Primary maternal preoccupation. In *Through Paediatrics to Psycho-Analysis* (Collected Papers). London: Karnac Books.

Winter, H., Moncrieff, J., & Speed, E. (2015). "Because you're worth It": A discourse analysis of the gendered rhetoric of the ADHD woman. *Qualitative Research in Psychology, 12*(4), 415–434.

Wittgenstein, L. (1980). *Remarks on the Philosophy of Psychology* (Vols. 1–2). Oxford: Basil Blackwell.

Wooffitt, R. (1992). *Telling Tales of the Unexpected: The Organisation of Factual Discourse*. Hemel Hempstead: Harvester Wheatsheaf.

Woolgar, S. (1988). *Science: The Very Idea*. Chichester: Ellis Horwood/London: Tavistock.

World Health Organisation. (1992). *ICD-10 Classifications of Mental and Behavioural Disorder: Clinical Descriptions and Diagnostic Guidelines*. Geneva: World Health Organisation.

World Health Organisation. (2010). *ICD-10 Version 2010 Classifications of Mental and Behavioural Disorder: Clinical Descriptions and Diagnostic*

Guidelines. Geneva: World Health Organisation. http://apps.who.int/classifications/icd10/browse/2010/en#/F90-F98.

Wynne, L. C., Sheilds, C. G., & Sirkin, M. I. (1992). Illness, family theory, and family therapy: I. conceptual issues. *Family Process, 31,* 3–18. https://doi.org/10.1111/j.1545-5300.1992.00003.x.

Yarwood, G. A. (2011). The pick and mix of fathering identities. *Fathering, 9*(2), 150–168.

Young, S., Bramham, J., Gray, K., & Rose, E. (2008). The experience of receiving a diagnosis and treatment of ADHD in adulthood: A qualitative study of clinically referred patients using interpretative phenomenological analysis. *Journal of Attention Disorders, 11*(4), 493–503.

Young, S., Chesney, S., Sperlinger, D., Misch, P., & Collins, P. (2009). A qualitative study exploring the life-course experiences of young offenders with symptoms and signs of ADHD who were detained in a residential care setting. *Criminal Behaviour and Mental Health, 19,* 54–63.

Young, S., & Gudjonsson, G. H. (2008). Growing out of ADHD: The relationship between functioning and symptoms. *Journal of Attention Disorders, 12*(2), 162–169. https://doi.org/10.1177/1087054707299598.

Young, S., Toone, B., & Tyson, C. (2003). Comorbidity and psychosocial profile of adults with attention deficit/hyperactivity disorder. *Personality and Individual Differences, 35*(4), 743–755.

Zhongdang, P., & Kosicki, G. (1993). Framing analysis: An approach to news discourse. *Political Communication, 10*(1), 55–75.

Zverina, M., Stam, H. J., & Babins-Wagner, R. (2011). Managing victim status in group therapy for men: A discourse analysis. *Journal of Interpersonal Violence, 26*(14), 2834–2855.

Index

M. Horton-Salway and A. Davies, *The Discourse of ADHD*, The Language of Mental Health, https://doi.org/10.1007/978-3-319-76026-1

The manufacturer's authorised representative in the EU is Springer Nature Customer Service Centre GmbH, Europaplatz 3, 69115 Heidelberg, Germany. If you have any concerns regarding our products, please contact ProductSafety@springernature.com

Printed and bound by CPI Group (UK) Ltd, Croydon, CR0 4YY
30/09/2026
02225660-0012